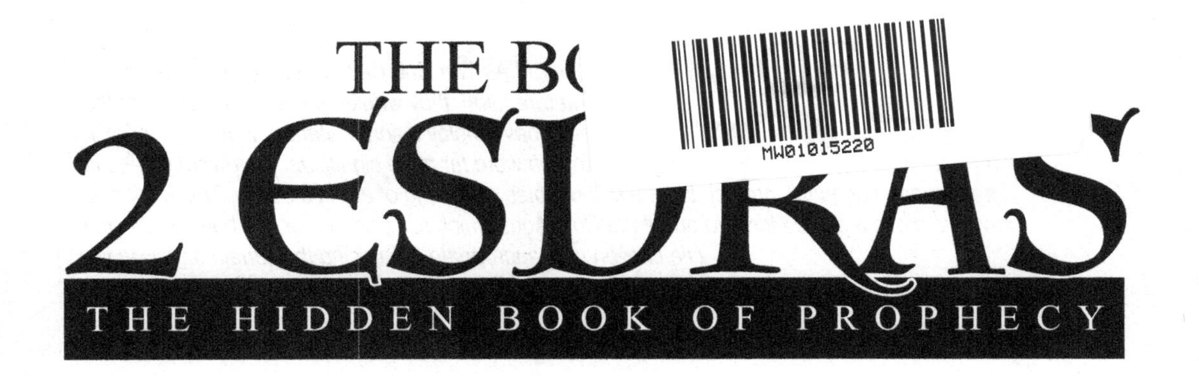

WITH 1ST ESDRAS - FIRST EDITION

Adapted From The Original, Authorized

1611 King James Version

Revised English with Restored Name of YHWH

Edited, Compiled, Commentary, Charts and Research By
Timothy Schwab, Anna Zamoranos
and The God Culture Team

NOTE: Why Foreward vs. the traditional foreword? As The God Culture represents an adjusting of traditional history, geography and bible interpretation, they wanted something more from the opening words that sets the tone appropriately. They employ a sort of literary double entendre in using the word Foreward reviving an Old English word far more significant. Foreward means to keep, guard, vanguard, protect, tend, etc. It denotes a warding of evil in a sense. This work also strives to move a people forward out of the Dark Ages which still persist. For this book, that is the title chosen very appropriately in raising the curtain on this work.

Library Of Congress Control Number: 1-10500202551
Library of Congress Registration Number: TXu002263795
ISBN Number: 979-8-510-54953-9

To order additional copies of this book, contact:

The Levite Bible By The God Culture
TheGodCulture@gmail.com
Facebook: The God Culture - Original
www.LeviteBible.com
www.OphirInstitute.com
www.TheGodCulture.com

CONTENTS

Foreward 7
Introduction 13
Who Lived In Qumran? 13
The Essenes of Ein Gedi Not Qumran! 21
Temple Priest Associations in the Dead Sea Scrolls 22
Who Defiled the Temple? 24
The Hanukkah Hoax? 26
Pharisee Fruits According to the Bible 28
Pharisees and Hasmoneans in the Dead Sea Scrolls 30
Messiah in 1st and 2nd Esdras 32
John the Baptist in Qumran? 34
The Torah Test 35
The Name of God, YHWH in Esdras 74

2nd Esdras Full Text Begins **77**
1: YAHUAH'S JUDGMENT OF ISRAEL
1: The Genealogy of Ezra *(1-3)* *78*
1: Ezra's Prophetic Call *(4-11)* *78*
1: Yahuah's Mercies to Israel *(12-23)* *78*
1: Israel's Disobedience and Rejection *(24-40)* *79*
1: Messiah Quotes 2 Esdras *(30-33 in Mt. 23:37-38)* *81*
2: SON OF YAHUAH REVEALED IN THE END TIMES
2: Yahuah's Judgment on Israel *(1-14)* *82*
2: Exhortation to Good Works *(15-32)* *83*
2: Ezra on Mount Horeb *(33-41)* *84*
2: Ezra Sees the Son of Yahuah in the End Times *(42-48)* *84*
3: EZRA MEDIATES FOR ISRAEL
3: Ezra's Prayer of Complaint *(1-27)* *86*
3: Babylon Compared with Zion *(28-36)* *87*
4: UNDERSTANDING THE END TIMES
4: Limitations of the Human Mind *(1-12)* *89*
4: Parable of the Forest and the Sea *(13-21)* *90*
4: The New Age Will Make All Things Clear *(22-32)* *90*
4: When Will the New Age Come? *(33-43)* *91*
4: How Much Time Remains? *(44-52)* *92*

CONTENTS

5: SIGNS OF THE END TIMES

5: Signs of the End *(1-13)* *93*
5: Conclusion of the Vision *(14-20)* *93*
5: Ezra's Second Prayer of Complaint *(21-30)* *94*
5: Response to Ezra's Complaints *(31-40)* *95*
5: Why Successive Generations Have Been Created *(41-49)* *95*
5: When and How Will the End Come? *(50-56)* *96*

6: THE WORKS OF CREATION

6: The Dividing of the Times *(7-9)* *97*
6: More Signs of the End *(11-28)* *97*
6: Conclusion of the Second Vision *(29-34)* *99*
6: The Third Vision *(35-37)* *99*
6: Yahuah's Work in Creation *(38-54)* *99*
6: Why Do God's People Suffer? *(55-59)* *100*
15% of Pre-Flood World Was Water *101*
Map of Rivers from Eden *102*
Map of Garden of Eden *104*
Garden System in the End Times *105*

7: MESSIAH REVEALED

7: Response to Ezra's Questions *(1-16)* *106*
7: The Fate of the Ungodly *(17-25)* *108*
7: The Temporary Messianic Kingdom *(26-35)* *108*
7: No Intercession for the Ungodly *(36-45)* *110*
7: Lamentation over the Fate of Most People *(46-61)* *110*
7: Ezra Appeals to God's Mercy *(62-70)* *112*

8: EZRA'S APPEALS FOR MERCY

8: Ezra Again Appeals to God's Mercy *(4-19)* *114*
8: Ezra's Prayer *(20-36)* *115*
8: Response to Ezra's Prayer *(37-45)* *116*
8: Ezra's Final Appeal for Mercy *(46-63)* *117*

9: MORE REVELATION OF THE END TIMES

9: More about the Signs of the End *(1-13)* *118*
9: The Argument Recapitulated *(14-25)* *118*
9: The Abiding Glory of the Mosaic Law *(26-37)* *120*
9: The Vision of a Weeping Woman *(38-47)* *121*

10: EZRA'S LESSON FROM THE VISIONS

10: The Vision of a Weeping Woman Continued *(1-28)* *122*
10: Uriel's Interpretation of the Vision *(29-59)* *124*

CONTENTS

11: VISION OF THE FINAL EAGLE EMPIRE

11: The Vision of the Eagle *(1-35)* *126*

11: A Lion Roused from the Forest *(36-46)* *127*

Eagle Empire Revealed *129*

12: EAGLE EMPIRE DESTROYED

12: The Interpretation of the Vision *(7-39)* *130*

12: The People Come to Ezra *(40-51)* *132*

13: TRAIL OF ISRAEL'S NORTHERN KINGDOM

13: The Man from the Sea *(1-13)* *134*

13: The Interpretation of the Vision *(14-38)* *135*

13: Trail of the Lost Tribes *(39-58)* *136*

Map of Northern Lost Tribes Migration into Assyria *137*

Map of Northern Lost Tribes Year and a Half Journey *138*

Isaiah 11 Migrations of Lost Tribes of Israel *139*

Destination: Isles of Sinim, Sinae (not the mountain) *140*

History: First World Globe of 1492 Shows Location *142*

14: RESTORATION OF TORAH

14: Yahuah Commissions Ezra *(1-18)* *144*

14: Ezra's Concern to Restore the Scriptures *(19-26)* *146*

14: Ezra's Last Words to the People *(27-36)* *146*

14: The Restoration of the Scriptures *(37-48)* *147*

15: VEGEANCE ON THE WICKED

15: Vengeance on the Wicked *(1-27)* *149*

15: A Terrifying Vision of Warfare *(28-33)* *150*

15: Judgment on Babylon *(34-45)* *151*

15: Judgment on Asia *(46-63)* *152*

16: THE END TIMES BATTLE

16: Further Denunciations *(1-17)* *155*

16: The Horror of the Last Days *(18-34)* *155*

16: Yahuah's People Must Prepare for the End *(35-50)* *156*

16: The Power and Wisdom of Yahuah *(51-67)* *157*

16: Impending Persecution of Yahuah's People *(68-73)* *158*

16: Promise of Divine Deliverance *(74-78)* *159*

1st Esdras Full Text Begins **161**

1: DESTRUCTION OF THE FIRST TEMPLE

1: Yosiah Celebrates the Passover *(1-22)* *162*

1: The End of Yosiah's Reign *(23-33)* *163*

1: The Last Kings of Yahudah *(33-46)* *164*

1: The Fall of Yerusalem *(47-58)* *165*

2 : RETURN OF THE SOUTHERN KINGDOM
2: Cyrus Permits the Exiles to Return *(1-15)* *167*
2: Opposition to Rebuilding Yerusalem *(16-30)* *168*
3 : THE WISDOM DEBATE
3: The Debate of the Three Bodyguards *(1-17)* *170*
3: The Speech about Wine *(18-24)* *171*
4 : SECOND TEMPLE TO CONTINUE CONSTRUCTION
4: The Speech about the King *(1-12)* *172*
4: The Speech about Women *(13-32)* *172*
4: The Speech about Truth *(33-41)* *174*
4: Zerubbabel's Reward *(42-57)* *174*
4: Zerubbabel's Prayer *(58-63)* *176*
5 : SECOND TEMPLE FOUNDATION LAID
5: List of the Returning Exiles *(1-46)* *177*
5: Worship Begins Again *(47-55)* *180*
5: The Foundations of the Temple Laid *(56-73)* *181*
6 : OVERCOMING OBSTRUCTION OF THE TEMPLE
6: Work on the Temple Begins Again *(1-22)* *184*
6: Official Permission Granted *(23-34)* *185*
7 : THE TEMPLE IS COMPLETED & DEDICATED
7: The Temple Is Dedicated *(1-9)* *187*
7: The Passover *(10-15)* *187*
8 : EZRA ARRIVES IN YERUSALEM WITH REBUKE
8: Ezra Arrives in Jerusalem *(1-7)* *189*
8: The King's Mandate *(8-24)* *189*
8: Ezra Praises Yahuah *(25-27)* *191*
8: The Leaders Who Returned *(28-49)* *191*
8: Ezra Proclaims a Fast *(50-53)* *192*
8: The Gifts for the Temple *(54-60)* *193*
8: The Return to Yerusalem *(61-67)* *193*
8: Ezra's Prayer *(69-90)* *194*
8: The Plan for Ending Mixed Marriages *(91-96)* *195*
9 : THE RESTORATION OF THE LAW
9: The Expulsion of Foreign Wives *(1-36)* *197*
9: Ezra Reads the Law to the People *(37-55)* *200*

Bibliography 202

FOREWARD

By Timothy Schwab
Author, Publisher, Researcher, Speaker, Singer/Songwriter, Founder of The God Culture, Non-Pharisee and proudly so...

In our extensive research restoring Biblical geography and scripture through exhaustive testing and supporting detail, we have often visited the Books of 1st and 2nd Esdras. Esdras is simply the Latin and Greek form of Ezra, the Prophet who actually wrote at least four books. The Rabbis catalogue these as:

1 Ezra = Ezra *(Modern Old Testament Canon)*
2 Ezra = Nehemiah *(Modern Old Testament Canon)*
3 Ezra = 1 Esdras *(Mislabeled as Apocrypha, a meaningless classification)*
4 Ezra = 2 Esdras *(Mislabeled as Apocrypha, a meaningless classification)*

Understand 1st and 2nd Esdras are translated into English, a major undertaking in that day especially, and published in the Original, Authorized 1611 King James Bible as well as the Original 1560 Geneva Bible. They would not have gone to such trouble to translate these just as they did scripture unless they viewed these as useful whether separated into a different category or not. They are in the 1611 KJV and 1560 Geneva Bibles period thus we should know them and publishing them would be a waste of a massive amount of time and resources otherwise. Yet they did.

The Geneva Bible separates these and notes that they are for edification which connotation is an endorsement of their value whether they even call it scripture or not. Let's cut thru the modern political correctness nonsense in scholarship. If the 1560 Geneva and 1611 KJV Bibles translated these works into English and published them, they read and used these books. Why don't we? Why doesn't every church? Who censored these and how could they be dropped from most modern Bibles?

Even the KJV only crowd seems to be largely unaware, these books were published in the original 1611 KJV yet many act as if they are not. They are not sticking to the King James Version if they are not using 1st and 2nd Esdras. So they need to reclassify themselves as partial KJV only. 2nd Esdras is even anchored to Messiah's quoting it even. Can someone explain how it is that something Messiah quoted could be eliminated from publishing?

Even the Geneva Bible's diminutive language still definitively offers evidence these are useful books to be read along with scripture and there is no debating that because they are there published in 1560 and 1611 period. It matters not whether a Catholic council branded them with their seal of approval. They have no authority to change what the Temple Priests already kept and we will unveil research in this book which makes such connection with 1st and 2nd Esdras to the Dead Sea Scrolls. Many will find this enlightening and well proven.

Also, the Catholic claim of "compiling the Bible" is not accurate in regards to the Old

Testament which, we now know, was already compiled in Qumran as every book in the modern Old Testament Canon was found in the Dead Sea Scrolls with the exception of Esther. The question remains, who do any of these counsels think they are in usurping authority to change what was definitively kept as the Old Testament. That cannot change! The fact they keep changing it is a sign of the presence of Pharisee leaven. Only in their paradigm is it acceptable to add and remove books. In the Bible's, that act brings dire consequences. They even marginalize the entire Old Testament in ignorance but what brazen gall it takes for any group to claim such authority they do not have even to remove the very name of YHWH over 6,800 times in the Old Testament in order to replace it with their Samaritan practice of calling their god Lord or in Hebrew, Ba'al. How could we lose books that were read as scripture whether equated as Genesis or not? How can we be missing books the exiled Temple Priests called Torah and inspired scripture even? Why on Earth isn't the church and ALL of scholarship seeking answers to these questions? They dare not.

1st and 2nd Esdras are categorized as Apocrypha which is a meaningless description of books that are considered by the Rabbis as outside of their Canon. Yes, the Catholic Church is essentially following Pharisee doctrine and using their terms in ignorance which is no surprise as the Catholic Church appears a Pharisee infusion of the Persian/ Babylonian religion with that of YHWH just as the Rabbis did in Samaria before attacking and conquering the Temple in 165 B.C. This attempt is always rebuked in scripture. The Pharisee Canon is impertinent as they are not and never were the Biblical keepers of scripture nor is the Catholic Church, especially not for the Old Testament in which they and the Pharisees changed and we now possess such proof of their fraud. We have the original Bible from Messiah's day. However, amazingly even the Protestant Church looks to these Pharisees as if they were Levites and they were not, are not and never will be. Changing their name to Cohen or even Netanyahu from his family's Polish name, does not change that fact.

That role was entrusted to the Aaronic Levite Priests whom they exiled and illegally replaced defiling the Temple according to these writings. These Levites would manage the Temple worship appointed by Yacob in Jubilees 45:16 and by Moses in Deuteronomy 31:24-26. From the days of Solomon, this Temple leadership were the sons of Zadok specifically within such lineage with other Levite families serving in courses approximately two weeks per year plus Feasts. That is what the Qumran documents identify in regards to these inhabitants never Essenes which we will prove is the most illiterate scholarship in history. They were not Pharisees nor Rabbis then nor now and we prove this. In the beginning of the Introduction, we will disseminate our research again identifying Qumran as the Temple Priest's headquarters for Temple worship and the library of scripture we would call the Old Testament which was no longer in Yerusalem. This is after they were exiled from the Temple in Yerusalem by the Hasmoneans and Pharisees who replaced them in leadership illegally. Those imposters never have a say in what is or is not scripture. They are impertinent then and now.

The Dead Sea Scrolls identify those factions who were new to Yerusalem and foreigners, not Hebrews, as the "sons of darkness," the "Wicked Priest," "those who seek smooth things," and "liars" even. They place them at war spiritually with the Bible keepers and we listen to these "Sons of Darkness" today which is why we know little about this community and the church loses track of the Bible keepers in ignorance. Of course, the Protestant Church is so busy marginalizing the Old Testament in willing ignorance, it cannot even see this narrative yet this is one of the most important issues of our era. The days of increasing knowledge Daniel predicted are upon us and they will render themselves obsolete as they are left behind clinging to what are now proven to be the doctrines of men injected and certainly not scripture and there are many.

In our introduction we publish our research proving the Qumran community is not Essene which we find an illiterate proposition. There is no mention of Essenes a single time in all the many writings from Qumran yet over a hundred identifying the inhabitants of this community as the exiled Temple Priests who are the sons of Zadok from Levi from Aaron. We cover the history and archaeology of the Essene headquarters well-entrenched 25 miles South of Qumran in Ein Gedi. We also prove Qumran is the Biblical Bethabara where John the Baptist, a son of Zadok and the Great Prophet even, lived and operated and baptized Messiah there. Messiah even visited this community again placing his endorsement on their practices including their Bible.

These are the Biblical keepers of scripture and never once are they on record as operating as such frauds as to make up their own writings and call it scripture. They do not pretend to be prophets falsely. That is the practice of the Rabbis not the Temple Priests whom Moses and even Yacob entrusted as the curators of scripture. What an insane accusation for a so-called Bible scholar to level at an Aaronic Levite Temple priest whose lineage went before the very presence of Yahuah in His Holy of Holies. The opinion that these curators lost their passion and sense of responsibility in their calling is ludicrous and unscholarly. Most seem to forget that though Israel and the Southern Kingdom rebelled, the sons of Zadok who led the Temple worship, continued to remain holy. This is not only evidenced in the abundant Qumran scrolls of their local community writings in application and interpretation, but even in Ezekiel's days of prophecy, these remained truly pious.

> ***Ezekiel 40:46 KJV***
> *And the chamber whose prospect is toward the north is for* ***the priests, the keepers of the charge of the altar****: these are the* ***sons of Zadok*** *among the sons of Levi, which come near to the LORD to minister unto him.*
> ***Ezekiel 44:15 KJV***
> *But* ***the priests the Levites, the sons of Zadok****, that* ***kept the charge of my sanctuary when the children of Israel went astray from me, they shall come near to me to minister unto me****, and* ***they shall stand before me*** *to offer unto me the fat and the blood, saith the Lord GOD:*

Ezekiel 48:11 KJV
It shall be for ***the priests that are sanctified of the sons of Zadok; which have kept my charge,*** *which* ***went not astray when the children of Israel went astray,*** *as the Levites went astray.*

Here we are in the Last Days in which knowledge is increasing – ancient knowledge we have lost largely. We now have the writings of these holy priests who ran the Temple and kept the Bible. Some might find a passage about Levites going astray but read this. The Sons of Zadok did not. They are the inhabitants of Qumran continuing this same holy practice following the Law of Moses and keeping scripture. Ezekiel is late in the game for the Southern Kingdom exiled at the time to Babylon already yet these Priests still remained pious until then. He spends much of his book on the future. He identified for us the faction who connects it all. The Old Testament and the New Testament melt together in their writings and practices. This is the home of John the Baptist who was a son of Zadok himself qualified to be High Priest.

What we see in scripture is Messiah's endorsement of John as there was "none greater" before him, the last great "prophet" in a line of prophets, "Elias *(Elijah)*, which was for to come" *(Mt. 11:11-14)*. This included the practices of his community in Qumran/ Bethabara which Yahusha observed Himself even participating as He chose to be baptized there in the place where scripture was kept. Where else would He who is the Word choose to launch His ministry? The very place He would preserve on the Dead Sea that we would rediscover in 1947. Yes, His promise to preserve His Word is truth.

Why search first century Rabbi babble when we have an extensive library of scripture, their official canon of indisputable renown and historicity, their commentaries, their hymns, their community laws based on scripture with references even, their calendars, etc. Yet over 70 years later, we are still asking questions like what was the original canon? It was found already. Are the Nephilim truly giants and the offspring of angels and humans? They answer that affirmative. What modern scholar could possibly even attempt to overrule and especially marginalize and even obscure the significance of this find which actually represents one of the greatest discoveries in history. The very restoration of the Word is sitting right there and we hear illiterate language from hordes of scholars who behave as elementary dunces on this topic.

In the case of Jubilees which we published in full, the sons of Zadok label it and use it as Torah. If the Temple Priests used it as Torah, who cares what any scholar nor Pharisee would ever have to say about it's authenticity as scripture. They have no permission to overrule the Biblical authority and it does not matter what the illegitimate usurpers of the Temple, the Pharisees *(modern Rabbis)*, perceived as their canon which was rebuked by Messiah in Mark 7 and elsewhere. We find the same with 2nd Esdras which we publish The Torah Test in this introduction following. When we can find a text which appears to be the basis of quotes from Messiah Himself even identified as such in the 1611 King James and 1560 Geneva Bibles, as well as direct connections to the Dead Sea Scrolls, we have very strong reservations about scholarly criticism which then questions the written date of the books placing them much later than the text clearly identifies. Again, they operate as scoffers representing the position that the Sons of Zadok were liars when they are the ones listening to the ancient liars according to scripture. They sit in the seat of the scornful and ridicule in ignorance and prove they are challenged to read and comprehend.

For instance, anyone can read this text and see that it could not have been written during nor after the time of the Apostles. After defining the End Times in what is clearly the origin of Revelation language, Yahuah Himself tells Ezra He has not revealed these things to anyone before. If this was written in 50 A.D. or after, those scholars are calling Yahuah a liar. This cannot be the case. We will explore this further but it also affirms that Ezra prophesied the coming of Messiah dating it very closely to about 0 B.C. and he knew His name would be Yahusha. This is firmly prophecy and accurate.

2 Esdras 13:53-54

This is the interpretation of the dream which you saw, and whereby ***you only are here lightened****.*
For you have forsaken your own way, and applied your diligence unto my law, and sought it.

Though the connection to the Dead Sea Scrolls with these books is not as definitive as Jubilees which is identified in their writings as Torah specifically, we find 1st and 2nd Esdras extremely well-written in matching scripture as well as some Dead Sea fragments mislabeled which we will explore. More importantly, when we read prophesies that would be future even if this dating was accurate as late as 218 A.D. or so, these test as powerful and true. When a work that vets as scripture even quoted by Messiah, reveals itself as truth and accurate in prophecy, this is the very definition of inspired. Then, to call into question such inspired writing as scripture, seems a mischaracterization of an incpt paradigm who is not even attempting to find the truth.

As we will cover, the prophecy of the Eagle that clearly identifies the Holy Roman Empire which did not exist at the time of the writing regardless of dating, we firmly believe this inspired. When, then, the text says it was written by Ezra the Prophet, that also rings true. The alternative again, is to accuse the exiled Temple Priests of falsifying. We will produce evidence that takes this dating back to at least 100 B.C. Many times, those same scholars will level such accusation and then, continue to discuss the book as potential scripture in theology yet they already undermined it in ethics. Of course, they'll float back and forth but the whole process appears double-minded. If the book vets as truth, then, what it says in terms of authorship as well is truth. Otherwise, the whole thing would be false and of little value. They take what they don't know and draw conclusions as if one can do so, with what they don't know. In other words, they merely tell what they don't know and they have no conclusion. The main reason is they do not wish to believe 2nd Esdras especially represents prophecy because if so, then, the Pharisees must produce their Messiah at the time of Yahusha whose name must be Yahusha because this book foretells such with accuracy by date and name.

In the Torah Test, we will cite fragments we believe to be mislabeled. The first belongs to "Proto-1st Esdras" grossly mislabeled as "Proto-Esther." We will prove this is an obvious and blatant fraud in which the story of Esther matches practically none of the fragments involved. Anyone who can read and understand the story, could never claim they belong to Esther.

We will then cite a scholarly review of 2nd Esdras that demonstrates a connection in thought of 2nd Esdras and the Qumran texts which is fascinating though unproven. In their mindset, 2nd Esdras belongs with the Qumran genre. However, we will then go into the Dead Sea Scrolls themselves and firmly identify two fragments in which 2nd Esdras is used to render such commentary and interpretation of the Qumran/Bethabara theology. This is extremely significant as no one has done so.

Once you review these, even if you do not agree, the historicity of these books rises to the occasion of inspired scripture in large part. We find them from the days of Qumran including a fragment from the 1st century B.C., meaning the Rabbi dating is wrong, with ancient inclusions in Orthodox Tewahedo Biblical Canon, Codex Vaticanus, Codex Sinaiticus, Codex Alexandrinus, Latin Vulgate, Greek Septuagint, 1560 Geneva Bible, 1611 Original, Authorized, King James Version, and even some modern canons to today. We will specify which periods as well. There is a reason why 1st and 2nd Esdras have withstood such long-standing and it matters not what Pharisee nor Church decides to overrule what is precedence in scripture as only the sons of Zadok kept the Old Testament and only their canon matters in terms of what is or is not scripture.

We also will obliterate the Essene theory with the very Qumran texts themselves next. Additionally, in our Introduction, we will cover the Messianic Prophesies, The Name of YHWH, the identity of the Qumran Priests in their writings, Who Defiled the Temple, test The Hanukkah Hoax and firmly link John the Baptist to Qumran.

Following the Introduction, we have curated 2nd Esdras as our main highlight with 1st Esdras after. In examining the Original, Authorized 1611 King James Version, we have revised the English and added several margin notes in cross-reference especially as we find this book in several portions of the New Testament. Throughout the text, we expound on the antediluvian cosmology including the Rivers from Eden, chart the vision of the Eagle Empire with our interpretation, and most especially, we provide a foundation in creating maps using 2nd Esdras along with other scripture and history to locate the Lost Tribes of the Northern Kingdom of Israel. If this book was written between 70 A.D. and 218 A.D. as some scholars assert, it still remains an incredibly valuable tool in these respects though we will prove that date wrong. This restored knowledge is full of revelation – too full to ignore and too accurate to minimize.

It is time to prove all things (1 Th. 5:21). Review this research and this will change your life. May this bless all who read. Yah Bless.

INTRODUCTION Who Lived in Qumran?

In 1947, the voice in the wilderness cried out yet again. Did you hear it? The entire modern Old Testament canon was found in Qumran with the exception of the Book of Esther in what is inappropriately labeled and expanded in scope as the Dead Sea Scrolls as the find was specific to the Qumran area and truly remains so. This included other books as well. For many of these books, these are the oldest copies found and some were complete such as the 24-foot long Isaiah Scroll. After over 70 years, we still know little about this community yet the archaeology, writings of the community and the large compound found there confirm these were the Aaronic Levite Priests, the sons of Zadok, who had been exiled to the Wilderness of Yahudea by the Hasmoneans and Pharisees. They were the Temple High Priests replaced by a new unbiblical order.

However, today, the world allows the Pharisees who defiled the Temple to teach us about this community. No wonder we know so little about them or at least we are taught so. This was the base of operations for John the Baptist and his disciples where he baptized Jesus*(Yahusha)* and was visited by Him later privately. It is among the most well-documented New Testament communities on record and the church does not even know because it is too busy defending a control narrative that the other books found with the Old Testament are somehow cursed when Yahusha and John set this library as a time capsule to preserve His Word.

Note: This "Who Lived In Qumran?" section of this Introduction only is the same as The Book of Jubilees: The Torah Calendar. The rest of the book is new.

Photo: Stone Sundial from Qumran site. The Qumran community were the keepers of the Biblical calendar based on the sun and the canon of scripture according to the decrees from Yacob and Moses.

Several other books were found among these scrolls which must be considered and tested. We will even discuss the possibility of 1st and 2nd Esdras included as well. Clearly important among that community of Levite priests, this tells us much as the Temple Levites were the keepers of scripture. Yacob entrusted Levi with this role in Jubilees 45:16 and Moses authorized these same Aaronic Levites in Deuteronomy 31:24-26 to do the same. If one truly wanted to know what books were and were not included in the Bible canon at the time of Messiah, they need not look far as this preserved the Old Testament canon of scripture up until His time. There were no books yet, just scroll libraries like the one found in Qumran.

Some attempt to force the books in the Septuagint that can be a useful publishing indeed in comparison but never as a standalone text as inerrant scripture. In fact, it too was a scroll library created in Egypt and the Aaronic Levites were not in Egypt at that time. They were in the Temple where they should be soon to be driven out into the Wilderness of Yahudea. They would take their Bible, scroll library in that time, with them. This was rediscovered in 1947 and immediately the Catholic Church and Pharisees moved to redefine the Bible that was found to protect the fraud they perpetrated in those days and since. The sect that created the Septuagint Greek translation in Egypt were not Aaronic Levite priests. These were Essenes in their attempt to hijack scripture which they would later write what they would call scripture in the Gnostic Gospels also found in Egypt. Not one Gnostic Gospel was found in Qumran nor do they coalesce with the New nor Old Testaments.

Essene is a name not found in the Bible even in the Greek Septuagint version demonstrating that cult has nothing to do with the Bible. The Qumran community never uses it nor anything similar. It is derived from the writings of Pliny, Josephus and others as ESSENOI, or ESSAIOI. As this is not a Bible word, we must go to an occult source to learn this originates in Egypt. In 2007, the Rosicrucian Digest weighs in on this.

> *Origins of the Word "Essene"*
> *The word truly comes from the Egyptian word kashai, which means "secret." And there is a Jewish word of similar sound, chsahi, meaning "secret" or "silent"; and this word would naturally be translated into essaios or "Essene," denoting "secret" or "mystic." Even Josephus found that the Egyptian symbols of light and truth are represented by the word choshen, which transliterates into the Greek as essen. Historical references have been found also wherein the priests of the ancient temples of Ephesus bore the name of Essene. A branch of the organization established by the Greeks translated the word Essene as being derived from the Syrian word asaya, meaning "physician," into the Greek word therapeutes, having the same meaning. [9]*

Again, this is an occult source and they take credit for the Essenes as a secret cult of sorcerers. To them, that is a good thing where those of us believers know better. However, what they do not connect is the "chsahi" *(kashaph: כָּשַׁף: H3784)* were the sorcerers and magicians in which Moses and Aaron faced in Egypt*(Ex. 7:11)*. Some of them exited Egypt in the Exodus and settled in Ein Gedi in ancient times and not Qumran. Pliny notes they are a very ancient cult. This same sorcery and witchcraft is recorded in Canaan*(Dt. 18:10)*, in Israel*(2 Chr. 33:6)* and even in Babylon*(Dan. 2:2)*. It is the enemy of the Bible.

Some even further connect this Aramaic word "asaya" as the origin of the word Hasmonean. These are the conquerors of the Temple in 165 B.C. who exiled the Levite Temple priest system who are rebuked by their Qumran community as the "sons of darkness." What a world in which we live. This word is the origin of the Hasidim or Hasidic Jews of today. They are Essenes. The breakdown of the factions still exists as Rabbinic Judaism generally are Pharisees essentially with a sect of Hasidim, Essenes. Sure, they call themselves pious but they do not even remotely know the relationship of Torah. This is why we find them referring to their god as Hashem. This name is a variant of Ashima, the god of the Samaritans from whom they originate. Who would replace the name of Yahuah 6,800+ times with Lord or Ba'al in Hebrew? These Samaritans would. Any attempt to associate them with Messiah and John the Baptist is ridiculous. We were warned in the end times evil would be called good and good, evil.

One of the main reasons employed by many is this assumption that Essenes lived in Qumran which they never did. Attempts are even exercised claiming Jesus*(Yahusha)* and John believed in resurrection and somehow that is supposed to be equated to the reincarnation doctrine of the Essenes which is among the most illiterate of positions. The two doctrines are opposites as are the Essenes from the Qumran community. In fact, human spirits cannot reincarnate. The only spirits who do are demons or spirits of Nephilim when they die. They wander the dry places and when invited, they can enter a human and possess it or even an animal as Messiah cast demons into swine. Reincarnation is literally a doctrine of demons as only they reincarnate possessing the body of another.

Essenes originated from Egypt, though perhaps truly Mesopotamian origins ultimately thus the Aramaic, where they were known as physicians or alchemists of sort. There, they were called the Therapeutae in Greek. In Biblical terms they were sorcerers such as the false prophet identified as from Yahudea, Barjesus, an Essene*(Acts 13:6)*, the "child of the devil" according to Paul, Elymus*(Acts 13:8)* and the bewitching Simon the sorcerer*(Acts 8:9)*. In Greek, Paul calls this pharmakeía*(φαρμακεία: G5331)* meaning medication *("pharmacy")*, i.e. *(by extension)* magic *(literally or figuratively)*:—sorcery, witchcraft."

Revelation tells us this is the end times deception in fact playing out as "by thy sorceries were all nations deceived"*(Rv. 18:23)*. This same sorcery is exactly what has happened with this entire narrative. Only a fool would claim Essenes lived in Qumran with no evidence, writings identifying themselves as Levites and incredibly significant Essene finds 25 miles South in Ein Gedi matching Pliny's directions to their headquarters. No scholar could logically draw such conclusion yet the mantra is vast. This false story permeates Judaism(Pharisaism according to the Jewish Encyclopedia) and those who manage the Rockefeller-funded museum doling out the idiotic control line. The church has bought this especially in seminaries. It is a lie.

The other list of Bible canon immediately thrown out there is that of Josephus who propagated a closed canon according to him of course. Josephus was an admitted Pharisee, Hasmonean and he was Essene trained by Banus in the wilderness*(Ein Gedi) [11: The Life of Flavius Josephus]*. Realize his "closed canon" which some Christians actually cite would mean the entire New Testament is not scripture and was already rebuked as ignoring part of the law or Torah according to Messiah*(Jn. 5:46-47)* and what they did use, they turned against scripture according to Him*(Mark 7:9)*. That is an oxymoron many do not even think through. His listing of what the Pharisees considered scripture educate us all on the paradigm at the time of Messiah and shortly after when the New Testament was just written as it already censored Jubilees especially. That is no canon.

However, whom did Yacob and Moses entrust with the keeping of scripture, Torah and what we would call Bible? The Temple Levite Priests of Aaron and Josephus was not nor were the Rabbis/Pharisees or Hasidim/Essenes. We have now found this scroll library which is the only which qualifies as the Bible canon for the entire history up until the time the Temple was destroyed. The question is, whom was ever given authority to overrule these Levites? Who was given their responsibility to keep scripture? Who was given authority to overturn Messiah's endorsement of this canon as well? Certainly not Pharisees who already threw out the Book of Jubilees in the days of Messiah. Most certainly not the cowardly general, Josephus, who ordered all of his troops to commit suicide while he failed to do so himself. Josephus is useful for history and geography to a point. However, he was no authority on scripture and his list is a spouting of Pharisee doctrine rebuked by Messiah many times. Only the Levite library records canon. Any Catholic council changing that was usurping Biblical authority it never had.

This community left history and scripture behind so that we would all know just what was and was not considered canon. They even include commentaries on different books, additional prophecy especially of the war of the "sons of darkness" versus the "sons of light," hymns, calendars, etc. The Hasmoneans*(Essenes)* and their priests*(Pharisees and Sadducees)* who exiled the true Aaronic Priests from the Temple are called the "sons of darkness" as they conquered the Temple and Yahudea in 165 B.C. This battle will last until the very end times in their writings. The Temple was the center of worship in Yerusalem. Though the Second Temple no longer housed the ark of the covenant with Yahuah's presence, it still received His blessing until that time. Priestly courses continued such as that of Zacharias, father of John the Baptist, in the course of Abiyah*(Abia)* but the leadership in the Temple, in all of Yahudea and essentially the world in a spiritual sense had been usurped by these "sons of darkness." This was a fulfillment of the Psalm 83 war in which David predicted the Temple, not even built at the time of his prophecy, would be defiled by neighboring enemies in this exact sense.

For the Hasmoneans did not attack just the Greeks nor did they originate in Yahudea. They inhabited an area called Modi'in which is across the border into Dan controlled by Samaria and the Philistines. They were not Hebrews nor Israelites. They were Samaritans who were the replacements of the Northern Tribes of Israel when they were taken captive into Assyria since around 700 B.C. This is why even in Messiah's parable of the Good Samaritan*(Lk. 10:25-37)*, what was unthinkable in the paradigm of that day, was that a Samaritan could be good. These replacements were brought into the Northern Kingdom of Samaria and kept the name. They then attempted to infuse the worship of Yahuah into pagan religions of their gods Ashima*(Hashem)*, Adrammelech *(Melech/Molech/Ba'al)* and others. However, this was never a sincere gesture. It was a response to the land that had been rejecting them as they were being attacked by wolves. They brought in a Levite Priest to teach them the rituals of the Bible. Yahuah rejected this infusion *(2 Ki. 17)*.

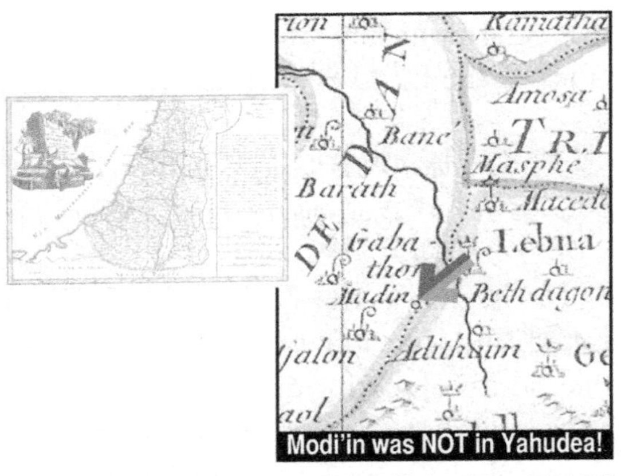

1770, Bonne Map of Israel. Rigobert Bonne 1727 – 1794. [12]

The Pharisees and Sadducees did not exist in Yerusalem until the so-called Hasmonean Revolt in 165 B.C. You will find the Books of Maccabees as well as Esther were not found among the Qumran scrolls because neither are scripture. Both are the stories of what would become Zionism today. This was predicted not only by David but identified in Revelation as Messiah discusses the Synagogue of Satan who say they are Jews and are not but do lie*(Rev. 2:9, 3:9)*. Even the term Jew is fraud and it never should be used in scripture as it is not of Ancient Hebrew,

Aramaic, Greek, Latin, Old French, Old German nor Old English origin. The name of Yahuah's people includes His own and such tribes would never remove His name from theirs. His people in the Old and New Testament are the Yahudim in Hebrew and Greek really. The shortened form of this word is Yah's never Jews as there is no "J" in any of the languages in which the Bible has been interpreted through. The first two letters are YH*(יה)* and that is Yah not Jew or Yah's not Jews. This fraud wraps into the rest of this false narrative coming from the modern Pharisees and the Catholic Church who changed scripture and attempt to cover it up.

Many do not realize that Qumran is identified in the Bible. However, Qumran is it's Muslim name oddly continued by Pharisees and modern Israel. Why would they do so when the Bible identifies this area by the name as Bethabara*(Greek)* or Betharabah*(Hebrew)*. Joshua*(Yahushua)* identifies the Western coastline of the Dead Sea geographically when he outlines a list in North to South progression of the cities of the Dead Sea wilderness.

> *Joshua 15:61-62 KJV: In the wilderness,* ***Betharabah****, Middin, and Secacah, And Nibshan, and the city of Salt, and Engedi; six cities with their villages.*

He begins in the North with Betharabah on the Northwestern tip. That is called Qumran today. Joshua continues as he heads South to Middin which is due South of Qumran, then further South all the way to Ein Gedi. He defined a 25-mile distance from North to South. Notice there are several cities between Betharabah*(Qumran)* and Ein Gedi so even if somehow Pliny meant just North instead of just above in the mountains, which is obvious, he still would not be identifying Qumran as the headquarters of the Essenes. Of course, Ein Gedi has the archaeology called "The Essene Find."

Above: Jordan. Madaba (biblical Medeba) - St. George's Church. Fragment of the oldest floor mosaic map of the Holy Land - the Jordan River and the Dead Sea. [13]

The Madaba Mosaic Map*(left)*, c. 6th century A.D., contains the oldest surviving original map of especially the Dead Sea and right on the intersection where the Jordon meets the Dead Sea, is labeled in Greek as Βηθαβαρά or Bethabara. This is right where Joshua placed it and it is modern Qumran.

The reason this is important as well is John the Baptist baptized Messiah at Bethabara. This was not some random journey into the wilderness but a visit to the very compound and library designed similar to the Temple where scripture was now kept outside of the Temple. Messiah Himself visited it more than once. Jesus*(Yahusha)* grew up and initially operated in Galilee*(Mt. 2:22)*. He came from there, headed South to beyond Jordan. The Jordan is not simply the Jordan River in scripture but the entire Jordan Plain or Jordan Valley *(Gn. 13:10)*. This does not indicate crossing the river but into the Wilderness of Yahudea at Qumran right on the border.

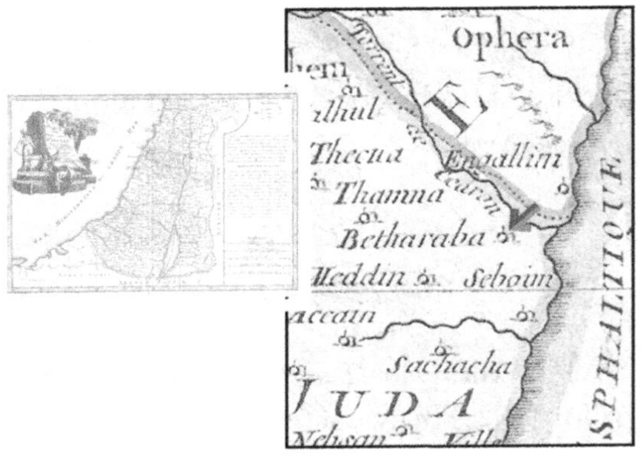

1770, Bonne Map of Israel. Rigobert Bonne 1727 – 1794 [12].

Luke 3:2-4 KJV: ...the word of God came unto John the son of Zacharias in the wilderness. And he came into all the country about Jordan, preaching the baptism of repentance for the remission of sins; As it is written in the book of the words of Esaias the prophet, saying, The voice of one crying in the wilderness, Prepare ye the way of the Lord, make his paths straight.

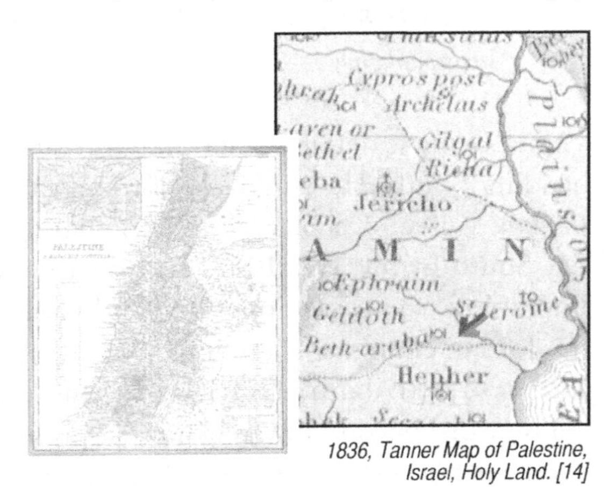

1836, Tanner Map of Palestine, Israel, Holy Land. [14]

Matthew 3 KJV 1: In those days came John the Baptist, preaching in the wilderness of Judaea...
5-6: Then went out to him Jerusalem, and all Judaea, and all the region round about Jordan, And were baptized of him in Jordan, confessing their sins.

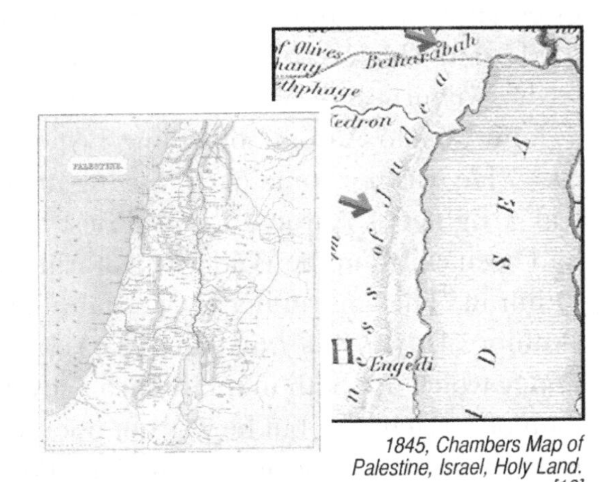

1845, Chambers Map of Palestine, Israel, Holy Land. [16]

The Wilderness of Yahudea *(Chambers Map, right)* is very specifically the area along the West coast of the Dead Sea. It is not nor ever has referred to the Jordan Plain or Valley nor River other than before

Inset of 1852, Philip Map of Palestine, Israel, Holy Land. [17]

there was a Dead Sea perhaps which was likely created by the destruction of Sodom. This has been known all along even on many maps until the 20th century *[previous page]*.

> ***Matthew 3:13 KJV:*** *Then cometh Jesus from Galilee to Jordan unto John, to be baptized of him.*

Where did Jesus *(Yahusha)* come from? Galilee. He travels South to Jordan. Where in Jordan? This verse is not specific.

> ***John 1:28 KJV:*** *These things were done in Bethabara beyond Jordan, where John was baptizing.*

Now, we have details rather than a general area. Jesus *(Yahusha)* came from Galilee heading South. He enters the Jordan Valley region and he travels "beyond" the Jordan Valley to a place called Bethabara. Where is this? The Jordan ends to the South at the Dead Sea and on the Northwest corner of the Dead Sea is Bethabara where John operated and baptized Messiah. It does not say he crossed the Jordan changing directions to go to the East. It says he travels South beyond Jordan to Bethabara. This is very clear and maps agree. This is Qumran.

The word beyond in Greek here is peran *(πέραν)* meaning "other side, beyond, over, farther side." This is where many scholars go wrong by forgetting the orientation of the region from Galilee South which does not enter the East side of the Jordan which is still the Jordan Valley. It progresses beyond the Jordan Valley to the Wilderness of Yahudea where John is said to be based. There is a reason.

John was an Aaronic bloodline Levite Priest qualified to be of High Priestly caste. He was not some hermit living under a tree eating locusts and honey. He was a righteous Aaronic Levite Priest operating in the place where his people had been exiled in the Wilderness of Yahudea in Bethabara which today is called Qumran. This forerunner to Messiah, the Elijah come again, wore camel's hair clothing *(Mt. 3:4, Mk. 1:6)* akin to sackcloth as in mourning. John ate locusts and honey which are both in the Biblical, covenant diet. He was essentially living the oath of a Rechabite but he was not poor and he did not live under a tree. He also is in no way the same as Banaah from the Talmud though attempts are made as Banaah lived 2-3 centuries later. John the Baptist was no Essene nor Pharisee nor was anyone in the Qumran community. John baptized mostly in fresh springs in clean water not the muddy waters of the Jordan River that few would desire to participate. Bethabara *(Qumran)* had fresh water. There is no disputing Qumran is Bethabara where Messiah was baptized and John and the Levites operated. This is the new location of the Temple practice where scripture was kept thus Bible.

THE ESSENES OF EIN GEDI

"On the west side of the Dead Sea, but out of range of the noxious exhalations of the coast, is the solitary tribe of the Essenes..."
"Lying below the Essenes was formerly the town of Engedi..." "Next comes Masada..." [10]
– Pliny the Elder, Natural History (Book V)

Remnants of a Chalcolithic Temple (4th millennium BCE). [18]

Pliny, a geographer, indisputably located the Essenes in the mountains overlooking Ein Gedi, 25 miles South of Qumran. He even anchors it to Masada just to the South and that is the Southern tip not near Qumran.

This is affirmed in mass scale archaeology called "The Essene Find" in Ein Gedi. This included a very ancient temple identified as a Chalcolithic Temple, c. 4th millennium B.C., which was not built by the Essenes but likely part of their compound in the mountains.

Essene synagogue in Ein Gedi. [18]

Also, archaeologists discovered a synagogue with many symbols identifying these Essenes as the secret cult throughout history fitting to everything we know about the Essenes who never lived in Qumran.

Tile mosaic on synagogue floor in Ein Gedi. [18]

They were obsessed with peacocks as they worship the Peacock Angel*(Persian)* identified by many as the Nephilim deity known as Asmodeus. They etched swastika on the wall, very prominently display an 8-pointed star of Ishtar on the floor in tile, etc. They even offer what appears a very freemasonic warning on the wall.

Peacock symbols in Ein Gedi synagogue. [18]

There is no actual coherent data placing Essenes in Qumran.

TEMPLE PRIEST ASSOCIATIONS IN THE DEAD SEA SCROLLS

The Biblical keepers of scripture and the Temple marginalized, mischaracterized, and hidden in fraud!

SONS OF ZADOK = 20 times

From the days of King Solomon, these are the Temple Priests. They are Levites and sons of Aaron both. However, they were given charge of the Temple worship and are the only Biblical keepers of scripture. They never call themselves Essenes but they identify themselves over 100 times and any scholar confusing the two is no scholar. They remained holy according to Ezekiel:

Ezekiel 48:11 KJV
It shall be for the priests that are sanctified of the sons of Zadok; which have kept my charge, which went not astray when the children of Israel went astray, as the Levites went astray.

They remained faithful when exiled from the Temple to Qumran and they will stand again in the End Times.

"The sons of Zadok are the elect of Israel, the men called by name who shall stand at the end of days."
–The Damascus Document, p. 132

Scripture was found in their library meaning this was Bible canon kept by the Sons of Zadok as was Biblical tradition. Essenes are never mentioned in scripture and never a Biblical tribe nor found in or near Qumran. That is blatant fraud!

Moses in Deuteronomy 31:25-26 KJV (Cf. Jubilees 45:16)
That Moses commanded the Levites, which bare the ark of the covenant of the LORD, saying, Take this book of the law, and put it in the side of the ark of the covenant of the LORD your God, that it may be there for a witness against thee.

SONS OF AARON = 16 times
LEVITES = 71 times
SONS OF LEVI = 5 times
SONS OF LIGHT = 27 times
TEACHER OF RIGHTEOUSNESS = 53 times

"...this concerns the Wicked Priest who pursued the Teacher of Righteousness to the house of his exile..."
-COMMENTARY ON HABAKKUK, p. 515

"the city is Jerusalem where the Wicked Priest committed abominable deeds and defiled the Temple of God. The violence done to the land..."
-COMMENTARY ON HABAKKUK, p. 515

"Words of blessing. The M[aster shall bless] the sons of Zadok the Priests, whom God has chosen to confirm His Covenant for [ever]"
- The Blessing of the High Priest, p.388

"When God engenders (the Priest-) Messiah, he shall come with them [at] the head of the whole congregation of Israel with all [his brethren, the sons] of Aaron the Priests" - The Messianic Rule, p.161

*From a search of "The Complete Dead Sea Scrolls in English" by Geza Vermes. Some are his mentions in commentary but that further affirms he knew who these were and still ignorantly concluded in fraud that these were Essenes with 0 mentions, 0 archaeology and Pliny indisputably placing them in Ein Gedi confirmed in archaeology.

ESSENES = 0 times

When groups of scholars make themselves so stupid as to say this group were Essenes, you know they are only offering propaganda.

WHO DEFILED THE SECOND TEMPLE?

The Books of Maccabees, not found in the Dead Sea Scrolls make the claim Greece defiled the Temple. That is a lie!

Greece Did NOT Defile the Temple

From the account of the Temple Priests which appears within their commentaries of prophetic interpretation of events that had already occurred in their time, they record that Greece did not defile the Temple nor even attack Yahudea with their military. This is consistent with Greek history that does not mention this Maccabees account which is not history nor Bible. This is a major problem for modern Judaism which has only this claim to link it to their being Hebrews. They are not.

"Whither the lion goes, there is the lion's cub, [with none to disturb it] (ii, 11b).
[Interpreted, this concerns Deme]trius king of Greece who sought, on the counsel of those who seek smooth things, to enter Jerusalem. [But God did not permit the city to be delivered] into the hands of the kings of Greece, from the time of Antiochus until the coming of the rulers of the Kittim. But then she shall be trampled under their feet..." –COMMENTARY ON NAHUM, p. 505

Thus, from the time of Demetrius to the time of Antiochus I including the time of Antiochus Epiphanes and until the time of the Kittim takeover which is the Roman Empire, Yahudea is not subdued with Greece's military. Even Alexander the Great was welcomed in a peaceful takeover not military conquest especially in the Temple where he even burnt the sacrifice of the Temple. Greece wanted the tax revenues and Israel agreed to that in all accounts even Josephus, Tacitus, Origen and others agree on that. However, who trampled Yahudea? Who defiled the Temple? This community did not keep that a secret...

"[For the violence done to Lebanon shall overwhelm you, and the destruction of the beasts] X II shall terrify you, because of the blood of men and the violence done to the land, the city, and all its inhabitants (ii, 17).
Interpreted, this saying concerns the Wicked Priest, inasmuch as he shall be paid the reward which he himself tendered to the Poor. For Lebanon is the Council of the Community; and the beasts are the simple of Judah who keep the Law. As he himself plotted the destruction of the Poor, so will God condemn him to destruction. And as for that which He said, Because of the blood of the city and the violence done to the land: interpreted, the city is Jerusalem where the Wicked Priest committed abominable deeds and **defiled the Temple of God**. The violence done to the land: these are the cities of Judah where he robbed the Poor of their possessions." –COMMENTARY ON HABAKKUK, p. 515

The Wicked Priest is not one man but the Hasmoneans including their priests, the Pharisees and new Sanhedrin that was new to Yerusalem and neither faction ever mentioned in the entire Old Testament as they did not exist in Yerusalem until installed by the Hasmoneans around 165 B.C. These exiled the Aaronic, Levite Temple Priest leadership of antiquity to Qumran replacing them with a new unbiblical order in Yerusalem. That is the defiling of the Temple not Greece. They conquered as they maintained control of it and changed the religion to their Samaritan infusion of Persian basis with attempted worship of YHWH that He rejected then and rejects now. This is clear and indisputable and this is actual history from the First Century ignored and untold by the church generally as they maintain willing ignorance as 2 Peter 3 warned. Who do they listen to? The very ones who defiled the Temple.

*Excerpts from "The Complete Dead Sea Scrolls in English" by Geza Vermes. One will notice multiple injections from Vermes and many scholars since of the Maccabees story as fact when these very writings of this community condemn the Hasmonean Revolt as the defiling of the Temple. That is dishonest and fraudulent!

The Maccabees Did!

THE HANUKKAH HOAX

The Feast of Dedication of modern Judaism also originates in the Books of Maccabees, yet Greece did not defile the Temple. However, worse, the Bible gives dates for the Dedication of the First and Second Temples and neither are December.

FIRST TEMPLE FEAST OF DEDICATION:

Feast of Tabernacles. 7th Hebrew Month (Ethanim)
Modern Calendar: Between Sept. 15 - Oct. 15

1 Kings 8:63, 1 Kings 8:2, 2 Chronicles 5:3

SECOND TEMPLE FEAST OF DEDICATION:

Adar 3 or 23. 12th Hebrew Month (Not December)
Modern Calendar: Between Feb. 15 - Mar. 15

Ezra 6:15-17, 1st Esdras 7:5-8 (Note: March 15 is still Winter)

The Second Temple stood until 70 A.D. Therefore, it's Feast of Dedication remained Late February to Early March. The history used to redefine this as a rededication proves to be fraud according to the Qumran community *(previous page)*. What the Maccabees did was celebrate their pagan, Persian Winter Solstice Festival and they called it Hanukkah which is the Hebrew word for dedication. However, they defiled the Temple on that date. It is a rather disgusting display in fraud. Some attempt to claim Messiah was celebrating the Hasmonean Hanukkah but that as well is a lie.

EXPOSED IN 1st ESDRAS!

Matthew 15:12-14 KJV
Then came his disciples, and said unto him, Knowest thou that the Pharisees were offended, after they heard this saying? But he answered and said, Every plant, which my heavenly Father hath not planted, shall be rooted up. Let them alone: they be blind leaders of the blind. And if the blind lead the blind, both shall fall into the ditch.

Messiah Was In The Temple In Adar (February) NOT December!

John 10:22 KJV
And it was at Jerusalem ***the feast of dedication****, and it was* ***winter****. And Yahusha walked in the Temple in Solomon's porch.*

This is consistent with the Second Temple Feast of Dedication in the Winter in Late February to Mid-March. Messiah did NOT celebrate the Hasmonean Hanukkah nor does He ever embrace their story on any level. He rebukes their priests, their religion and even their lineage. It is time we correct this for good.

Pharisee Fruits

These Fruits Match Satan's from John 10:10 not Yahusha's

"Vipers"	"Hypocrites"	"Expand the Word with Leaven"
Matt. 3:7, 12:34, 23:33 Luke 3:7	Matt. 6:2, 6:5, 15:7, 16:3, 22:18, 23:13, 14, 15, 23, 25, 27, 28, 29, 24:51 Mark 7:6 Luke 11:44, 12:56	Matt. 15:6, 16:6, 11 Mark 7:13, 8:15 Luke 12:1
"Lead People to Hell"	**"Operate Against His Commandments"**	**"Blind" "Vain"**
Matt. 23:13, 23:15, 24:51 Luke 11:52	Matt. 15:3-6, 23:4, 23 Mark 7:5-13 Rom. 2:17-20	Matt. 15:12-14, 23:16-17, 23-26 Mark 7:7 John 9:39-41 Rom. 1:21, 2:17-20
"Condemned to Hell Generally"	**"Unclean" "Self-Righteous"**	**"Murderers"**
Matt. 5:20, 23:13-15, 24:51	Matt. 6:5, 23:5, 15, 23-27, 28 Luke 7:29-30, 36-50, 18:9-14 John 8:39-59, 12:42	Matt. 12:14, 21:45-46, 23:31, 26:4 Luke 6:11, 11:47 John 8:44, 11:45-57 Acts 3:14-15, 7:52

"Pharisaism shaped the character of Judaism and the life and thought of the Jew for all the future."
–Jewish Encyclopedia [60]

According to the Bible

Why Ignore What the Bible Says to Support a False Paradigm?

"Seed/ Synagogue of Satan"	"Devour Widow's Houses/Poor"	"Pray/Give to Be Seen" "Haughty"
John 8:44 Rev. 2:9, 3:9	Matt. 23:14 Mark 12:40 Luke 7:36-50, 20:47, 21:1-6	Matt. 6:2, 5, 16, 23:5-6, 14, 17-22 Mark 12:40 Luke 11:43,16:14, 20:45-47
"Don't Know Prophecy" "Seek Signs"	**"Don't Know Scripture"**	**"Thieves" "Extort"**
Matt. 12:14-37, 16:1-4, 27:40-43 Mark 8:11-12 Luke 7:29-30, 11:29-32 John 5:18, 10:24-39	Matt. 16:6-12, 21:23-27, 22:34-46, 23:23-24 , 26:62-68 Mark 3:6; Acts 1:6 Luke 7:29-30, 22:2 17:20-21 John 5:18, 10:24-39	Matt. 21:13, 23:25 Mark 11:17 Luke 19:46
"Stand in the Way of Knowledge"	**"Accusers and Liars"**	**"Fools"**
Matt. 23:34-35 Luke 11:52, 22:2 John 12:42	Matt. 12:1-2, 13-17, 22-24, 22:15-22, Mark 3:22 Luke 6:7, 7:39, 11:53, 19:39, 20:20-26 John 8:13; Rev. 2:9	Matt. 23:17, 19 Luke 11:40, 24:25 Rom. 1:22, 2:17-20

**Pharisaism Became Rabbinic Judaism After 70 A.D.
Pharisees Are Modern Rabbis, Modern Jews.**

Who Were the Pharisees and Hasmoneans?

*Page Number in Paranthesis.

"Sons of Darkness" "Men of the Pit"	"Sons of Belial/ Satan" "Lot of Belial"	"Wicked Priests"
War Scroll, (165-182) Dam. Doc. (134, 144) 4Q548 (573) Comm. Rule (111) 4Q258 (121) Hymn 9 (265)	4Q286 (394), 4Q386 (613) Dam. Doc. (133) Temple Scroll (212) War Scroll (176) Comm. Rule (99) Hymn 7 (263)	4Q394-9 (221) 4Q448 (340) iQpHab (509-515) 4QpPsa (519)
"Defilers of the Temple"	**"Theives" "Rob the Poor" "Prey on Widows"**	**"Unclean"**
iQpHab (513, 515) Dam. Doc. (133, 137, 148) 4Q174 (525) Temple Scroll (212)	iQpHab (509-515) Dam. Doc. (134) 4Q163 (499) Hymn 13 (273) Comm. Rule (113)	iQpHab (513) 4Q174 (525) Dam. Doc. (133-134) 4Q286 (394)
"Vain"	**"Strangers" "Men of Perdition"**	**"Flouters of the Law"** *(Disregard, Despise)*
iQpHab (514) Dam. Doc. (134) 4Q174 (526) Comm. Rule (103, 119) War Scroll (171, 176) Hymn 14 (276)	4Q174 (525) 4Q501 (328) Comm. Rule (113) 4Q 171 (522)	iQpHab (509-512) Dam. Doc. (133) 4Q163 (499) 4Q174 (525) 11Q13 (533)

"Pharisaism shaped the character of Judaism and the life and thought of the Jew for all the future."

–Jewish Encyclopedia [60]

According to the Dead Sea Scrolls

From "The Complete Dead Sea Scrolls in English. Revised Edition" By Geza Vermes. [1]

"Liars" "Spouter of Lies"	"Those Who Seek Smooth Things"	"Scoffers"
4QpPsa (37) iQpHab (510-515) Dam. Doc. (137) 4Q 171 (519, 522) 4Q501 (328) Hymn 14 (278)	Dam. Doc. (129-130) Thanksgiving Hymns (262-269) 4Q163, (499) 4Q169, (505-7) 4Q177, (536)	Dam. Doc. (129, 137) iQH, 1Q36,4Q427-32 Hymn 6 (262) 4Q162 (499)
"Abomination" "House of Guilt"	**"Enemies"**	**"Oppressive" "Overbearing"**
iQpHab (511, 513) Dam. Doc. (133) 4Q175 (528) Temple Scroll (212) 4Q387 (603) 4Q389 (604)	iQpHab (514-515) Dam. Doc. (133) 4Q174 (525) War Scroll (176-177, 184) Temple Scroll (215-217)	iQpHab (509-514) 4Q448 (341) 4Q508 (383) 4Q504 (378) 4Q 171 (522)
"Unfaithful" "Rebellious"	**"Vipers, Spiders, Serpents, Dragons"**	**"Men of Violence" "Instruments of Violence"**
iQpHab (509-510, 513) Dam. Doc. (133) 4Q306 (243), 11Q13 (533) Hymn 14 (278) 4Q332 (405) Comm. Rule (99)	Dam. Doc. (133) Hymn 14 (275) Hymn 13 (273)	Hymn 14 (276, 278) Hymn 7 (263) 4Q 171 (520-522) Comm. Rule (113) iQpHab (509-515) 4Q175 (528), 4Q379 (585)

Pharisaism Became Rabbinic Judaism After 70 A.D.
Pharisees Are Modern Rabbis, Modern Jews

THE COMING OF MESSIAH IN 2ND ESDRAS

The Book of 2nd Esdras especially contains a massive amount of Revelation-style prophecy that we highlight throughout. However, as it deals with The Creation to the time of Messiah all the way to the End Times, this prophetic book precedes and becomes the origin of many of the concepts of Revelation and the New Testament. John saw a vision and it matched what he already read in 2nd Esdras in large detail. For Ezra knew when Messiah would arrive and even His name.

> *7:28 For **my son YAHUSHA** shall be revealed with those that be with him, and they that remain shall rejoice **within four hundred years**.*

Ezra lived about 400 B.C. which places the coming of Messiah's birth around 0 B.C. which is the most accurate prophecy of such. He, then, tells us His name would be called Yahusha. Again, this is a problem for Judaism who would then have to produce a Messiah named Yahusha in that era of which they have none. This is why this book was censored by them and they remain ignorant of it's concepts as well as the Only Messiah named Yahusha whom they rejected.

Then, Ezra further identifies Messiah's death that all men may have life. We know this well from the New Testament and some prophesies of the Old but this is exact and specific like no other. Ezra, the Prophet, knew these things.

> *7:29 After these years shall **my son Messiah die, and all men that have life**.*

Ezra saw the vision of Messiah, then, ascending into Heaven as well as His Second Coming. This, too, is a major conundrum for Judaism who cannot produce anyone.

> *13:32 And the time shall be, when these things shall come to pass, and the signs shall happen which I showed you before, and then shall **my son be declared**, whom you saw as **a man ascending**.*

Following these incredible prophesies, Esdras elaborates on the role of Messiah in His Second Coming. Once again, Judaism has nothing to offer in these regards.

> *The son of Elohim being confessed in the world... (2:47)*
> *After 7 days, the world will be raised up... (7:31)*
> *Mass resurrection of those who are asleep... (7:32)*
> *The Judgment Seat... (7:33)*
> *Evil will disappear... (7:35)*
> *The road to salvation is a narrow gate... Few are saved... (7:12-14, 8:1)*
> *The Garden of Eden and Tree of Life are opened in the end... (8:52)*
> *He is not willing that any should perish... (8:59)*
> *The signs of the end times and origin of Matthew 24 in part... (9:1-7)*
> *The Lion of Yahudah will consume the Final Empire... (11:36-46)*
> *Consuming His enemies with fire from His mouth... (13:10-11)*
> *The Lost Tribes return... (13)*
> *Every eye shall see Him... (13:52)*
> *Handing out crowns and giving palms... (2:45)*

The transition from the Old Testament to the New is fully defined in Esdras and the Qumran/Bethabara community of exiled Temple Levite Priests. There is no gap and Revelation is not a book of new concepts but originates largely in theology from Esdras. Messiah is all over these books and yet we are taught not to read them. This is what we call Dark Age Theology. Anyone who ever tells you, you cannot read something is teaching censorship not discernment. The church or really, ekklesia in the Bible, is to teach discernment instead and we are all to prove all things *(1 Th. 5:21)* for ourselves. Messiah begins His discourse in Matthew 24 with *"Take heed that no man deceive you..."* and He, then, lays out the end that Ezra defined 400 years earlier. Our Torah Test will vet this date and content.

PRECISE PROPHECY REVEALED 400 YEARS BEFORE HIS BIRTH?

JOHN THE BAPTIST IN QUMRAN? He Likely Grew Up There *(Luke 1:80)*

John's Rare Diet found there

"You may eat [the following] flying [insects]: every kind of great locust, every kind of long-headed locust, every kind of green locust, and every kind of desert locust."
–The Temple Scroll, P. 207

"And as for locusts, according to their various kinds they shall plunge them alive into fire or water, for this is what their nature requires."
–The Damascus Document, P. 143

Prophecy of John Blessing Messiah

The Blessing of the Prince of the Congregation (100 B.C.) [56]

"The ***Master (John the Baptist) shall bless the Prince of the Congregation (Yahusha)*** . . . and shall ***renew for him the Covenant of the Community*** that he may establish the ***kingdom of His people for ever***, [that he may **judge the poor** with righteousness and] **dispense justice** with {equity to the oppressed} of the land, and that he may walk perfectly before Him in all the ways [of truth], and that ***he may establish His holy Covenant*** at the time of the affliction of those who seek God. May the Lord raise you up to everlasting heights, and as a fortified tower upon a high wall! [May you ***smite the peoples***] with the might of your hand and ravage the earth with ***your sceptre***; may you ***bring death to the ungodly with the breath of your lips***! ...The ***rulers ... [and all the kings of the] nations shall serve you***. He shall strengthen you with ***His holy Name*** and you shall be ***as a [lion***; and you shall not lie down until you have devoured the] prey which naught shall deliver"

–Calendars, Liturgies and Prayers, p. 389-390.

Prepare the Way in the Wilderness...

Zacharias' prophecy at John's birth: *Luke 1:79*

"To Give Light..."

Qumran Identification:

"Sons of Light"

John baptized Yahusha in Qumran/ Bethabara fulfilling these 2 Qumran prophesies and Isaiah. These exiled Temple Priests knew their community would play such a role. This is the link between the Old and New Testaments.

And when these become members of the Community in Israel according to all these rules, they shall separate from the habitation of unjust men and shall go into the wilderness to prepare there the way of Him; as it is written, Prepare in the wilderness the way of..., make straight in the desert a path for our God (Isa. xl, 3). This (path) is the study of the Law which He commanded by the hand of Moses, that they may do according to all that has been revealed from age to age, and as the Prophets have revealed by His Holy Spirit.
–The Community Rule, P. 109.

Are 1st and 2nd Esdras Scripture, Inspired and Canon?

Criteria set forth by Blue Letter Bible with our additions. [1]

1. Prophetic Authorship

"For a book to be considered canonical, it must have been written by a prophet or apostle or by one who had a special relationship to such (Mark to Peter, Luke to Paul). Only those who had witnessed the events or had recorded eyewitness testimony could have their writings considered as Holy Scripture."

2. Witness of the Spirit

"The appeal to the inner witness of the Holy Spirit was also made to aid the people in understanding which books belonged in the canon and which did not." BLB quotes Pinnock who claims the canon is a matter of "historical process" (Clark Pinnock, Biblical Revelation, Grand Rapids: Baker Book House, 1973, p. 104). [2] We would agree but Pinnock ignores the most obvious such history. The Levite Library or Bible canon found in Qumran serves as a time capsule for the Old Testament canon long before the Catholic Church nor councils. Every book in the modern Old Testament canon was found there except Esther. It is Levite Priests who were the keepers of scripture and the Qumran community identifies as such over 100 times. We will examine certain fragments in Qumran that place 1st and 2nd Esdras there at least in "Proto" form and used for interpretation of prophecy.

3. Acceptance

"The final test is the acceptance of the people of God." BLB notes this is to accept Jesus and the Apostles which we agree for New Testament but this would also be to accept His people in the time of Ezra which is the return of Southern Israel especially. 2nd Esdras still prophesies of Messiah though and serves to bridge the gap between the Old and New Testaments.

4. Quoted As Doctrine In Scripture (Our Addition)

Our added test in which we will apply to Esdras will assess whether or not these books are quoted in scripture for significant doctrine. This is not some arbitrary word or phrase but does doctrine derive from these two books which one does not find specifically in other Old Testament writings? This is the ultimate exam. As 1st Esdras charts much like Ezra and Nehemiah already matching, we will fully vet 2nd Esdras on this point.

5. In Agreement With the Whole of Scripture (Our Addition)

Does it agree with scripture in whole? Even the Gospels have minor details to iron out in understanding, but how do 1st and 2nd Esdras compare? The conclusion may surprise many.

1. Prophetic Authorship: Who Wrote 1st and 2nd Esdras and When?

1st and 2nd Esdras both identify their writer as the Prophet Ezra, or in Latin Esdras as an eyewitness or relating a fairly recent era in his time around 400 B.C. It does not do so in speculation but even identifies the exact Ezra to whom it refers with detailed lineage. In modern scholarly circles, many hold to the paradigm that somehow those in Qumran just wrote whatever they wanted and called it scripture claiming they wrote in the name of a prophet in fraud. The fact that they do not even realize they are undermining the actual Levite Temple Priests who cared for and curated scripture with their very lives, demonstrates the paradigm is illiterate of the Biblical keepers of scripture up until the time of Messiah. They did not write scripture arbitrarily, they kept it copying it over for many centuries in order to preserve it.

The prophet would typically employ the assistance of a Levite scribe to write his words down but they did not just make up whatever they wanted nor add to it nor wait centuries to write. That is not established and irresponsible. It is certainly not scholarly to claim they just made up texts and attributed them to the prophets just because they wanted to teach the people a lesson. This would undermine their authority in every sense and such practice is not recorded anywhere among the Temple Priests nor would it be acceptable in any sense then nor today. It is unthinkable anyone calling themselves a scholar would even enter such false paradigm.

This demonstrates a disrespect from the scholarly community for scripture and it's writers and keepers. If a text says Ezra or Moses wrote it, then, either they wrote it, at most with the assistance of a scribe, or the whole thing is a lie. If it is a lie, then there is little to be learned from it. This vets very easily by merely reading the content as such research will reveal whether the writing offers truth or not. Notice, you will not learn this from reading a blog and scoffing. Does it align with scripture? Is it quoted in scripture? As we executed with The Book of Jubilees, it is time to apply The Torah Test to 1st and 2nd Esdras. Many may be surprised at what we find.

The Qumran/Bethabara exiled Temple Priests are the only documented source for scripture as to what was in the Old Testament and what was not up until the time of Messiah. Anything found there should be assessed with literacy and not by such scoffers. Anything not found there, should also be examined as to whether it should even qualify as scripture. Every book of the Old Testament canon was found in Qumran with the exception of Esther which tells us much. Esther must be examined as well. Notice too, Maccabees of similar Zionist tone to Esther also was not found among these Temple Priests. These are questionable and must be vetted. This is not a new thought. We will show you Martin Luther's comments on this topic.

Ezra wrote these two books that bear his name as they not only test as scripture in theme and content but they are quoted in the New Testament and by Messiah Himself.

In fact, the Original, Authorized 1611 King James Version even anchors Messiah's words to 2nd Esdras that we will cover. We had a pastor argue on this even sending us the page from his copy of the 1611 KJV, of course, with the margin note cut off. We then produced the 1611 King James itself from King James Bible Online to reveal the margin note which is firmly anchored to 2nd Esdras as the origin of Messiah's words also showing where he cut the page off. However, Yahusha did not only quote 2nd Esdras once but many times and the themes are an obvious match for anyone who knows scripture. We will fully vet this.

2. Witness of the Spirit: The Historical Process

In modern times, there are Bibles that maintain 1st and 2nd Esdras in their publishing. As we mentioned in our Foreward, these books were also published in the 1560 Geneva Bible and the Original, Authorized 1611 King James Version. The KJV translators even anchor Messiah's words in one instance as originating from 2nd Esdras which we will cover. However, how is it that 1st and 2nd Esdras were included in the Bible Canon as Apocrypha over such a long period when many other books, even some found in the Dead Sea Scrolls, were omitted? Unfortunately, most view all things history through the lens of only a Western perspective when no Bible writer was from the West.

What is telling is one of the first Christian communities in their canon, the Ethiopian Orthodox Tewahedo Biblical Canon, approximated to the 4th century, included 1st and 2nd Esdras though titles get confusing as they are listed as 1 Ezra (Ezra-Nehemiah as 1 book), 2 Ezra (1st Esdras or Ezra 3 to the Rabbis) and Ezra Sutuel (2nd Esdras or Ezra 4 to the Rabbis). Even the Codex Vaticanus and Codex Sinaiticus both of the 4th Century as well as the Codex Alexandrinus of the 5th century included 1st Esdras (labeled as 3 Esdras or Ezra 3 and some Ezra 2 but all are 1st Esdras). Also, though not included in Jerome's original Vulgate, the Latin Vulgate includes 1st and 2nd Esdras since the 9th century or so.

However, copies of the Greek Septuagint also include 1st Esdras (Esdras A) as well as Ezra-Nehemiah as one book (Esdras B). This publishing originated in Egypt around 300- 200 B.C. or so but few fragments have been found from that era thus we do not know whether 1st Esdras was included that far back. Many have made such assumption with Maccabees having it published before the events of Maccabees even occurred and they do not seem to realize many times. It is probable that 1st Esdras was included in the original publishing and there is no evidence to the contrary.

Then, we have the Dead Sea Scrolls which list does not appear to include 1st nor 2nd Esdras (Ezra 3 and 4). However, deeper study reveals that may not be the case. We believe a connection can be made.

1st Esdras in the Dead Sea Scrolls?

In the Dead Sea Scrolls, we find what appears misrepresentation on yet another topic from those controlling these narratives. We already found they defrauded Essenes into the story in illiterate fashion in which they should be embarrassed. Not a single reference is found to the Essenes in any literature in Qumran but they call themselves Aaronic Levite priests, the sons of Aaron, the sons of Zadok, the very Temple Priests exiled by the Pharisees (modern Rabbis) who control the illiterate narrative today. There is no archaeology, not one piece, and no history supporting Qumran as the Essene Headquarters but both "The Essene Find" in archaeology and the historic placement by Pliny, the only one to do so, located them in Ein Gedi 25 miles South not Qumran.

Worse, Qumran is a new Muslim name and shouldn't Israel be restoring the Biblical name of this area? We prove in the Introduction of this book that Qumran has an ancient name on the Oldest Map of Israel, the Madaba Tile Map showing Bethabara as Qumran supported by several maps over the centuries all the way up until 1901. But somehow between 1901 and 1947, the name was lost and forgotten in willing ignorance. In fact, Messiah was baptized there in freshwater springs and go to Israel and they'll take you to the muddy, nasty Jordan River to baptize you in error. Certainly, they are laughing in the back room. These Pharisees are cunning though this is incredibly inept and uneducated and again very embarrassing for those calling themselves scholars to make themselves so stupid, but they have fooled us indeed. No longer.

Are we sure, then, that 1st and 2 Esdras were not found among the Dead Sea Scrolls? Are they even looking for it since these are not in their interest? Let's take a good look at these so-labeled "Proto-Esther" fragments from the Dead Sea Scrolls, of which there are two. See, Esther was the only text of the modern Old Testament canon which was not found in Qumran/Bethabara in this library of the Temple Priests. Those were the keepers of scripture and they kept the Bible of that time which did not include Esther nor it's festival and that is quite damning. It was simply not there. This is the historic catalogue of the true Old Testament and again all texts were found there except Esther. Then, several books were found that have continued throughout the ages just not in the Pharisee canon which is an impertinent paradigm as they are not the keepers of canon.

First, the so-labeled Proto-Esther[d] fragment reads:

> *"The **Most High** whom you (Jews) fear and worship rules o[ver the whole e]arth. Everyone whom He wishes (comes) near. **Bagasro** ... Whoever speaks an evil word against **Bagasro** [will be] put to death for there is no-o[ne to destroy h]is good for [e]ver..."*
> *–Proto-Esther[d], p. 620 [49]*

Let us begin with the Most High title for the Elohim of Yahudea. Esther never mentions that title once. However, King Darius himself uses this title "Most High" to refer to Yahuah in 1st Esdras in a similar decree more fitting to this fragment.

> ***1 Esdras 6:31-33***
> ***(Darius refers to Yahudea's God As "Most High." Esther does not.)***
> *That offerings may be made to the* ***Most High*** *Elohim, for the king (Darius) and for his children, and that they may pray for their lives. And he commanded, that whosoever should transgress, yes, or make light of any thing afore spoken or written, out of his own house should a tree be taken, and he thereon be hanged, and all his goods seized for the king. 33* ***Yahuah therefore whose Name is there called upon, utterly destroy every king and nation,*** *that stretches out his hand to hinder or damage that house of Yahuah in Yerusalem.* ***I Darius the king*** *have ordained, that according unto these things it be done with diligence.*

The "Most High" as the reference to Yahuah is used regularly, 29 times, throughout 1st and 2nd Esdras and in this case by Darius himself as a well-established precedent matching the fragment as this is a decree from a king. It is never used even once in the Book of Esther nor is Yahuah used even once nor is there a single reference to Him in any of Esther. We do not find Esther giving Yahuah credit for any of her story and even the fasting portion is also a pagan practice of the Persians that does not specifically even identify which religion she even represented. Her entire story is one of a supposed Jewess who slept her way to gaining influence as a concubine not a Queen initially, which is also greatly misrepresented in the recent movie "One Night With the King" retelling Esther based on these fragments claiming Esther just read to the King. No, she slept with him and the reading of the law he requests much later not on the evening in which he slept with her outside of marriage. This fragment appears to be stretched away from 1st Esdras where it is far more likely a match to that story than that of Esther.

In fact, those wishing to try to force this fragment as Artaxerxes' era in the time of Ezra and Esther both, in Esther no one ever uses Most High but in 1st Esdras, even Artaxerxes himself uses Most High for Yahuah for that matter. He was fully aware of this people, their laws, and their God yet we find the writer of Esther clearly was not. Esther misrepresents all three and demonstrates a complete ignorance of Yahuah, scripture and both Biblical and Persian history. It is difficult to imagine how anyone would defend a book clearly not Bible in any sense and very obviously of Pharisee origin as it was not kept by the Temple Priests in Qumran nor the New Testament thus it was not in the Bible. Only Pharisees propagated it which appears to originate with Josephus at the end of the 1st century. Maybe he wrote that fiction. Certainly, no prophet nor Biblical scribe did.

1 Esdras 8:19 -21
And I, king Artaxerxes, have also commanded the keepers of the treasures in Syria and Phoenicia, that whatsoever Ezra the priest, and the reader of the law of the ***Most High*** *Elohim shall send for, they should give to him with speed, 20 To the sum of an hundred talents of silver: likewise also of wheat even to an hundred cors, and an hundred pieces of wine, and other things in abundance. Let all things be performed after the law of Elohim diligently unto the* ***Most High*** *Elohim, that wrath come not upon the kingdom of the King and his sons.*

How is it that King Artaxerxes, the Persian king, knew "Most High" for Yahuah yet Esther cannot seem to pray to Him, give Him credit, nor acknowledge Him? Is this not supposed to be scripture? She is clearly applying Pharisee/Samaritan doctrine especially not pronouncing nor even mentioning YHWH. This also disproves that the Yahudim were being persecuted in a nation which protected them by royal decree even for at least three generations. Artaxerxes did not proclaim such and then turn around and set up a mafia scandal to take back from the Yahudim in which he freed and his father even renewed such pledge assisting them to complete the Second Temple even. Artaxerxes decreed the final migration of the return of the Lost Tribes which occurred the same year before Esther even entered his palace in her story. He favored Ezra and gave him all of his requests including a mandate to restore the law of Yahuah not just in Yerusalem but in Syria and Phoenicia (Samaria). However, we are then to believe he forgot what a Hebrew was, forgot he committed even significant financial resources to them specifically to restore Yah's law only to turn against them in ignorance because some advisor hated Jews. Note that is not even a Hebrew word being forced into scripture in fraud as it is Yahudim or Yah's for short, never Jews except in Yiddish infusion changing the language of the Bible.

The incredible leap over planets into another universe by scholars claiming Bagasro must be Mordecai, Esther's Uncle, fails any test of logic. There is no such etymology nor association in name. Certainly, Mordecai was protected and such warning was given in Esther. However, the assumption that represents the only time such warning occurs even in Persia by that king is erroneous. In 1st Esdras, there is a very similar relationship with Zerubabel and King Darius in which a similar declaration is made. Three bodyguards of the king enter into a contest in which the winner will be given in reward royal robes, protected by the king, given from the treasury even, etc. The winner is Zerubabel and he received an edict of overwhelming support in a true Bible story returning to Yerusalem to continue construction on the Second Temple with the second wave of Southern Kingdom Lost Tribes.

In assessing the different names especially in the Latin, it is not rare for 1st or 2nd Esdras to render names even in the 1611 King James Version somewhat scrambled and backwards in letters. Having reconciled such throughout these books, we have found that often. Zerubbabel: ZRBBL (לֶבָּבֻרְז: 2216) has much more affinity to BGSR (Bagasro) than does Mordecai: MRDKY (יַכֳּדְרָמ). Mordecai has 1 letter in common with Bagasro and yet, Zerubbabel has 75% of Bagasro's same letters.

Both men, Mordecai from Esther and Zerubbabel from 1st Esdras were honored and protected by the Persian king with royal decrees with penalty of death for those who oppose them. Again, this is not exclusive to Esther nor does Esther fit. Darius elevates Zerubabel to family as the status of a cousin.

> ***1 Esdras 4:42 (King Darius to Zerubbabel)***
> *42 Then said the king unto him,* ***Ask what you will****, more than is appointed in the writing, and we will give it to you, because you are found wisest, and you shall sit next to me, and shall be called* ***my cousin****.*
> ***1 Esdras 6:32 (Darius in Protection of Zerubbabel and Yahudea)***
> *32 And he (Darius) commanded, that whosoever should transgress, yes, or make light of any thing afore spoken or written, out of his own house should a tree be taken, and he thereon be hanged, and all his goods seized for the king.*

Therefore, our first fragment, Proto-Esther[d], should be retitled as Proto-1st Esdras as that is a far better match. The second fragment has a bit more detail but really has similar issues as it too appears a telling of the 1st Esdras account not Esther. Right from the beginning, it has massive problems for Esther that is a ludicrous guess from one who seems unaware of the basic storyline of Esther nor the Greek language nor Persian history.

> *"... [and they li]sten to Patireza, your father ..." –4QProto-Esther[a], p. 619 [48]*

Somehow, it is assumed that only Esther is the E-Z-A here ignoring the rest of the word even. We have a very well known title in the word in which scholars well know and ignore in claiming such. Well, she is not a father and her father's name was not Patireza thus no match. The Book of Esther records her father's name as Abihail *(Est. 2:15, 9:29)*. So the mention of this name as someone's father, a name never mentioned in any scripture for anyone for that matter does not lead to Esther but proves this is not about Esther at least this portion definitively. So who could Patireza be?

Those claiming Patireza could be Esther are not linguists or certainly not acting like it. This is of Greek origin and the word Pater with an "E" not an "I" simply means "father" used hundreds of times in Greek translations including the New Testament. What remains... Eza. E-Z-A cannot be Esther but far more likely Ezra and the first part demonstrates this. Pater is also the name for a Priest in Persia as Catholicism's "Father" originates there from Mithraism not the Bible which rebukes that title in fact in the New Testament. It was one of the 7 grades of initiates in Mithraism in fact. [57] The Mithraic Pater Patrum was the high priest in Persia as well thus the title was for a Priest. [58] However, in Ezra's days, he was a Priest of Yahuah but in service of the King of Persia before returning to Yerusalem. The king knew him and he found favor with the king who even refers to him as Priest Ezra. In other words, Pater Ezra (EZA) makes perfect sense. Pater Esther is nonsense. She was no father nor a priest but a concubine whose story doesn't even have a Biblical foundation in any sense as her God is never even identified. A secular story that somehow was included in canons which follow the Pharisees not the Biblical historical tradition. One would think this obvious.

> *"...and amid the officials of the royal apparel..." –4QProto-Esther[a], p. 619 [48]*

Though Esther says "that Esther put on her royal apparel" *(Est. 5:1)*, and Mordecai is later paraded in "royal apparel" this fragment says the officials of royal apparel not Esther nor Mordecai. This, again, sounds like the story in 1st Esdras of the Three Bodyguards who compete as to whom is wisest. Whoever wins will be given royal apparel for one, but they also appear before the counsel who would be arrayed in such as well and that is the context of this fragment as the officials are the one's arrayed not Esther nor Zerubbabel. Frankly, this portion tells us again, this is not specific to Esther.

> ***1 Esdras 3:4-7***
> *"Then three young men that were of the guard, that kept the kings body, spoke one to another: Let every one of us speak a sentence: he that shall overcome, and whose sentence shall seem wiser than the others, unto him shall the king Darius give great gifts, and great things in token of victory: As to be clothed in purple, to drink in gold, and to sleep upon gold, and a chariot with bridles of gold, and an head-tire of fine linen, and a chain about his neck: And he shall sit next to Darius, because of his wisdom, and shall be called, Darius his cousin.*
> ***(Darius agrees to this and more in 1st Esdras 3:13-15)***

1st Esdras presents an exact match to these fragments in which Esther fails.

> *"...to work in the service of the king in accordance with all that you have received..."*
> *–4QProto-Esther[a], p. 619 [48]*

This applies in both stories perhaps but more so in 1st Esdras than Esther. Neither is a direct quote verbatim but this is a "proto" fragment not an exact quote. For Zerubbabel in 1st Esdras, one of the King's bodyguards in his service, was a contest winner in which this makes the most sense in context. With his winnings, he would be required to still remain in the service of the King. It fits Mordecai from Esther too but not with Patireza whom cannot be Mordecai or anything else we reviewed thus far.

> *"In that hour the king could not go to sleep (literally, his spirit was stretched)"*
> *–4QProto-Esther[a], p. 619 [48]*

Though this appears in Esther's story indeed *(Est. 6:1)*, this also matches 1st Esdras which says the same as Darius could not sleep.

> ***1 Esdras 3:3***
> *"And when they ate and drank, and being satisfied were gone home,* ***then Darius the king went into his bed chamber, and slept, and soon after awakened.****"*

Thus the king could not sleep in both stories and the assumption that this detail again only exists in the Esther saga is incomplete and erroneous. 1st Esdras also fits this fragment as well as the first especially Patireza (Priest Ezra) where Esther already failed.

The remaining portion of this fragment attributed to Esther does no more to bolster the case for Esther which already fails and here it falls flat on it's face. This also coalesces with 1st Esdras. Scholars insert portions into this fragment in assumption as well which we feel are likely inaccurate but anyone claiming this represents Esther is ignoring the story completely. They don't even know it. King Artaxerxes never calls for his father's scrolls in Esther. He calls for his own law from recent years and discovers Mordecai's reporting his attempted assassination during his own administration. How can that be missed by someone calling themselves a scholar?

> *"[and he commanded that the b]ooks of his father be read before him. And among the books there was a scroll [the mou]th of which [was] s[ealed] with seven seals by the signet-ring of his father Darius the heading of which ... [Dar]ius the king to the officials of the kingdom, Peace. It was opened and read and in it was found: [... Dar]ius the King to the kings who will reign after me and to the officials of the kingdom, Pe[ac]e. It should be known to you that every tormentor and liar..." –4QProto-Esther[a], p. 619 [48]*

This is not Esther. In the story of Esther, the King seeks the scroll that he commissioned not his father's nor does he have his father's read but his own (Est. 6:1-2). He was affirming Mordecai was the one whom reported the plot against him and his response is to honor Mordecai as a result. So Esther is wrong for this no matter what.

You can see two of the three times Darius is mentioned here, the fragment is not complete nor is that clear. There is enough to determine this is not Esther and better matches Esdras. However, the very odd omissions both times in this fragment for the name of the King on the Decree here may be revealing.

It first identifies "his father Darius" which confusion arises often in all four books of Ezra really including the two in the modern canon *(Ezra and Nehemiah)*. This is a telltale sign this is Esdras as well. The Persian kings get confused in those writings as scholars have observed. However, this is far more likely Cyrus the King's decree as he is the origin of the monumental decree to rebuild the Temple in favor of the Yahudim and Darius is recorded requesting such whereas Artaxerxes is not. Only "ius or yus" appears on the fragment both times as the brackets reflect and scholars are assuming this is DARius yet that is not likely.

Then, notice the second time, who succeeded Darius, and this is telling? Xerxes did, and there is no tie in name to "ius or yus" there when it says "[...]*ius (or ...yus) the King to the kings who will reign after me*." That is not Xerxes and Artaxerxes is the next generation after that as he is grandson of Darius I and his name also does not match. However, Cyrus who made the decree and fits, handed his rule to his son Cambyses also known by his Chaldee name Ahasuerus which matches the "[...]*ius*" or yus. This is the 2nd Persian king and there is a story of an imposter who replaced him for a short time as well so it gets confusing but that imposter claimed to be Cambyses thus still the same rule in name and position. Darius I would then take rule as the third king of Persia and the Temple is completed under his rule. Darius ordered the scrolls of Cyrus be read especially concerning the Yahudim in Persia in answering a complaint from the Samaritans who hated the Temple and Yahudea and would defile it in 165 B.C. Artaxerxes orders his own law to be read and discovered a recent event from his own law not his father's. Esther cannot coalesce.

> ***1 Esdras 6:21 -22***
> *Now therefore if it seem good unto the king,* ***let search be made among the records of King Cyrus****, And if it be found, that the building of the house of Yahuah at Yerusalem has been done with the consent of King Cyrus, and if our lord the king be so minded, let him signify unto us thereof.*

> ***1 Esdras 6:23 (Affirmed in Ezra 6:1-3)***
> ***Then commanded king Darius to seek among the records at Babylon:*** *and so at Ecbatana the palace which is in the country of Media,* ***there was found a rule wherein these things were recorded.***

We believe this is Darius who sought the scrolls and not likely his grandson as it must be since the Temple was completed under his rule and a fit to Zerubbabel, who returned to Yerusalem with a decree of protection in this same manner. Those wishing to say this is Artaxerxes still fail in forcing Esther. It cannot fit but one will also find Ezra returned to Yerusalem in the 7th year of Artaxerxes, before Esther's story takes off in fact, with a royal edict as well not only for protection but ordering Syria and Phoenicia to give to the Temple project. It even includes a threat of penalty of death as does Zerubbabel's thus both eras are covered and could fit in 1st Esdras and neither would fit Esther.

It cannot be Esther in either sense as Artaxerxes was not seeking the scroll of his father, he was seeking his own scroll from his recent reign even. The scroll would not have been decreed by his father in any sense but by him. There would likely be no mention of Darius' son as 1st Esdras records that specific decree to continue Temple construction which does not have such language.

Even worse for Esther is that the timing of her story also begins with her being made queen later in this same 7th year in which Ezra already returned and with many Lost Tribes in the final mass migration. Why did Esther not return as well? Why did she along with Mordecai even remain in Persia? In fact, Artaxerxes well knew who the Jews *(Yahudim)* were, had a good relationship with them and loved Ezra in fact. He signed a decree allowing ALL of Yahudea to return before Esther was taken into his palace in her story. However, we are supposed to believe that King forget what a Hebrew was 5 years later and decided to play along with a mafia racket for money when he gave to the Temple and supported Yahudea with protection including a decree for them to restore the same law of their people that supposedly Haman now convinced him to hate. Nonsense.

The timeline is clear Cyrus decrees the Second Temple to be built. The Southern Kingdom begins to return at that time in part and they begin construction on the Second Temple. Then, the Samaritans, the true enemy of Israel who will attack them in 165 B.C. defiling the Temple, successfully petition against the rebuilding and the project is placed on hold under Cambyses (Ahasuerus) who is misunderstood as Artaxerxes, grandson of Darius I by many. He cannot be as the Temple is completed under Darius so it's construction cannot be halted under his grandson two generations after it was already built. Thus, no one needs a scholar to waive their wand here for that era, Artaxerxes in this story when Temple construction was halted, is Cambyses by his Chaldean name period both in Ezra and in 1st Esdras. He has to be. The real Artaxerxes, grandson of Darius I does not appear until later in Ezra's final return. That King is actually the same one from the story of Esther but Esther has a major challenge. We know it is firmly the same King Artaxerxes as Ezra (Esdras) as his palace was in Shushan/Susan which was not moved until the days of Darius I thus this cannot be the son of Cyrus who bore similar Chaldean name *(Est. 1:2)*. He was earlier.

We are to believe this same Artaxerxes who loved Ezra who served him as a Priest in Persia much like Daniel, had a very poor memory. He decrees for Ezra's protection and return to Yerusalem with thousands of Lost Tribes from the Southern Kingdom. He even previously clarified to Ezra ALL who wished to return there had his permission to do so. Ezra's migration in return with Lost Tribes begins in Artaxerxes' 7th year of reign in the 1st month and they arrive in the 5th month.

Ezra and the Final Wave of Yahudim Return to Yerusalem: Left Babylon: Abib (1st Month/Mar.-Apr.), 7th Year of Artaxerxes

1 Esdras 8:6-7
In the ***seventh year of the reign of king Artaxerxes, in the fifth month, (this was the king's seventh year) for they went from Babylon in the first day of the first month****, and came to Yerusalem, according to the prosperous journey which Yahuah gave them. For Ezra had very great skill, so that he omitted nothing of the Law and Commandments of Yahuah, but taught all Israel the Ordinances and Judgments.*

1 Esdras 8:9-10
King Artaxerxes *unto Ezra the Priest and reader of the Law of Yahuah, send greeting. Having determined to deal graciously, I have given order, that such of* ***the nation of the Yahudim, and of the Priests and Levites being within our Realm, as are willing and desirous, should go with you unto Yerusalem****.*

Esther's Story Beginning: Sleeps With Artaxerxes: Tebeth (10th Month/Dec.-Jan.), 7th Year of Artaxerxes (9 months later):

Esther 2:16 KJV
So ***Esther was taken unto king Ahasuerus*** *into his house royal in the* ***tenth month****, which is the month* ***Tebeth****, in the* ***seventh year of his reign****.*

Let us break this down. Ahasuerus is Artaxerxes, grandson of Darius I in this narrative for both. These are the same era of his reign even the same year, the 7th year. Ezra and the Lost Tribes leave Babylon/Persia that year in the 1st month (Abib, Mar.-Apr.). Esther's story had begun as she was in the king's harem at that time preparing to meet him. She would not be brought to the King until the 10th month (Dec.-Jan.) of the same year (7th year). However, she began such preparation one year prior.

Esther 2:12 KJV
Now when every maid's turn was come to go in to king Ahasuerus, after that she had been ***twelve months****...*

Let us not forget though that Esther was brought in as a concubine. This is not the story of a virtuous woman nor one who ever acknowledges Yahuah and his practices nor keeps such as there is no mention of Sabbath and not a single mention of YHWH even once in her entire story. Her story even adds a Feast Day of Purim which has no Biblical foundation nor track. This is not scripture nor accurate to history.

Esther 2:14 KJV

In the evening she went, and on the morrow she returned into the second house of the women, to the custody of Shaashgaz, the king's chamberlain, which kept the ***concubines****:*

Did Artaxerxes know at that point what a Hebrew was? What they looked like even? Of course he did. Did they look like Persians? Not according to scripture as they would be dark-skinned. Artaxerxes, however, would be from Japheth or white skinned as his grandfather was Darus the Mede *(Dn. 11:1)* from Media or the lineage of Madai who likely stole that land from Shem *(Jb. 10:35-36)*. It certainly is odd that the two encroachers from Jubilees Canaan and Madai continue to enter the narrative or at least the lands in which they stole *(Jb. 10:28-36)*. David was ruddy meaning "red" or medium brown *(Strong's #H122: 1 Sam. 16:12, 17:42, Lam. 4:7)* and Solomon's countenance or skin tone was medium brown as cedars *(S.Sol. 5:15, 5:10)*. Some of the Southern Kingdom were even considered black as Yahudah married a Canaanite from Ham *(1 Chr. 2:3)*, likely black, as well as having a child with Thamar of Aram *(1 Chr. 2:4)*, likely medium brown. Hebrews generally are not white in scripture and that is another false paradigm thrust upon us in willing ignorance.

Was he fully aware of who they were as a people? Not only was he aware, he decreed their return and demanded Syria and Phoenicia pay tribute to their Temple in Yerusalem even. Mordecai and Esther should no longer even be in Persia for that matter. The fact they are there if even true, demonstrates they are not worshipping Yahuah. In fact, Ezra gathered the people, "ALL them that were of the captivity" into Yerusalem. One could attempt to say this was just those who had returned perhaps but this appears to tell us that all returned at that point in that final migration. Anyone who did not was not serving Yahuah and Esther's story takes place after this.

1st Esdras 9:3-5

And there was a ***proclamation in all Jewry and Jerusalem*** *to* ***all them that were of the captivity****, that they should be* ***gathered together at Jerusalem****: And that whosoever met not there within two or three days according as the elders that bare rule appointed, their cattle should be seized to the use of the temple, and himself cast out from them that were of the captivity. And* ***in three days were all they of the tribe of Judah and Benjamin*** *gathered together at Jerusalem the twentieth day of the* ***ninth month****.*

Ezra tells them that anyone not coming to Yerusalem within 2-3 days, meaning they were already there or near, would be cast out and their cattle seized for use in the Temple. Within three days, ALL they of Yahudah and Benyamin were in Yerusalem. Again, one can attempt that this only means those who returned yet it certainly seems to reference this was the final migration and at this point, during Artaxerxes' time and before Esther was even brought into the King's Palace the first time, Yahudea already returned. In addition, the text appears to remain in that same year at this progression and this is the 9th month of the 7th year of Artaxerxes which is still a month before Esther is even taken into the King's palace in Persia if so. If this is the case, then Esther was not likely a Yahudim nor was Mordecai but likely imposters whom Ezra even identifies such usurpers of the priesthood even attempting to mix into Yahudea's return pretending to be Yahudim but they were not. That sounds like Revelation 2:9 and 3:9 in Messiah's rebuke of the synagogue of satan – Pharisees/Pharsees/Farsees/Persians.

> ***1st Esdras 5:37-39***
> ***Neither could they show their families, nor their stock, how they were of Israel***: the sons of Delaiah, the sons of Tobiah, the sons of Nekoda, six hundred fifty and two. And of the ***Priests that usurped the office of the Priesthood***, and were not found, the sons of Habaiah: the sons of Hakkoz, the sons of Yaddus, who married Agia one of the daughters of Barzillai, and was named after his name. ***And when the description of the kindred of these men was sought in the Register, and was not found, they were removed from executing the office of the Priesthood.***

However, at the very least, they were not worshipping Yahuah or they would not have remained in Persia. Also, this exposes that the masses of Yahudim supposedly in Persia at the time of Esther is also likely false as they already migrated before then. It was about 5 years later in the 12th year of Artaxerxes that Haman made his move against the "Jews" (Yahudim) who weren't even there. The story seems erroneous.

> ***1 Esdras 9:3-5***
> *And there was a proclamation in all Yahudea and Yerusalem,* ***to all them that were of the captivity****, that they should be gathered together at Yerusalem: And that* ***whosoever met not there within two or three days*** *according as the Elders that bare rule, appointed,* ***their cattle should be seized to the use of the Temple, and himself cast out from them that were of the captivity****. And in* ***three days were all they of the tribe of Yahudah and Benyamin gathered together at Yerusalem*** *the twentieth day of the ninth month.*

That is a major problem for this story in Esther which doesn't even mention YHWH nor give Him credit for anything. The fasting is a pagan practice as well thus not specific. When Ezra fasts during this same time, he is extremely clear it is to Yahuah and why. There is no question yet with Esther the absence of such is telling. Worse, they then claim that during this time, Artaxerxes forgot what a Hebrew was, forgot that portion of his kingdom and his commitment to them and decided to have them slain in a racket that this narrative proves false. The plan was hatched by Haman in mafia-style and Artaxerxes just went along in ignorance of his extensive history with the Yahudim whom he gave as did his grandfather. It makes no sense and it is out of time in sequence. This is problematic for Esther as the story is riddled with challenges as lies typically are.

> ***Esther 3:7-11 KJV***
> *In the first month, that is, the month Nisan, in the* ***twelfth year of king Ahasuerus,*** *they cast Pur, that is, the lot, before Haman from day to day, and from month to month, to the twelfth month, that is, the month Adar. And Haman said unto king Ahasuerus,* ***There is a certain people scattered abroad and dispersed among the people in all the provinces of thy kingdom;*** *and* ***their laws are diverse from all people; neither keep they the king's laws: therefore it is not for the king's profit to suffer them.*** *If it please the king, let it be written that* ***they may be destroyed:*** *and I will pay ten thousand talents of silver to the hands of those that have the charge of the business, to bring it into the king's treasuries.* ***And the king took his ring*** *from his hand, and gave it unto Haman the son of Hammedatha the Agagite, the Jews' enemy. And* ***the king said unto Haman, The silver is given to thee, the people also, to do with them as it seemeth good to thee.***

> ***1st Esdras 8:8-24 Artaxerxes' Decree***
> *Now the copy of* ***the Commission which was written from Artaxerxes the King,*** *and came to Ezra the priest and reader of the* ***Law of Yahuah,*** *is this that follows. King Artaxerxes unto Ezra the Priest and reader of the* ***Law of Yahuah,*** *send greeting. Having* ***determined to deal graciously,*** *I have given order, that such of* ***the nation of the Yahudim,*** *and of the Priests and Levites being within our Realm, as are willing and desirous,* ***should go with you unto Yerusalem. As many therefore as have a mind thereunto, let them depart with you,*** *as it has seemed good both to me, and my seven friends the counselors, That they may look unto the affairs of Yahudea and Yerusalem,* ***agreeably to that which is in the Law of Yahuah.*** *And carry the* ***gifts unto Yahuah of Israel to Yerusalem, which I and my friends have vowed,*** *and* ***all the gold and silver that in the country of Babylon can be found, to Yahuah*** *in Yerusalem, With that also which is given of the people, for the* ***Temple of Yahuah*** *their Elohim at Yerusalem: and that silver and gold may be collected for bullocks, rams and lambs, and things thereunto appertaining, To the end that they may* ***offer sacrifices unto Yahuah,*** *upon the* ***Altar of Yahuah*** *their Elohim, which is in Yerusalem. And whatsoever you and your brethren will do with the silver and gold, that do* ***according to the will of your Elohim.*** *And the* ***holy vessels of Yahuah***

> ***which are given to you****, for the use of the* ***Temple of your Elohim*** *which is in Yerusalem, you shall set before your Elohim in Yerusalem.* ***And whatsoever thing else you shall remember for the use of the Temple of your Elohim, you shall give it out of the king's treasury****. And* ***I, king Artaxerxes****, have also commanded the* ***keepers of the treasures in Syria and Phoenicia, that whatsoever Ezra the priest, and the reader of the law of the Most High Elohim shall send for, they should give to him with speed****, To the sum of an hundred talents of silver: likewise also of wheat even to an hundred cors, and an hundred pieces of wine, and other things in abundance.* ***Let all things be performed after the law of Elohim diligently unto the Most High Elohim, that wrath come not upon the kingdom of the King and his sons****. I command you also that you* ***require no tax, nor any other imposition of any of the Priests or Levites****, or holy singers, or porters, or ministers of the temple, or of any that have doings in this temple, and that* ***no man have authority to impose anything upon them****. And* ***you, Ezra, according to the wisdom of Elohim, ordain judges, and justices, that they may judge in all Syria and Phoenicia, all those that know the law of your Elohim, and those that know it not you shall teach****. And* ***whosoever shall transgress the law of your Elohim, and of the king, shall be punished diligently, whether it be by death or other punishment, by penalty of money, or by imprisonment****.*

We are to believe the same king who even decreed for Ezra to restore the law of his people which he well knew was different from Persia, forgot his commitment and edict. This is a king who blessed the Yahudim with freedom, gave them gifts, offered to the Temple, approved of their worship and especially their law, offered penalty of death for those in their area who did not keep their law which he was familiar and embraced. The same king who desired the protection of Yahuah and feared His wrath who declared that any nation that rises against the Yahudim will be destroyed, now changes his mind, loses his fear and conviction for a God he called Most High even above his Persian gods. You can now see why Esther needed to be fraudulently forced into this fragment as to admit it is 1st Esdras endorses the book which completely exposes Esther, Purim and the Pharisee paradigm as false.

However, Esther's issues are even more glaring. For instance, Esther meaning "star" is the same name as the goddess Isthar/Astarte/Ashteroth/Asherah. Some even equate this name to Ashima, the god or goddess of the Samaritans who replaced the Northern Tribes of Israel which would be likely and they were Persians/Medians/Assyrians. Modern Judaism does not worship YHWH whom they blot out but Hashem that derived from Ashima etymologically. Esther's Hebrew name is impertinent as it is a side note in the story and she does not behave as a Hebrew serving Yahuah. Ishtar as well was a consort or concubine to the gods just as Esther to the King. Ishtar's legend focuses on the 10th month of Tebeth (Dec.-Jan.) in which the modern Christmas celebration also originates just as Esther does. That is her story and her son Tammuz not Yahusha's and it is hypocritical to attempt to celebrate His birthday on the day of this sun god's birth and rebirth. There are many more such issues as this story is an occult legend retold as a Bible story including the god Marduk *(MRDKY, Mordechai)* and the goddess Ishtar *(Esther)* of Akkadian legend commemorating their lore on their timelines.

There is no Biblical value to the Book of Esther and it is not Yahuah's but that of Ishtar. Even the celebration of Purim includes a beauty contest many times which is never Biblical nor a focus on Yahuah but it fits Isthar, the goddess of fertility and sex. She was consort or concubine to the gods just as Esther was the same to the king. Even the word "Pur" in Purim means "lot" according to the Bible but that is an Akkadian word not even Persian also linked to Ishtar, the Akkadian goddess known as the Queen of Heaven rebuked three times in Jeremiah. If this were a Biblical Feast, the name would be rendered in Hebrew not Akkadian. It is no surpirse the same Samaritans, originally Persians/Medians/Babylonians/Assyrians who replaced the Northern Tribes of Israel when taken away captive, who infused their Persian gods such as Ishtar, Ashima and Molech into the worship of YHWH and who defiled the Temple in 165 B.C., found a way to insert their Persian myth into the Bible. The Catholic Church embraced this.

Many do not realize, this was not just rejected by the Qumran/Bethabara community but even by some Rabbis in that era, there is no mention of Purim nor Esther in the New Testament, the early church strongly questioned its authenticity and inspiration especially those in Turkey where the 7 ekklesias of Revelation were, and even Martin Luther wrote:

> *"I am so great an enemy to the second book of the Maccabees, and to Esther, that I wish they had not come to us at all, for they have too many heathen unnaturalities. The Jews much more esteemed the book of Esther than any of the prophets; though they were forbidden to read it before they had attained the age of thirty, by reason of the mystic matters it contains."*
> *–Martin Luther (1483-1546), Table Talk [59]*

Martin Luther knew even the Jews in the 1500s had issues with the Book of Esther being read among the youth due to mystic matters meaning there is hidden Kabbalistic meaning embedded in this book which demonstrates it is not scripture. That clarifies this is a Pharisee writing with hidden Pharisee messages to the initiated among the Pharisees. It is not for us and we need not read it. It is not scripture. However, let's be clear, she was a concubine who slept with the King prior to marriage and the story should be adults only really as the Jews of the 1500s even knew.

If the Qumran/Bethabara community embraced this story as scripture not only would it be found there with every other book of the modern Old Testament canon, but the Book of Esther sets forth a new Feast which the community rejected as it is not found on any of their extensive calendars which were discovered. Their rejection of the Feast of Purim is also a rejection of the Book of Esther and let us not forget the New Testament also rejects Purim and never once does Messiah nor any Apostle write in endorsement of Esther. We could go even deeper into this story but Esther is not found in the Dead Sea Scrolls and instead these liars have propagandized these two fragments in fraud. This needs to be addressed and the church should have caught this and addressed it long ago. However, they give this New Testament era find over to the Pharisees who defiled the Temple and defile scripture still. As long as the church listens to them, they will remain in willing ignorance. This is Proto-1st Esdras not Esther.

2nd Esdras In The Dead Sea Scrolls:

The general conclusion of those managing the Qumran narrative who are Pharisees (modern Rabbis) not Aaronic Levite Priests nor even Hebrews, is that 1st and 2nd Esdras are not found among the Qumran fragments. We have identified a sort of "Proto-1st Esdras" and now let us consider 2nd Esdras at least in mindset of the community that aligns heavily with 2nd Esdras. New information has been brought to light which one must consider in making at least a connection in thought. Then, we do the research ourselves and we find two fragments worthy of note.

> *"4 Ezra is universally acknowledged to be an apocalypse and therefore the literary genre of book is apocalyptic. However, we are convinced that an apocalypse cannot be reduced to the literary genre of apocalypse, and therefore we consider 4 Ezra to be one of the witnesses of thought in the Jewish apocalyptic tradition at the end of the 1st century. We are equally convinced that the theological ideas of the Qumran Community have their roots in an apocalyptic tradition that was flourishing in Palestine at the close of the 3rd c. B.C.E."*
> *– Studies on the Texts of the Desert of Judah, Volume: 63, 2007. [43-44]*

> *"The second factor which prompted our inquiry was the publication of the first fragments of a previously unknown Qumran composition: Second Ezekiel. As the editors of the text have noted, the similarities of this apocalypse with 4 Ezra are surprising, and a recent article has shown that in fact one of the sentences of The Epistle of Barnabas, usually considered to have originated in 4 Ezra, comes from the Second Ezekiel recovered from Qumran."*
> *– Studies on the Texts of the Desert of Judah, Volume: 63, 2007. [43]*

If nothing else, this denotes the synergy between the tenor and tone of 2nd Esdras especially and the Dead Sea Scrolls community in fact, potentially as the origin of certain texts such as what is labeled as 2 Ezekiel or at least a very similar mindset. We find such connection as not strong enough as these scholars should have completed their research before releasing speculation. We agree 2 Ezekiel has language which matches 2nd Esdras and that is not really debatable but that is not enough nor is that language as strong as other connections we have found. However, we encourage everyone to read this entire finding but unfortunately, they do not prove this out. One is left with a maybe or ammunition to scoff which is the likely intention unfortunately. If only these scholars then conducted true research seeking other fragments that may actually be a match to 2nd Esdras, then, this might be compelling. We did and we find more direct references.

Direct Proof Qumran Was Reading and Applying 2nd Esdras:

One must merely read the community writings and commentaries especially from these Aaronic Temple Priests to quickly realize they were reading and applying the prophesies of 2nd Esdras which the aforementioned scholars do perceive. One of the greatest examples of this synergy is Ezra's Prophetic Vision of the Eagle Empire, the Final Empire *(2 Esd. 11-12)*. Ezra tells us this is a continuation of Daniel's Fourth Beast thus this must be the Final Empire which Daniel describes in interpretation of the statue from Nebuchadnezzar's dream from Yahuah *(Dan. 2)* as well as the Four Beasts *(Dan. 7)*. We fully break this Eagle Empire down at the end of Chapter 11 of 2nd Esdras with diagram even identifying the three heads in the end.

In their commentary on Habakkuk, these sons of Zadok of Qumran/Bethabara clearly apply this 2nd Esdras vision in their interpretation. They were aware that the Final Empire was the Eagle associated with Rome *(the Kittim)* and really this prophecy is future even if this were written as late as 218 A.D. which is nonsense and unscientific as it says Ezra wrote it because he did. The next fragment will also prove this. It would remain prophecy and it has come to pass in large part since. That is the best measure of inspired scripture – a Prophet who was accurate as Ezra was. Even this commentary is prophetic and proves 2nd Esdras was around prior to the first century as well as it is used by Qumran/Bethabara.

Habakkuk 1:8-9 Fragment from Dead Sea Scrolls

"Their horses are swifter than leopards and fleeter than evening wolves. Their horses step forward proudly and spread their wings; they fly from afar like an eagle avid to devour. All of them come for violence; the look on their faces is like the east wind (i, 8~9a)."

Prophetic Commentary in Qumran, (0-100 A.D. or Earlier, Not A Scientific Dating)

"[Interpreted, this] concerns ***the Kittim*** *who trample the earth with their horses and beasts. They come* ***from afar****, from the* ***islands of the sea****, to devour all the peoples* ***like an eagle*** *which cannot be satisfied, and they address [all the peoples] with anger and [wrath and fury] and indignation." [53]*

Kittim = Roman Empire Which Becomes the Holy Roman Empire = Final Eagle Empire (Iron/Rome mixed with miry clay)

As this is the continuation of Daniel's Fourth Beast in more detail, this is the new Roman Empire called the Holy Roman Empire which moves it's capitals and hides it's power also possessed by a powerful demon *(Gog of Magog, Ez. 38)* who speaks from inside the body even as evidenced in Ezra's vision. There is only one final empire and it is a mixture with the Roman Empire *(miry clay mixed with the legs of iron/Rome. Dan. 2)* as it superseded it and must still remain until the end as there is no lapse of days in any of these empires. However, Daniel does not call it an Eagle and that comes from 2nd Esdras which understanding is applied here.

The Holy Roman Empire moves it's seat at least in appearance but the islands from Greece and Turkey to the rest of the Mediterranean to the British Isles as well as their coastal nations have been these power structures as these 'islands of the sea" which "come from afar" largely throughout history until today. They established such pattern from the beginning when Constantine essentially declared Turkey as the seat of the new Roman Empire. He is the origin of the Holy Roman Empire *(Final Empire)* as he established the control religion that remains the largest in the world to this day. He did so "where satan's seat is" *(Rev. 2:13)* and the synagogue of satan worked *(Rev. 2:9, 3:9)* That restored the role of Priest King, Pontifex Maximus *("greatest priest," title of the Pope also deriving from Persia not the Bible)* originating in the Nephilim Atlantis and prominent in Persian history. That role is NEVER a Biblical one and it's history is lined in blood no different from that of Mohammed who was no prophet but a warlord both better aligning with the acts of the Beast and fruits of satan as they steal, kill and destroy *(Jn. 10:10)*. This was the origin of his religion as well as he was High Priest of Mithraism, a Persian religion. Constantine was repeating the same Samaritan hijacking of Yahuah's worship infusing it with their Persian/Babylonian gods *(2 Ki. 17)* which is why Catholicism is so foreign to the Bible in practice most of the time.

One must wonder how he and his father called themselves Flavians yet were not considered such by blood. The Flavian Dynasty took power in the days of Josephus who was oddly adopted into their family taking the name Flavius Josephus. He was a Pharisee, Hasmonean and Essene-trained by his own admission. It appears likely this new brand of Flavians, who were not by blood, were the progeny of one who was adopted into the Flavian household. Perhaps this might have been an Hasomean Pharisee such as Josephus as they followed the same strategy as the replacements of the Northern Kingdom of Israel did. They were infusing the Biblical religion *(really relationship)* with their Persian gods or in this case, specifically Mithraism or sun worship found throughout Catholic dogma. It would certainly explain their obsession with forcing a Trinity, a term not found in the Bible but well-documented in Persian worship. It would also explain the elevation of the statue called Mary that is the exact image of Isis/

Semiramis/Ishtar from 500 years in archaeology worshipped *(venerated derives from the Latin word "to worship")* before Mary was born and bears a Persian image not a Hebrew. She is the ancient Queen of Heaven rebuked by Jeremiah the prophet three times *(Jr. 7:18, 44:17-19, 44:25)*. That's not Mary but a continuation of that same goddess worship.

Let us not forget Messiah pinpointed Turkey as the seat of satan's throne *(Rev. 2:13)* and from where the Synagogue of Satan *(Rev. 2:9, 3:9)* would come from and their presence as the enemy of the true ekklesia even to the end. Constantine rose from that province establishing the Final Eagle Empire now mixed with an infused religion pretending to be that of the Bible and the Nephilim government even with Nephilim bloodlines mixed into the leadership. Somehow, the church lost track of them yet they are very easy to chart in migration and they are still infiltrating the Protestant church today. This is a spiritual war verses these "Sons of Darkness" from the time the Dead Sea Scrolls were written until the end times perfectly matching Messiah's warning in Revelation 2:9 and 3:9 also in His time and to the very end times. However, there is no Book of Revelation at this time, but 2nd Esdras embodies the same message.

Who mixes with Roman Empire leadership in Daniel? It is they who "mingle themselves with the seed of men" *(Dan. 2:43)*. They are not human or there would be no "mingling of seed" but Nephilim bloodlines *(Gen. 6)*. They are not difficult to place in history as they claim blood of gods such as Poseidon in their own writings and those are the Watcher Fallen Angels who bred Nephilim with human women. Those are largely much of the world elite bloodlines today who claim divine rule by blood, a Nephilim doctrine.

Esdras even notes this Empire is presumed to have disappeared and it's true power hidden much like the Holy Roman Empire and the overarching role of Pope, as well as it's demonic presence with a voice from inside the body and not the heads. However, it remains in power to the very end when it reveals itself, Messiah rebukes it and it then disappears.

Qumran understood this and they did not write false writings which is illiterate scholarship of the inept who commit propaganda knowingly or not. 2nd Esdras is prophetic no matter the dating from the Pharisees which is erroneous and unscientific anyway as we will prove next especially. This evidence injecting Ezra's Eagle Empire in interpretation in this commentary demonstrates Qumran was reading 2nd Esdras with the same understanding and even here, their commentary remains prophetic as the Holy Roman Empire is still centuries away. This is the prophecy of the Eagle from Ezra used to interpret Habakkuk. 2nd Esdras was used by the Dead Sea Scrolls community indeed. Can we find a 2nd witness?

Fragment of John the Baptist and Messiah Quotes 2nd Esdras' Prophecy:

> ***The Blessing of the Prince of the Congregation (100 B.C.) [56]***
> "The ***Master (John the Baptist) shall bless the Prince of the Congregation (Yahusha)*** . . . and shall ***renew for him the Covenant of the Community*** that he may establish the ***kingdom of His people for ever***, [that he may **judge the poor** with righteousness and] **dispense justice** with {equity to the oppressed} of the land, and that he may walk perfectly before Him in all the ways [of truth], and that ***he may establish His holy Covenant*** at the time of the affliction of those who seek God. May the Lord raise you up to everlasting heights, and as a fortified tower upon a high wall! [May you ***smite the peoples***] with the might of your hand and ravage the earth with ***your sceptre***; may you ***bring death to the ungodly with the breath of your lips***! [May He shed upon you the spirit of counsel] and everlasting might, the spirit of knowledge and of the fear of God; may righteousness be the girdle [of your loins] and may your reins be girdled [with faithfulness]! May He make your horns of iron and your hooves of bronze; may you toss like a young bull [and trample the peoples] like the mire of the streets! For God has established you as ***the sceptre***. The ***rulers ... [and all the kings of the] nations shall serve you***. He shall strengthen you with ***His holy Name*** and you shall be ***as a [lion***; and you shall not lie down until you have devoured the] prey which naught shall deliver"
> –Calendars, Liturgies and Prayers, p. 389-390.

What did John the Baptist preach? Repentance from sin and the coming Messiah. What exactly was one to repent from? Breaking the Law of Moses and the Covenant which is the definition of sin or lawlessness and exactly what the Master who blesses Messiah does in this fragment – renews covenant with Messiah, the same covenant. Yahusha then, walks perfectly in that covenant and establishes His covenant (based on the same). John was not propagating a new law but keeping of the current Law of Moses in which he was preaching people to return. Was he wasting his time? Oddly, Messiah did the same in Matthew 5:17-20 though the church changes the definition of fulfill to include "pass away" which is illiterate. We are told it passed away yet the Bible expresses a renewal of covenant that John preached and this fragment serves to breach the gap between the Old and New Covenants in fact. Messiah represented the Covenant period – Old and New.

What did John say Messiah's purpose was? He declared: "Behold the Lamb of God, which taketh away the sin of the world" *(Jn. 1:29)*. The only way to take away lawlessness or sin is to restore the law. This is exactly what John preached and when you read the many writings of the Qumran community, this is an exact match. Yes, we are under a new covenant as Yahuah has further advanced his portion of that same covenant. You will find this same doctrine in 2nd Esdras with exclamation points as even the fire which proceeds from the mouth of Messiah that consumes the ungodly is the Law.

> ***2 Esdras 13:38***
> ...and he (Messiah) shall destroy them without labor, by the law which is like unto fire...

However, Messiah said that same covenant, every letter of it, remains until the Day of Judgment when Heaven and Earth pass thus, the New Covenant includes EVERY letter of the Old. Also, His promises to Abraham, Isaac and Yacob as well as in Daniel, Isaiah, Ezekiel and the Prophets are not complete in this age yet nor is His greatest work. It is a fallacy to claim all of His purpose was completed at the Cross. He continues to complete His work even today. How can we ignore especially Revelation?

Only Messiah fits this Prince of the Congregation as he is judge of all *(2 Esd. 12:33, 8:18, 7:33, 7:44, 7:69, 8:18, 13:37, 11:46)*. He has a kingdom established forever *(2 Esd. 9:1-8)* and He established His covenant which fits no prophet *(2 Esd. 13:38)*. Yahusha is the Scepter in prophecy *(Gn. 49:10, Nm. 24:17, Hb. 1:18)* who smites the ungodly peoples in the end *(2 Esd. 9:9-13)* and all kings will only serve Messiah and no one else *(Psalm 72:11, Is. 45:22-25, Phil. 2:10, Rom. 14:11)*. Literally, He came in the name of Yahuah *(Yahusha, Jn. 5:43)* and no one can deliver those whom He judges and condemns to Hell *(2 Esd. 7:45, 13:38)*. Only Yahusha brings death spiritually and in finality to the ungodly *(2 Esd. 13:11, 49)* and with His breath or as 2nd Esdras is being represented there, with fire from His mouth *(2 Esd. 13:4, 10, 27, 38)*. Remember, Revelation is not written yet, this is quoting 2nd Esdras in large part with a clear understanding of prophecy in general. Even the Lion Messiah is mentioned prominently in 2nd Esdras *(2 Esd. 11:37, 12:31-32)*.

We all know His forerunner, the Aaronic Priest from Qumran/Bethabara even baptizing and blessing Him right there in fact – John the Baptist. John is the Master in this fragment blessing and baptizing Messiah as this serves as evidence that John is mentioned in Qumran as well. He was from the Sons of Zadok at Qumran/Bethabara and this is well-recorded in the Gospels as he executed this prophecy. Because the Qumran community was reading 2nd Esdras' prophesies, they knew this and even that they would play such a role in fact. They also knew that Messiah was coming very soon because Esdras pinpoints a dating for Messiah's birth even. They mention Him several times. This prophetic fragment is dated to the 100 B.C. era before Messiah and John and proves to be accurate prophecy thus inspired yet it originates in the prophesies of 2nd Esdras which are inspired as well.

One will truly find even local community documents, though not scripture necessarily, in Qumran also wield inspiration in accurate interpretation such as these fragments. Qumran/Bethabara knew in the end this Messiah would consume His enemies with His breath that again Revelation is about 200 years in the future, not written yet.

Therefore, that originates from 2nd Esdras and nowhere else. Also, the mention of the lion in this same context appears to originate from 2nd Esdras Vision of the Eagle Empire. We see the Lion of Yahudah in other places of course in prophecy but in 2nd Esdras this is very specific to the Lion Messiah who rebukes and consumes that Final Eagle Empire with fire from His mouth along with all the ungodly, fitting this fragment with exactness. Nothing else really does at that time. This is specific and Qumran was reading and applying 2nd Esdras for doctrine and as this is dated 100 B.C., this serves as evidence 2nd Esdras was indeed already written prior to 100 B.C. *[J. T. Milik (DJD, I, 118 - 29)]*. Their unscientific guess in date is wrong.

Again, 1st and 2nd Esdras both say they are written by Ezra the Prophet around 400 B.C. or so when he lived. It either was or it is a lie. The Temple Priests at Qumran/ Bethabara were not liars. The Pharisees who control this narrative today are known, documented liars in scripture by the Son of Yahuah Himself and throughout these community writings found there. What they kept as scripture such as Jubilees, they did not misrepresent themselves as writing in any instance. They never pretend to be a prophet by precedence in the whole of the Old Testament unless they were a prophet. The notion is illiterate, inept and a lie from liars who approve of such false actions.

This is enough to establish 1st Esdras as the "Proto-Esther" claimed fragment, really as Proto-1st Esdras instead and 2nd Esdras at least in tone and content being quoted and used in interpretation, whether direct fragments were found or not as Dead Sea Scrolls. This connection is strong and this is why we chose to publish these two books in The Levite Bible that represents the rest of the Bible or scroll library of the only qualified community to keep scripture Biblically. They were reading and applying these two books in Qumran/Bethabara.

We firmly believe they belong in this library and it certainly affirms the thinking and content generally and specifically which we will test even further. This is why you see this continued even in Bible canons in publishing all the way through history even as late as the 1560 Geneva Bible and 1611 King James Version with yet some Bible versions continuing this practice to this very day. The historicity of 1st and 2nd Esdras is unquestionable as it has been used as inspired all along regardless of an erroneous classification of Apocrypha which is a term that originates from the Pharisees who have no authority to determine such and whose canon is impertinent. These are linked to the Dead Sea Scroll community in which scripture was kept. Pharisees are not.

3. Acceptance

Esdras not only aligns with the Old Testament view of Israel very strictly as he mourns for Yerusalem's destruction and intercedes on behalf of both the Northern and Southern Kingdom's of Israel, but the New as well. He speaks of Messiah's birth, death, ascension and Second Coming, the re-gathering, the Day of Judgment and beyond as well which gels with scripture.

1st Esdras is specific to the Old Testament and 2nd Esdras aligns with both the Old and New Testaments as the source of several New Testament concepts which we will cover next. Esdras views the end times very similar to Revelation before it was written.

2nd Esdras identifies Messiah's coming and that He is the salvation of the world for those who confess Him. *(2:47)* It tells of the End Times remnant ekklesia in very similar terms to Revelation as well as Peter and Paul but most especially of Messiah Himself in which Matthew 24 largely originates in 2nd Esdras. *(9:1-7)* It even nails Messiah's Second Coming in detail akin to Revelation as it is the likely origin of such.

> *The son of Elohim being confessed in the world... (2:47)*
> *After 7 days, the world will be raised up... (7:31)*
> *Mass resurrection of those who are asleep... (7:32)*
> *The Judgment Seat... (7:33)*
> *Evil will disappear... (7:35)*
> *The road to salvation is a narrow gate... Few are saved... (7:12-14, 8:1)*
> *The Garden of Eden and Tree of Life are opened in the end... (8:52)*
> *He is not willing that any should perish... (8:59)*
> *The signs of the end times and origin of Matthew 24 in part... (9:1-7)*
> *The Lion of Yahudah will consume the Final Empire... (11:36-46)*
> *Consuming His enemies with fire from His mouth... (13:10-11)*
> *The Lost Tribes return... (13)*
> *Every eye shall see Him... (13:52)*
> *Handing out crowns and giving palms... (2:45)*

1st and 2nd Esdras serves to fill the gap between the Old Testament and the New Testament answering tons of questions from Creation to the Second Temple to the Day of Judgment, and offering deep revelation in even still future prophecy. It also exposes Esther and Maccabees as false stories as such is affirmed in the Qumran community in detail. These books identify as inspired scripture.

4. Quoted As Doctrine In Scripture (Our Addition)

In this portion of The Torah Test, we will identify several scriptures from the New Testament in which 2nd Esdras is the likely origin. We are aware the current scholarly dating of 70-218 A.D. remains an illiterate guess as to when this book was written. No scientific dating has occurred thus they are only guessing. As we proved earlier in this test, we can find 2nd Esdras being used to interpret prophecy as early as 100 B.C. and 1st Esdras in 100 A.D. at least. There is a high likelihood 1st Esdras was in the original Septuagint of 300 B.C. or so. We covered the historicity which waxes solid.

2nd Esdras was written at the very least in 100 B.C. well before the whole of the New Testament thus any concepts we find in the New Testament for that book, proves Messiah and the Apostles were quoting it. Of course, that still is far later than the book says and once you find this vets as scripture in doctrine especially, 2nd Esdras was written when it says it was around 400 B.C. by the Prophet Ezra himself or perhaps his scribe though he originally was a scribe so certainly would not have needed one necessarily. This will affirm 2nd Esdras as inspired scripture or not. Let's begin with Messiah's words even recognized in the 1611 King James Version as originating in 2nd Esdras.

Messiah Quoted 2nd Esdras:

According to the Original, Authorized 1611 King James Version, 2nd Esdras is anchored in the Margin Note for Matthew 23:37-38 as Messiah quoting 2 Esdras 1:30-33. He certainly was as is obvious.

> ***Matthew 23:37-38***
> *O Jerusalem, Jerusalem,* ***thou that killest the prophets****, and stonest them which are sent unto thee, how often would I* ***have gathered thy children together, even as a hen gathereth her chickens under her wings****, and* ***ye would not!*** *Behold,* ***your house is left unto you desolate****.*
>
> ***2nd Esdras 1:30-33***
> ***I gathered you together, as a hen gathers her chickens under her wings****: but now, what shall I do unto you? I will cast you out from my face. When you offer unto me, I will turn my face from you: for your solemn feast days, your new Moon, and your circumcisions have I forsaken.* ***I sent unto you my servants the Prophets, whom you have taken and slain****, and torn their bodies in pieces, whose blood I will require of your hands, says Yahuah. Thus saith the Almighty Yahuah,* ***Your house is desolate****, I will cast you out, as the wind does stubble."*

This is an endorsement of 2nd Esdras as inspired scripture. Messiah Himself quoted this book. Even if you do not desire to view this as Bible, no one should reject any book quoted by Messiah for doctrine. He is the Word and there is no overcoming that. In the Second Chapter after being quoted by Messiah, 2nd Esdras offers a paragraph that becomes the root of multiple New Testament verses regarding the End Times. This is significant doctrinal application that is irrefutable. The only attempt would be the dating which we already proved 2nd Esdras being used to interpret prophecy in the Qumran scrolls over 100 years before Revelation was written.

2nd Esdras 2:10-12

Thus says Yahuah unto Ezra, Tell my people that ***I will give them the kingdom of Yerusalem****, which I would have given unto Israel. Their glory also will I take unto me, and give these the* ***everlasting Tabernacles****, which I had prepared for them.* ***They shall have the Tree of Life for an ointment of sweet savor, they shall neither labor, nor be weary****.*

2nd Esdras 2:23

Wheresover you find the dead, take them and bury them, and I will give you the first place in my resurrection.

2nd Esdras 2:31

Remember ***your children that sleep****, for* ***I shall bring them out of the sides of the earth****, and show mercy unto them: for I am merciful, says Yahuah Almighty.*

2nd Esdras 7:32

And the ***earth shall restore those that are asleep in her****, and so shall* ***the dust those that dwell in silence****, and* ***the secret places shall deliver those souls that were committed unto them****.*

2nd Esdras 8:52

For unto you is Paradise opened, the tree of life is planted, the time to come is prepared, plentiousness is made ready, a city is built, and rest is allowed, yes perfect goodness and wisdom.

Revelation 2:7 KJV (Tree of Life Reopened)

He that hath an ear, let him hear what the Spirit saith unto the churches; To him that overcometh will ***I give to eat of the tree of life, which is in the midst of the paradise of God****.*

Revelation 22:2 KJV (Tree of Life Healing)

In the midst of the street of it, and on either side of the river, was there the ***tree of life****, which bare twelve manner of fruits, and yielded her fruit every month:* ***and the leaves of the tree were for the healing of the nations****.*

Revelation 22:14 KJV (Right to Tree of Life, Enter the Kingdom)

Blessed are they that do his commandments, that they may have ***right to the tree of life****, and may* ***enter in through the gates into the city****.*

Philippians 3:21 KJV (Everlasting Tabernacles Given)

Who shall change our vile body, that it may ***be fashioned like unto his glorious body****, according to the working whereby he is able even to subdue all things unto himself.*

2 Corinthians 5:1 KJV (Everlasting Tabernacles Given)

For we know that ***if our earthly house of this tabernacle were dissolved, we have a building of God, an house not made with hands, eternal in the heavens****.*

Here we have five passages from 2nd Esdras matched as the origin of Revelation as John was completely aware of this book as every book in Qumran where the Temple practice had relocated just before his time. Messiah is speaking in some of these passages of Revelation further proving Messiah quoted 2nd Esdras multiple times. The Tree of Life conceptually being opened to believers after Judgment Day is very prevalent in the New Testament but 2nd Esdras employs it first. Paul also was well aware of 2nd Esdras as the doctrine of our receiving new "tabernacles" or heavenly bodies originates in 2nd Esdras. What about the dead rising on the Day of Judgment? Once again, 2nd Esdras precedes all of these New Testament writings and becomes the catalyst for such important doctrine.

> ***2nd Esdras 2:16***
> *And* ***those that be dead will I raise up again from their places****, and* ***bring them out of the graves****: for I have known my Name in Israel.*
>
> ***1 Thessalonians 4:14-16 KJV***
> *For if we believe that Jesus died and rose again, even so* ***them also which sleep in Jesus will God bring with him****. For this we say unto you by the word of the Lord, that we which are alive and remain unto the coming of the Lord shall not prevent them which are asleep.* ***For the Lord himself shall descend from heaven with a shout, with the voice of the archangel, and with the trump of God: and the dead in Christ shall rise first:***
> ***John 5:28-29 KJV***
> *Marvel not at this: for the hour is coming, in the which* ***all that are in the graves shall hear his voice, And shall come forth****; they that have done good, unto the resurrection of life; and they that have done evil, unto the resurrection of damnation.*
> ***1 Corinthians 15:52 KJV***
> *In a moment, in the twinkling of an eye, at the last trump: for the trumpet shall sound, and* ***the dead shall be raised incorruptible,*** *and we shall be changed.*
> ***Acts 24:15 KJV***
> *And have hope toward God, which they themselves also allow, that there shall be a* ***resurrection of the dead, both of the just and unjust.***
> ***Revelation 20:13 KJV***
> ***And the sea gave up the dead which were in it; and death and hell delivered up the dead which were in them****: and they were judged every man according to their works.*

Once again, this is a significant doctrine and it originates in 2nd Esdras. Even Messiah's Second Coming in some details is first predicted with clarity in 2nd Esdras.

2nd Esdras 2:42
I Ezra saw upon the mount Sion a great people, whom I could not number, and they all praised Yahuah with songs.

Revelation 14:1-3 KJV
And I looked, and, lo, ***a Lamb stood on the mount Sion, and with him an hundred forty and four thousand****, having his Father's name written in their foreheads. And I heard a voice from heaven, as the voice of many waters, and as the voice of a great thunder: and I heard the voice of harpers harping with their harps: And* ***they sung as it were a new song before the throne****, and before the four beasts, and the elders: and no man could learn that song but the hundred and forty and four thousand, which were redeemed from the earth.*

Oh my! 2nd Esdras predicted Messiah's coming with the 144,000 atop Mt. Sion where they sing a new song before Revelation. It also foretells of his placing crowns on the head of the remnant believers in the end before Peter and Revelation.

2 Esdras 2:43
And in the midst of them there was a young man of a high stature, taller then all the rest, and ***upon every one of their heads he set crowns****, and was more exalted, which I marvelled at greatly.*

1 Peter 5:4
And ***when the chief Shepherd shall appear, ye shall receive a crown of glory*** *that fadeth not away.*
Revelation 2:10 KJV
...and I will give thee a crown of life.

We all know the New Testament informs us to confess Messiah but did you know that first appears in 2nd Esdras 400 years before His birth?

2nd Esdras 2:47
So he answered, and said unto me, It is the ***son of Elohim, whom they have confessed in the world.*** *Then I began greatly to commend them, that stood so stiffely for the Name of Yahuah.*

Matthew 10:32 KJV
Whosoever therefore shall confess me before men, him will I confess also before my Father which is in heaven.

Luke 12:8 KJV
Also I say unto you, ***Whosoever shall confess me before men, him shall the Son of man also confess before the angels of God:***
Romans 10:9 KJV
That if thou shalt confess with thy mouth the Lord Jesus*, and shalt believe in thine heart that God hath raised him from the dead, thou shalt be saved.*
Philippians 2:11 KJV
And that ***every tongue should confess that Jesus Christ is Lord****, to the glory of God the Father.*
1 John 1:19 KJV
Whosoever shall confess that Jesus is the Son of God*, God dwelleth in him, and he in God.*

Do you recall the term the first Adam? It does not appear in scripture often but Paul was very likely reading and applying the term from 2nd Esdras.

2nd Esdras 3:21
For ***the first Adam*** *bearing a wicked heart transgressed, and was overcome; and so be all they that are born of him.*

1 Corinthians 15:45 KJV
And so it is written, The first man Adam *was made a living soul; the last Adam was made a quickening spirit. Howbeit that was not first which is spiritual,* ***but that which is natural****; and afterward that which is spiritual.* ***The first man is of the earth, earthy: the second man is the Lord from heaven.***

Just two verses later, Paul identifies in the same vein as 2nd Esdras that Adam was natural or fleshly or earthy. He then, describes Yahusha as the second Adam or man. We all know the earth groans in travail for His return. However, did you know that concept originates in 2nd Esdras? Paul and Messiah are quoting 2nd Esdras.

2nd Esdras 4:42
For ***like as a woman that travails, makes haste to escape the necessity of the travail: even so do these places haste to deliver those things that are committed unto them.***

Romans 8:22 KJV
For we know that the ***whole creation groaneth and travaileth in pain together until now.***

Matthew 24:8 NIV
All these are the beginning of birth pains.

For wickedness will increase in the last days says Messiah. However, Ezra wrote it first in 2nd Esdras. Once again, Yahusha quotes 2nd Esdras. How could anyone say that which Messiah quoted could ever be anything but inspired?

2nd Esdras 5:2
But iniquity shall be increased above that which now you see, or that you have heard long ago.

Matthew 24:12 KJV
***Because of the increase of wickedness**, the love of most will grow cold,*
Matthew 24:37 KJV (Luke 17:26)
As it was in the days of Noah, so it will be at the coming of the Son of Man.

Did you know that Revelation is not the first to mention several concepts which you will find in 2nd Esdras in origin. We will not cover them all because the list would be massive. Here is a very specific such passage after the Third Trumpet which would be the Fourth.

2nd Esdras 5:4
*But if the Most High grant you to live, you shall see **after the third trumpet, that the Sun shall suddenly shine again in the night, and the Moon thrice in the day.***

Revelation 8:12 KJV
And the fourth angel sounded, and the third part of the sun was smitten, and the third part of the moon, and the third part of the stars; so as the third part of them was darkened, and the day shone not for a third part of it, and the night likewise.

How did Ezra know 400 years before Messiah and 500 years before Revelation that the Fourth Trumpet would lead to the sun, moon and stars darkening? He even specifically knew a third part even. Ezra truly had an encounter of like experience to John and John was well aware of Ezra's visions. Messiah lays out a profound doctrine that the path to salvation is a narrow one. The same language and concept in greater detail derives from 2nd Esdras.

2nd Esdras 7:12-14
Then were the ***entrances of this world made narrow, full of sorrow and travail:*** *they are but few and evil, full of perils, and very painful. For* ***the entrances of the elder world were wide and sure,*** *and brought immortal fruit. If then they that live, labor not to* ***enter these straight and vain things,*** *they can never receive those that are laid up for them.*

Matthew 7:13-14 KJV
Enter ye in at the strait gate: for wide is the gate, and broad is the way, that leadeth to destruction, and many there be which go in thereat: Because strait is the gate, and narrow is the way, which leadeth unto life, and few there be that find it.

Esdras even expanded on that one and does so multiple times that entrances to salvation became narrow after the fall of Adam. They were wide previously. However, this one stands on it's own. There is no parallel in prophecy as 2nd Esdras gives a fairly exact timeframe for the birth of Messiah to come. In 400 B.C., he prophesies Yahusha by name, will be revealed or born on earth in 400 years around 0 B.C. Only the fraudulent dating based on nothing scientific, and we proved wrong earlier, could possibly lead one to question this one. With Ezra nailing the very birth of Messiah in era, that alone proves this an inspired writing and Ezra a true prophet that should be taken far more seriously than many have awarded.

2nd Esdras 7:28
For my son YAHUSHA shall be revealed with those that be with him, and they that remain shall rejoice within four hundred years.

In addition, Ezra saw Messiah's death, ascension, second coming and His righteous Judgment in the end. New Testament concepts found in the Old Testament. No wonder the Pharisees do not want this connection to be made.

2nd Esdras 7:33
And the Most High shall appear upon the seat of judgment, *and misery shall pass away, and the long suffering shall have an end.*

Romans 14:10 KJV
But why dost thou judge thy brother? or why dost thou set at nought thy brother? for we shall all stand before ***the judgment seat of Christ.***

2 Corinthians 5:10 KJV
For we must all appear before the judgment seat of Christ; *that every one may receive the things done in his body, according to that he hath done, whether it be good or bad.*

As with the narrow gate, we find 2nd Esdras further defining what we read in the New Testament from Yahusha once again. He was quoting 2nd Esdras.

2nd Esdras 8:1, 3
And he answered me, saying, ***The Most High hath made this world for many, but the world to come for few.***
...There be many created, but few shall be saved.

Matthew 20:16 KJV
So the last shall be first, and the first last: ***for many be called, but few chosen.***

Many of us have quoted many times that it is not Yahuah's will that any should perish. However, did you know that originates in 2nd Esdras?

2nd Esdras 8:59
For as the things aforesaid shall receive you, so thirst and pain are prepared for them; ***for it was not his will that men should come to nothing.***

2 Peter 3:9 KJV
The Lord is not slack concerning his promise, as some men count slackness; but is longsuffering to us-ward, ***not willing that any should perish, but that all should come to repentance.***

Peter is again referencing 2nd Esdras. We have heard many times that faith without works is dead. Of course, many forget that and claim faith only is all we need when the Bible says both so why preach dead faith?

2nd Esdras 9:7-8
And every one that shall be saved, and shall be able to escape by his works, and by faith, whereby you have believed, Shall be preserved from the said perils, and shall see my salvation, *in my land, and within my borders: for I have sanctified them for me, from the beginning.*

James 2:18-20, 26 KJV
Yea, a man may say, ***Thou hast faith, and I have works: shew me thy faith without thy works, and I will shew thee my faith by my works.*** *Thou believest that there is one God; thou doest well: the devils also believe, and tremble. But wilt thou know, O vain man,* ***that faith without works is dead?***
...For as the body without the spirit is dead, so faith without works is dead also.

Unfortunately, Messiah was clear there will be Christians who will be turned away from the Kingdom of Heaven because they know church but they do not know Him. They received benefits in their lives and even performed casting out demons, prophesying and miracles but they do not KNOW Him.

2nd Esdras 9:10
For such, as in their life ***have received benefits, and have not known me:***

Matthew 7:21-23 KJV
Not every one that saith unto me, Lord, Lord, shall enter into the kingdom of heaven; but he that doeth the will of my Father which is in heaven. Many will say to me in that day, Lord, Lord, have we not prophesied in thy name? and in thy name have cast out devils? and in thy name done many wonderful works? And then will I profess unto them, I never knew you: depart from me, ye that work iniquity.

In part of Matthew 24, Yahusha rattles off signs of the End Times. 2nd Esdras offers context for much of this. In this passage, we have earthquakes and uproars of people or nation against nation and kingdom against kingdom.

2nd Esdras 9:2-3
Then shall you understand, that it is the very same time, wherein ***the Highest will begin to visit the world which he made. Therefore when there shall be seen earthquakes and uproars of the people in the world:***

Matthew 24:7 KJV
For nation shall rise against nation, and kingdom against kingdom: and there shall be famines, and pestilences, and earthquakes, in divers places.

2nd Esdras conveys a continuation of the prophecy of Daniel's Four Beasts specifically the final empire. There is much to discuss and we will leave that for that chapter's charts. However, it is very telling that Daniel does not mention this Beast rising out of the sea as we see in Revelation. However, 2nd Esdras does and becomes the likely origin of Revelation again.

> ***2nd Esdras 11:1***
> *Then I saw a dream, and behold, **there came up from the Sea an Eagle, which had twelve feathered wings, and three heads.***
>
> ***Revelation 13:1 KJV***
> *And I stood upon the sand of the sea, and saw a **beast rise up out of the sea,** having seven heads and ten horns, and upon his horns ten crowns, and upon his heads the name of blasphemy.*

Again, just a reading of this book for prophecy will ring true for most and raise the hairs on the back of one's neck. There are many scriptures we could pair with this passage from 2nd Esdras alone. However, we will allow it to stand on it's own.

> ***2nd Esdras 12:31-33***
> ***And the Lion whom you saw rising up out of the wood, and roaring, and speaking to the Eagle, and rebuking her for her unrighteousness, with all the words which you has heard, This is the Anointed which the Highest has kept for them, and for their wickedness unto the end: he shall reprove them, and shall upbraid them with their cruelty. For he shall set them before him alive in judgment, and shall rebuke them and correct them.***

In Revelation, Yahusha will consume His enemies with a sword from His mouth. In 2nd Esdras, this is a flaming sword of fire. All of those who come to fight Yahusha will be turned to dust or ash and smoke. That phoenix will never rise again.

> ***2nd Esdras 13:4, 10-11***
> ***And whensoever the voice went out of his mouth, all they burnt, that heard his voice, like as the earth fails when it feels the fire. ...But only I saw that he sent out of his mouth, as it had been a blast of fire, and out of his lips a flaming breath, and out of his tongue he cast out sparks and tempests, And they were all mixed together; the blast of fire, the flaming breath, and the great tempest, and fell with violence upon the multitude, which***

> ***was prepared to fight, and burnt them up every one, so that upon a sudden, of an innumerable multitude, nothing was to be perceived, but only dust and smell of smoke: when I saw this, I was afraid.***
>
> ***Revelation 19:15 KJV***
> ***And out of his mouth goeth a sharp sword, that with it he should smite the nations:*** *and he shall rule them with a rod of iron: and he treadeth the winepress of the fierceness and wrath of Almighty God.*
> ***Revelation 19:21 KJV***
> ***And the remnant were slain with the sword of him that sat upon the horse, which sword proceeded out of his mouth: and all the fowls were filled with their flesh.***

For anyone wondering, a flaming sword in scripture has precedence all the way back to the angels who guard the entrance to the Garden of Eden. When Paul mentions the law of the spirit of life, it also appears he is quoting 2nd Esdras.

> ***2nd Esdras 14:30***
> *And received* ***the law of life*** *which they kept not, which you also have transgressed after them.*
>
> ***Romans 8:2 KJV***
> *For* ***the law of the Spirit of life*** *in Christ Jesus hath made me free from the law of sin and death.*

Notice, how 2nd Esdras bridges the gap between the Old Testament and the New. This is one of the most important purposes of this book that preserves the Old in the New in prophecy. Even the Book of Life concept is published in 2nd Esdras before Revelation though we do see that concept in the Book of Jubilees in true origin.

> ***2nd Esdras 14:30***
> *For after death,* ***shall the judgment come,*** *when we shall live again:* ***and then shall the names of the righteous be manifest, and the works of the ungodly shall be declared.***
>
> ***Revelation 20:12 KJV***
> ***And I saw the dead, small and great, stand before God; and the books were opened: and another book was opened, which is the***

book of life: and the dead were judged out of those things which were written in the books, according to their works.

Even the judgment of Babylon and its harlot are first foretold in 2nd Esdras long before Revelation was published.

2nd Esdras 15:44 (Judgment on Babylon)
They shall come to her, and besiege her, the star and all wrath shall they power out upon her, then shall the dust and smoke go up unto the heaven: *and all they that be about her,* ***shall bewail her.***

Revelation 18:8 KJV
Therefore shall her plagues come in one day, death, and mourning, and famine; and she shall be utterly burned with fire: for strong is the Lord God who judgeth her. And the kings of the earth, who have committed fornication and lived deliciously with her, shall bewail her, and lament for her, when they shall see the smoke of her burning

There are so many more examples. However, we feel we have enough here to determine that 2nd Esdras was quoted by Messiah and the Apostles as they were aware of the book and use it as inspired scripture for significant doctrine. There is far too much here to ignore and even for those who just do not wish to add it into their Bibles, they should at least be mindful of the messages contained in this book. Messiah used it and that pretty much settles it.

1st Esdras cross-references with the Old Testament especially the Book of Ezra and Nehemiah who are the same author. These cross-references are noted throughout. It does not become the origin however, of Old Testament passages as 2nd Esdras does for the New. Though we do not see it in the New Testament as we do 2nd Esdras, it's content is very consistent with scripture in the stories of the return from Babylon and the rebuilding of the Second Temple. Much is shared with Ezra and Nehemiah especially. We do find however, Josephus even quotes the story of the 3 bodyguards directly from 1st Esdras so he read it and used it in about 90 A.D. as well which also dates 1st Esdras well before the Rabbis have attempted in claiming an Egyptian Jew wrote it in the 2nd Century. That is illiterate and you would think they would know Josephus at least.

"After the slaughter of the Magi, who, upon the death of Cambyses, attained the government of the Persians for a year, those families which were called the seven families of the Persians appointed Darius, the son of Hystaspes, to be their King.

> *Now he, while he was a private man, had made a vow to God, that if he came to be King, he would send all the vessels of God that were in Babylon to the temple at Jerusalem. Now it so fell out, that about this time Zorobabel, who had been made governour of the Jews that had been in captivity, came to Darius, from Jerusalem: for there had been an old friendship between him and the King. He was also, with two others, thought worthy to be guards of the King's body; and obtained that honour which he hoped for." –Flavius Josephus, Antiquities of the Jews, Book XI, 3.1.*

As we proved earlier, there were at least two "Proto-1st Esdras" fragments found in the Dead Sea Scrolls as well also crushing the Rabbi dating.

5. In Agreement With the Whole of Scripture (Our Addition)

In these scriptures, one will observe an alignment in 1st and 2nd Esdras and the whole of scripture. It's prophesies are endorsed by Revelation especially. We find Messiah quoting the books, the Qumran Temple Priests using them in interpretation and as "Proto" fragments and the New Testament fully in agreement. Our assessment has yet to turn up anything we deem a challenge in the alignment of these two books with the rest scripture as evidenced by the previous section of abundant passages. These are in agreement with the Old and New Testaments and fitting to their message.

Having fully reviewed the 5 points of our Torah Test, some from Blue Letter Bible and our additions to strengthen such test, we feel confident in declaring 1st and 2nd Esdras as inspired scripture. We find the authorship of a prophet who writes accurate prophecy and doctrine from which many New Testament passages originate. We find these books applied in consistent historicity as inspired scripture from around 100 B.C. to present. Again, we demand the Pharisees and the Catholic Church produce their authority to overrule the legitimate, ordained Temple Priests who were exiled to Qumran. If they cannot, and none can, they have no such authority. We should all migrate to a position which places these Biblical keepers of scripture above any modern scholar.

1st and 2nd Esdras coalesce with the whole of scripture including the role of the Yahudim in the Old Testament and New as well as Messiah's purpose, birth, death, ascension and second coming. One can strain gnats to attempt a detail here or there but they do that with the Gospels even and they are wrong every time. The Bible never contradicts itself, man's interpretations do. This is very solid ground in which we can move forward in publishing 1st and 2nd Esdras in The Levite Bible of texts found in Qumran not currently in most modern canons. When assessing all of these books, one uncovers a clear agenda of manipulation which has led to their censorship at least in part for some. It is time we all awaken and test this increasing knowledge of ancient origin. Here is our report card for 1st and 2nd Esdras which prove as inspired scripture.

Conclusion: 1st & 2nd Esdras Are Inspired Scripture

Criteria set forth by Blue Letter Bible with our additions. [1]

1. Prophetic Authorship

Ezra, the Prophet wrote 1st and 2nd Esdras. As he was a prophet and this vets as his writing consistent with his other writings exactly as claimed in both books, it vets as inspired scripture even serving to prove the Book of Esther is a false story. The Qumran use of 1st and 2nd Esdras is evident and proves it was in circulation in at least the first century B.C. proving scholars guessing at a date of later authorship are unfounded. Ezra wrote these books.

2. Witness of the Spirit

1st and 2nd Esdras was found in the Temple Library kept at Qumran by the Sons of Zadok who were the only Biblically ordained keepers of scripture. We find the Proto-Esther Fragments found there are actually 1st Esdras not Esther and the prophesies of 2nd Esdras are used to interpret at least two fragments as well in the Dead Sea Scrolls. We see these books throughout history within scripture eventually mislabeled as Apocrypha meaning they were not in the Pharisee canon which is impertinent. They continued to be translated and published with scripture in the 1560 Geneva Bible and 1611 King James Version even remaining in some versions until today. The historicity of 1st and 2nd Esdras is undeniable.

3. Acceptance

The Books of 1st and 2nd Esdras set forth Israel as Yah's people and agrees with the Bible in it's importance while repeating prophecy that this relationship will be further extended to the Gentiles. The prophesies in 2nd Esdras include Messiah's coming by date, His role as Savior and Judge, His death, His Ascension, His Second Coming, the Day of Judgment, etc. It demonstrates the Biblical view basically as the origin of portions of the New Testament including Revelation.

4. Quoted As Doctrine In Scripture (Our Addition)

Messiah and the Apostles quote 2nd Esdras for significant doctrine. 1st Esdras reads as Ezra and Nehemiah and proves consistent with the Old Testament that it parallels.

5. In Agreement With the Whole of Scripture (Our Addition)

1st and 2nd Esdras agree with the whole of scripture even demonstrating the origin of portions of the New Testament which specifics we have reviewed in abundance.

The Name Of God in Esdras

We learn from Jubilees Hebrew is the language of Creation thus it must be simple and somehow for thousands of years, it was written with just consonants yet spoken without ever needing vowel points. Those were added in about 1000 A.D. by the Masoretes and at times serve to offer more confusion than clarity as they clearly were not honest about the name of Yahuah since it was their practice to hide His name. Therefore, this must be a phonetic language requiring no vowels and no fancy rules especially those changing even within a word illogically. What we call Hebrew today is Yiddish-infused not Ancient Hebrew.

Phonetically, YH is simple. H is AH *(see chart to right)*. That's YAH. The next combination is HW which we know by the names of the prophets is HU. Thus it's YAHU as with the prophets. Finally, we add the last H or AH for YAHUAH.

We recognize there is a whole church out there which stakes it's claim on the name Jehovah. Here's the largest problem with that word. It is not Ancient Hebrew, Aramaic, Greek, Latin, Old French, Old German nor Old English. In other words, every language in which the Bible has been interpreted through in origin cannot render J nor V until the Renaissance *(1500s or so)*. The Bible was already thousands of years old and never used J nor V in any ancient text. There is a Pharisee out there deceiving many by trying to make this fit but we have the Dead Sea Scrolls dating to as early as 300 B.C. with even entire books such as the Isaiah scroll of about 25 feet in length which never renders a J nor a V even once. There is no overturning that. One may ignore it but let us not pretend they would be interested in the truth.

This leads us to the name of Messiah as the same first 3 letters YHW or YAHU as set by Yahuah. Yes, He literally meant He came in His Father's name. His name ends with SH - SHIN, A - AYIN which is SHA. He is Yahusha with Yahushua also appearing as a variant in scripture. Joshua has this same name in Hebrew. His people are the YAHUdim never Jews but YAH's.

Finally, some focus on the one time in scripture that Yahuah says His name is HYH, HAYAH as His only name ignoring the 6,800 times it is recorded as YHWH, Yahuah. However, modern Yiddish renders this as EHYEH and similar in fraud. Ancient Hebrew is HA YAH or THE YAH. It is the same name. Yahuah is being specific in saying I am The Yah not to be confused with any other. He is still invoking His name Yahuah in that passage which matches. In fact, YAH is rendered in the Old Testament 45 times on a standalone basis.

PHOENICIAN	𐤉𐤄𐤅𐤄	*1100 B.C.*
PALEO-HEBREW	𐤉𐤄𐤅𐤄	*1000 B.C.*
HEBREW	יהוה	*300 B.C. - TODAY*

FATHER

YAHUAH

יהוה

HEY WAW HEY YAD

HaUHaY

YAHUAH

Hebrew reads right to left.

Ancient Semitic/Hebrew

Early	Middle	Late	Name	Picture	Meaning	Sound
		א	El	Ox head	Strong, Power, Leader	ah, eh
		ב	Bet	Tent floorplan	Family, House, In	b, bh(v)
		ג	Gam	Foot	Gather, Walk	g
		ד	Dal	Door	Move, Hang, Entrance	d
		ה	Hey	Man with arms raised	Look, Reveal, Breath	h, ah
		ו	Waw	Tent peg	Add, Secure, Hook	w, o, u
		ז	Zan	Mattock	Food, Cut, Nourish	z
		ח	Hhet	Tent wall	Outside, Divide, Half	hh
⊗	⊗	ט	Tet	Basket	Surround, Contain, Mud	t
		י	Yad	Arm and closed hand	Work, Throw, Worship	y, ee
		כ	Kaph	Open palm	Bend, Open, Allow, Tame	k, kh
		ל	Lam	Shepherd Staff	Teach, Yoke, To, Bind	l
		מ	Mem	Water	Chaos, Mighty, Blood	m
		נ	Nun	Seed	Continue, Heir, Son	n
		ס	Sin	Thorn	Grab, Hate, Protect	s
	o	ע	Ghah	Eye	Watch, Know, Shade	gh(ng)
		פ	Pey	Mouth	Blow, Scatter, Edge	p, ph(f)
		צ	Tsad	Trail	Journey, chase, hunt	ts
		ק	Quph	Sun on the horizon	Condense, Circle, Time	q
		ר	Resh	Head of a man	First, Top, Beginning	r
	w	ש	Shin	Two front teeth	Sharp, Press, Eat, Two	sh
+	×	ת	Taw	Crossed sticks	Mark, Sign, Signal, Monument	t
			Ghah	Rope	Twist, Dark, Wicked	gh

Ancient Hebrew Research Center 26

AH U

Y

SON

YAHUSHA

"YAHU IS SALVATION"

יהושע

AYIN SHIN WAW HEY YAD

AhS U HaY

YAHUSHA

NO "J"

NO "V"

NO VOWEL POINTS

YAHUdim יהודים
Yah's People (Never Jews, Yah's)

YAHUdah יהודה
"Yahu Be Praised" (Tribe of Judah)

Ha YAH היה
I AM or THE YAH

EliYAHU אליהו
"My God Is Yahu"

THE
Levite
BIBLE
THE
Levite
BIBLE
LeviteBible.com

THE BOOK OF 2 ESDRAS

THE HIDDEN BOOK OF PROPHECY

THE Levite BIBLE
LeviteBible.com

CHAPTER 1:

1 Ezra is commanded to reprove the people. 24 Yahuah threatens to cast them off, 35 and to give their houses to a people of more grace then they.

The Genealogy of Ezra

Esdras = Ezra the Prophet.

1 The second book of the Prophet Ezra the son of Seraiah, the son of Azariah, the son of Hilkiah, the son of Shallum, the son of Zadok, the son of Ahitub,

Cf. Ezra 7.1.

2 The son of Ahiyah, the son of Phinehas, the son of Eli, the son of Amariah, the son of Azariah, the son of Meraimoth, the son of Arna, the son of Uzzi, the son of Borith, the son of Abishua, the son of Phinehas, the son of Eleazar,

3 The son of Aaron, of the Tribe of Levi, who was captive in the land of the Medes, in the reign of Artaxerxes, king of the Persians.

Assyria, Media. Shallum.

Ezra's Prophetic Call

4 And the word of Yahuah came unto me, saying,

5 Go your way, and show my people their sinful deeds, and their children their wickedness which they have done against me, that they may tell their children's children,

Cf. Is.58.1.

6 Because the sins of their fathers are increased in them: for they have forgotten me, and have offered unto strange gods.

7 Am I not, even He that brought them out of the land of Egypt, from the house of bondage? but they have provoked me unto wrath, and despised my counsels.

8 Pull you off then the hair of your head, and cast all evil upon them, for they have not been obedient unto my law, but it is a rebellious people.

9 How long shall I forebear them unto whom I have done so much good?

10 Many kings have I destroyed for their sakes, Pharaoh with his servants, and all his power have I smitten down.

Cf. Ex.14:28; Nm. 21:24; Jos. 8:12.

11 All the nations have I destroyed before them, and **in the East I have scattered the people of two provinces**, even of Tyrus and Sidon, and have slain all their enemies.

Cf. 2 Esd. 13:38-49, 1:38. Is. 11:10-12. The Northern Kingdom was released from Assyria but did not return to Samaria. Some stayed in Assyria and the rest migrated farther East to the isles of Tarshish, Ophir and Sheba. The Southern Kingdom was still in Judaea at this point and not exiled yet.

Yahuah's Mercies to Israel

12 Speak you therefore unto them saying, Thus says

Yahuah,

13 I led you through the Sea, and in the beginning gave you a large and safe passage, I gave you Moses for a leader, and Aaron for a priest,

Cf. Ex.14:29, Or, street., Ex. 3:10. and 4:14.

14 I gave you light in a pillar of fire, and great wonders have I done among you, yet have you forgotten me, says Yahuah.

Cf. Ex.13:21.

15 Thus says the Almighty Yahuah, The quail were as a token for you, I gave you tents for your safeguard, nevertheless you murmured there,

Cf. Ex.16:13.

16 And triumphed not in my name for the destruction of your enemies, but ever to this day do you yet murmur.

17 Where are the benefits that I have done for you? When you were hungry and thirsty in the wilderness, did you not cry unto me?

Cf. Nm. 14:3.

18 Saying, Why have you brought us into this wilderness to kill us? It had been better for us to have served the Egyptians, then to die in this wilderness.

19 Then I had pity upon your mournings, and gave you Manna to eat, so you did eat Angels bread.

Cf. Wisd. 16:20. i.e. Manna.

20 When you were thirsty, did I not cleave the rock, and waters flowed out to your fill? for the heat I covered you with the leaves of the trees.

Cf. Nm. 20:11. Wisd. 11:4, Or, abundantly.

21 I divided amongst you a fruitful land, I cast out the Canaanites, the Pherezites, and the Philistines before you: what shall I yet do more for you: says Yahuah?

22 Thus says the Almighty Yahuah, when you were in the wilderness in the river of the Amorites, being athirst, and blaspheming my Name,

Cf. Ex. 15:23.

23 I gave you not fire for your blasphemies, but cast a tree in the water, and made the river sweet.

Or, at the bitter waters, or waters of Marah.

Israel's Disobedience and Rejection

Jacob = Yacob. Judah = Yahudah. There is no J in Ancient Hebrew, Greek, Aramaic, Latin, Old German, Old French nor Old English.

24 What shall I do unto thee, O Yacob? thou Yahudah would not obey me: I will turn myself to other nations, and unto those will I give my Name, that they may keep my Statutes.

Cf. Ex.32:8.

25 Seeing you have forsaken me, I will forsake you also: when you desire me to be gracious unto you, I shall have no mercy upon you.

26 Whensoever you shall call upon me, I will not hear you: for you have defiled your hands with blood, and your feet are swift to commit manslaughter.

Cf. Is.1:15.

27 You have not as it were forsaken me, but your own selves, says Yahuah.

28 Thus says the Almighty Yahuah, Have I not entreated you as a father his sons, as a mother her daughters, and a nurse her young babes,

Cf. Gen. 17:8; Jer. 24:7, 32:38; Ez. 11:20, 37:23, 37:27; Zec. 8:8; 2Cor. 6:16

29 That you would be my people, and I should be your Elohim, that you would be my children, and I should be your Abba?

Or, as I am your Elohim.

Cf. Mt.23:37-38. ***Messiah quoted 2 Esdras.*** *Note: This is the 1611 Original Authorized KJV Footnote both in 2 Esd. and Mt.*

30 I gathered you together, as a hen gathers her chickens under her wings: but now, what shall I do unto you? I will cast you out from my face.

31 When you offer unto me, I will turn my face from you: for your solemn feast days, your new Moon, and your circumcisions have I forsaken.

Cf. Is.1:13; Amos 5:21.

32 I sent unto you my servants the Prophets, whom you have taken and slain, and torn their bodies in pieces, whose blood I will require of your hands, says Yahuah.

33 Thus says the Almighty Yahuah, Your house is desolate, I will cast you out, as the wind does stubble.

34 And your children shall not be fruitful: for they have despised my Commandment, and done the thing that is evil before me.

35 Your houses will I give to a people that shall come, which not having heard of me, yet shall believe me, to whom I have shown no signs, yet they shall do that I have commanded them.

Cf. Jn. 20:29

36 They have seen no Prophets, yet they shall call their sins to remembrance, and acknowledge them.

Cf. Is. 60:9. ***Isles and Tarshish will usher in the return of the Lost Tribes with their gold and silver of Ophir and Tarshish.***

37 I take to witness the grace of the people to come, whose little ones rejoice in gladness: and though they have not seen me with bodily eyes, yet in spirit they believe the thing that I say.

Is. 40:31-41:2 ***Yahuah raises the righteous men of the isles of the East to judge and restore His law.***

38 And now brother, behold what glory: and see the people that **comes from the East**.

Is. 46:11 ***Eagle of the Far East will execute His counsel. This is the modern Philippines who has the largest eagle on Earth.*** *Cf. 1:11.*

39 Unto whom I will give for leaders, Abraham, Isaac, and Yacob, Hosea, Amos, and Micah, Yoel, Obadiah, and Yonah,

40 Nahum, and Habakkuk, Zephaniah, Haggai, Zechariah, and Malachi, which is called also an Angel of Yahuah.

Cf. Mal. 3:1. i.e. Messenger.

"30 **I gathered you together, as a hen gathers her chickens under her wings**: but now, what shall I do unto you? I will cast you out from my face.
31 When you offer unto me, I will turn my face from you: for your solemn feast days, your new Moon, and your circumcisions have I forsaken.
32 I sent unto you my servants **the Prophets, whom you have taken and slain**, and torn their bodies in pieces, whose blood I will require of your hands, says Yahuah.
33 Thus saith the Almighty Yahuah, **Your house is desolate**, I will cast you out, as the wind does stubble."

CHAPTER 2:

1 Yahuah complains of his people: 10 Yet Ezra is willed to comfort them. 34 Because they refused, the Gentiles are called. 43 Ezra sees the Son of Yahuah, and those that are crowned by him.

Yahuah's Judgment on Israel

1 Thus says Yahuah, I brought this people out of bondage, and I gave them my Commandments by my servants the prophets, whom they would not hear, but despised my counsels.
2 The mother that bare them, says unto them, Go your way you children, for I am a widow, and forsaken.
3 I brought you up with gladness, but with sorrow and heaviness have I lost you: for you have sinned before Yahuah your Elohim, and done that thing that is evil before him.
4 But what shall I now do unto you? I am a widow and forsaken: go your way, O my children, and ask mercy of Yahuah.
5 As for me, O father, I call upon you for a witness over the mother of these children, which would not keep my Covenant,
6 That you bring them to confusion, and their mother to a spoil, that there may be no offspring of them.
7 Let them be scattered abroad among the heathen, let their names be put out of the earth: for they have despised my Covenant.
8 Woe be unto you Asshur, you that hides the unrighteous in you, O you wicked people, remember what I did unto Sodom and Gomorrah.
9 Whose land lies in clods of pitch and heaps of ashes: even so also will I do unto them that hear me not, says the Almighty Yahuah.
10 Thus says Yahuah unto Ezra, Tell my people that I will give them the kingdom of Yerusalem, which I would have given unto Israel.
11 Their glory also will I take unto me, and give these the everlasting Tabernacles, which I had prepared for them.
12 **They shall have the Tree of Life for an ointment** of sweet savor, they shall neither labor, nor be weary.
13 Go and you shall receive: pray for few days unto you, that they may be shortened: the kingdom is already prepared for you: Watch.
14 Take heaven and earth to witness; for I have broken the

Sacrament or oath.

This addresses the Northern Kingdom left in Asshur/ Assyria. Those that migrated took the oath of a Rechabite renewing covenant. Nineveh, capital of Assyria, is destroyed.

Cf. Gn. 19:24.

Cf. 8:52, Rev. 2:7, 22:2, 22:14. ***Believers in the end will once again partake of the Tree of Life. 2 Esdras appears the origin of this doctrine.***

Cf. Mt. 24:22, Mar. 13:20. This is an end times context in the same fashion as Mt. 24 which quotes Esdras.

Cf. Dt. 4:26. Heaven and Earth witness.

evil in pieces, and created the good; for I live, says Yahuah.

Exhortation to Good Works

15 Mother, embrace your children, and bring them up with gladness, make their feet as fast as a pillar: for I have chosen you, says Yahuah.

Cf. 1 Thes. 4:14-17; Dn. 12; Jn. 5:28-29; Rev. 20:1, Acts 24:15.

16 And those that be dead will I raise up again from their places, and bring them out of the graves: for I have known my Name in Israel.

17 Fear not you mother of the children: for I have chosen you, says Yahuah.

Jeremiah = YirmiYahu in Hebrew with Yahu's name in his.

18 For your help I will send my servants Isaiah and YirmiYahu, after whose counsel I have sanctified and prepared for you twelve trees, laden with diverse fruits;

Rev. 22:2, Tree of Life has 12 kinds of fruits.

19 And as many fountains flowing with milk and honey: and seven mighty mountains, whereupon there grow roses and lillies, whereby I will fill your children with joy.

20 Do right to the widow, judge for the fatherless, give to the poor, defend the orphan, clothe the naked,

Cf. Jas. 1:27.

21 Heal the broken and the weak, laugh not a lame man to scorn, defend the maimed, and let the blind man come into the sight of my clearness.

22 Keep the old and young within your walls.

Cf. Is. 26:20-21.

23 Wheresover you find the dead, take them and bury them, and I will give you the first place in my resurrection.

Tob.1:17-18. Tobit buried them.

Cf. Rev. 20:5-6, 1 Thes. 4:14-17, "the first resurrection." ***Origin: 2 Esdras.***

24 Abide still, O my people, and take your rest, for your quietness shall come.

25 Nourish thy children, O you good nurse, establish their feet.

26 As for the servants whom I have given you, there shall not one of them perish; for I will require them from among your number.

27 Be not weary, for when the day of trouble and heaviness comes, others shall weep and be sorrowful, but you shall be merry, and have abundance.

The Tribulation.

28 The heathen shall envy you, but they shall be able to do nothing against you, says Yahuah.

29 My hands shall cover you, so that your children shall not see Hell.

30 Be joyful, O you mother, with thy children, for I will deliver you, says Yahuah.

31 Remember your children that sleep, for I shall bring them out of the sides of the earth, and show mercy unto them: for I am merciful, says Yahuah Almighty.

Cf. Rev. 20:5-6, 1 Thes. 4:14-17. ***Origin: 2 Esdras.***

32 Embrace your children until I come and show mercy unto them: for my wells run over, and my grace shall not fail.

Cf. 2 Cor. 12:9.

Ezra on Mount Horeb

33 I Ezra received a charge of Yahuah upon the mount Horeb, that I should go unto Israel; but when I came unto them, they set me at nought, and despised the commandment of Yahuah.

Or, preach.
i.e. Sinai.
i.e. Northern Kingdom only.

34 And therefore I say unto you, O you heathen, that hear and understand, Look for your shepherd, he shall give you everlasting rest; for he is near at hand, that shall come in the end of the world.

Messianic prophecy.

35 Be ready to the reward of the kingdom, for the everlasting light shall shine upon you for evermore.

36 Flee the shadow of this world, receive the joyfulness of your glory: I testify my Savior openly.

37 O receive the gift that is given you, and be glad, giving thanks unto him that has called you to the heavenly kingdom.

38 Arise up and stand, behold the number of those that be sealed in the feast of Yahuah:

Or, for.

39 Which are departed from the shadow of the world, and have received glorious garments of Yahuah.

40 Take your number, O Sion, and shut up those of yours that are clothed in white, which have fulfilled the Law of Yahuah.

Lat. conclude.

41 The number of your children whom you long for, is fulfilled: beseech the power of Yahuah, that your people which have been called from the beginning, may be hallowed.

In the End Times, believers will still be fulfilling His law. Cf. Rev. 22:14. Rev. 7:9 (the enumerable multitude. This is not the 144,000).

Ezra Sees the Son of Yahuah in the End Times

42 I Ezra saw upon the mount Sion a great people, whom I could not number, and they all praised Yahuah with songs.

Rev.7.9. The 144,000 sing on the Mt. of Olives. ***Origin of Revelation doctrine.***

43 And in the midst of them there was a young man of a high stature, taller then all the rest, and upon every one of their heads he set crowns, and was more exalted, which I marvelled at greatly.

Messianic prophecy.

44 So I asked the Angel, and said, Sir, what are these?

45 He answered, and said unto me, These be they that have put off the mortal clothing, and put on the immortal, and have confessed the Name of Yahuah: now are they crowned, and receive palms.

46 Then I said unto the Angel,

What young person is it that crowns them, and gives them palms in their hands?
47 So he answered, and said unto me, It is the **son of Elohim, whom they have confessed in the world.** Then I began greatly to commend them, that stood so stiffly for the Name of Yahuah.

Cf. Rom. 10:8-10.

48 Then the Angel said unto me, Go your way, and tell my people what manner of things, and how great wonders of Yahuah thy Elohim you have seen.

To him that overcometh will I give to eat of the tree of life, which is in the midst of the paradise of God.
Rev. 2:7 KJV (Messiah)

In the midst of the street of it, and on either side of the river, was there the tree of life, which bare twelve manner of fruits, and yielded her fruit every month: and the **leaves of the tree were for the healing of the nations**.
Rev. 22:2 KJV

Blessed are they that do his commandments, that they may have right to the tree of life, and may enter in through the gates into the city.
Rev. 22:14 KJV

For unto you is
Paradise opened, ***the tree of life is planted...***
2 Esdras 8:52

MESSIAH QUOTES 2 ESDRAS AGAIN

Origin: 2 Esdras 2:12

CHAPTER 3:

1 Ezra is troubled, 13 and acknowledges the sins of the people: 28 yet complains that the heathen were lords over them, being more wicked then they.

Ezra's Prayer of Complaint

1 In the thirtieth year after the ruin of the city, I was in Babylon, and lay troubled upon my bed, and my thoughts came up over my heart.

2 For I saw the desolation of Sion, and the wealth of them that dwelt at Babylon.

Yahuah and Yahusha created. Though we leave this insertion, it was not clear to the translators and this cannot overturn precedence. There were 2 Creators as Genesis refers to them as "Us" and "Our" and John 1 is clear Messiah created too. Elohim is plural. Elohim made not just El.

3 And my spirit was sore moved, so that I began to speak words full of fear to the Most High, and said,

4 O Yahuah, who bears rule, you spoke at the beginning, when you did plant the earth (and that yourself alone) and commanded the people,

5 And gave a body unto Adam without soul, which was the workmanship of your hands, and did breathe into him the breath of life, and he was made living before you.

Cf. Gn. 2:7.

6 And you led him into paradise, which your right hand had planted, before ever the earth came forward.

Paradise = Garden of Eden. Cf. Jub. 2:7. Garden was planted on Day 3. Right hand would be the East.

7 And unto him you gave commandment to love your way, which he transgressed, and immediately you appointed death in him, and in his generations, of whom came nations, tribes, people, and kindreds out of number.

Adam had Law or commandments he broke inviting the Law of Sin and Death which is never Yahuah's Law even in Paul. Cf. Rom. 7-8.

8 And every people walked after their own will, and did wonderful things before you, and despised your commandments.

Cf. Gn. 6:12. Yahuah still had Law after the Fall.

9 And again in process of time you brought the flood upon those that dwelt in the world, and destroyed them.

Cf. Gn. 7:10.

10 And it came to pass in every of them, that as death was to Adam, so was the flood to these.

11 Nevertheless one of them you left, namely Noah with his household, of whom came all righteous men.

Cf. 1 Pet. 3:20.

12 And it happened, that when they that dwelt upon the earth began to multiply, and had gotten them many children, and were a great people, they began again to be more ungodly than the first.

13 Now when they lived so wickedly before you, you did choose a man from among them, whose name was Abraham.

Cf. Gn.12:1, Gn.17:5.

14 Him you loved, and unto him only you showed your will:

15 And made an everlasting

covenant with him, promising him that you would never forsake his seed.

16 And unto him, you gave Isaac, and unto Isaac also you gave Yacob and Esau. As for Yacob thou did choose him to yourself, and put by Esau: and so Yacob became a great multitude.

Cf. Gn.21:2-3, Gn. 25:25-26; Mal.1:2-3; Rom. 9:13.

17 And it came to pass, that when you led his seed out of Egypt, you brought them up to the mount Sinai.

Cf. Ex. 19:1; Dt. 4:10.

18 And bowing the heavens, you did set fast the earth, moved the whole world, and made the depth to tremble, and troubled the men of that age.

19 And your glory went through four gates, of fire, and of earthquake, and of wind, and of cold, that you might give the law unto the seed of Yacob, and diligence unto the generation of Israel.

And to all the generations of Israel, that they should keep it with diligence.

20 And yet you took not away from them a wicked heart, that your law might bring forth fruit in them.

21 For the first Adam bearing a wicked heart transgressed, and was overcome; and so be all they that are born of him.

Cf. 1 Cor. 15:45. ***Origin of Paul's doctrine.***

22 Thus infirmity was made permanent; and the law (also) in the heart of the people with the malignity of the root, so that the good departed away, and the evil abode still.

23 So the times passed away, and the years were brought to an end: then did you raise up a servant, called David,

Cf. 1 Sam. 16:13.

24 Whom you commanded to build a city unto your name, and to offer incense and oblations unto you therein.

Cf. 2 Sam. 5:1 and 7:5.

25 When this was done many years, then they that inhabited the city forsook you,

26 And in all things did even as Adam, and all his generations had done, for they also had a wicked heart.

27 And so you gave the city over into the hands of your enemies.

Babylon Compared with Zion

28 Are their deeds then any better that inhabit Babylon, that they should therefore have the dominion over Sion?

29 For when I came thither, and had seen impieties without number, then my soul saw many evil doers in this thirtieth year, so that my heart failed me.

30 For I have seen how you suffer them sinning, and have spared wicked doers: and have destroyed your people, and have preserved your enemies, and have not signified it.

31 I do not remember how this way may be left: Are they then of Babylon better than they of Sion?

Or, I conceive.

32 Or is there any other people that knows you besides Israel? Or what generation has so believed your Covenants as Yacob?

33 And yet their reward appears not, and their labor has no fruit: for I have gone here and there through the heathen, and I see that they flow in wealth, and think not upon your commandments.

Or, abound.

34 Weigh therefore our wickedness now in the balance, and theirs also that dwell in the world: and so shall your Name no where be found, but in Israel.

35 Or when was it that they which dwell upon the earth, have not sinned in thy sight? or what people has so kept your commandments?

36 You shall find that Israel by name has kept your precepts: but not the heathen.

CHAPTER 4:

1 The Angel declares the ignorance of Ezra in Yahuah's judgments, 13 and advises him not to meddle with things above his reach. 23 Nevertheless Ezra asks diverse questions, and receives answers to them.

Limitations of the Human Mind

Cf. 1 En. 9:1, 1 En. 19:1. Angel Uriel.

1 And the Angel that was sent unto me, whose name was Uriel, gave me an answer,
2 And said, your heart has gone too far in this world, and you think to comprehend the way of the Most High?
3 Then I said, Yes my lord: and he answered me and said, I am sent to show you three ways, and to set forth three similitudes before you.
4 Whereof if you can declare me one, I will show you also the way that you desire to see, and I shall show you from whence the wicked heart comes.
5 And I said, Tell on my lord. Then he said unto me, Go your way, weigh me the weight of the fire, or measure me the blast of the wind, or call me again the day that is past.
6 Then I answered and said, What man is able to do that, that you should ask such things of me?
7 And he said unto me, If I should ask you how great dwellings are in the midst of the sea, or how many springs are in the beginning of the deep, or how many springs are above the firmament, or which are the outgoings of Paradise:

The deep is the ocean and the springs found there are hydrothermal vents. They are the fountains of the great deep found in the Mid-Ocean Ridge and Oceanic Trench systems.

8 Peradventure you would say unto me, I never went down into the deep, nor as yet into hell, neither did I ever climb up into heaven.
9 Nevertheless, now I have asked you but only of the fire and wind, and of the day where through you have passed, and of things from which you can not be separated, and yet can you give me answer of them.
10 He said moreover unto me, Your own things, and such as are grown up with you, can you not know.
11 How should your vessel then be able to comprehend the way of the Highest, and the world being now outwardly corrupted, to understand the corruption that is evident in my sight?

Or, incorruption.

12 Then I said unto him, It were better that we were not at all, then that we should live still in wickedness, and to suffer, and not to know wherefore.

Parable of the Forest and the Sea

13 He answered me and said, I went into a forest into a plain, and the trees took counsel,

Cf. Judg. 9:8. 2 Chr. 25:18.

14 And said, Come, let us go and make war against the Sea, that it may depart away before us, and that we may make us more woods.

15 The floods of the Sea also in like maner took counsel, and said, Come, let us go up and subdue the woods of the plain, that there also we may make us another country.

16 The thought of the wood was in vain, for the fire came and consumed it.

17 The thought of the floods of the Sea came likewise to nought, for the sand stood up and stopped them.

18 If you were judge now between these two, whom would you begin to justify, or whom would you condemn?

19 I answered and said, Verily it is a foolish thought that they both have devised: for the ground is given unto the wood, and the sea also has his place to bear his floods.

Or, the land, Or, waves.

20 Then he answered me and said, You have given a right judgment, but why judge you not yourself also?

21 For like as the ground is given unto the wood, and the sea to his floods: even so they that dwell upon the earth may understand nothing, but that which is upon the earth: and he that dwells above the heavens, may only understand the things that are above the height of the heavens.

The land. Is. 55:8-9; Jn. 3:31; 1 Cor. 2:13.

The New Age Will Make All Things Clear

22 Then I answered, and said, I beseech you, O Yahuah, let me have understanding.

23 For it was not my mind to be curious of the high things, but of such as pass by us daily, namely wherefore Israel is given up as a reproach to the heathen, and for what cause the people whom you have loved, is given over unto ungodly nations, and why the Law of our forefathers is brought to nought, and the written Covenants come to none effect.

Or, no where.

24 And we pass away out of the world as grasshoppers, and our life is astonishment and fear, and we are not worthy to obtain mercy.

25 What will he then do unto his Name, whereby we are called? of these things have I asked.

26 Then he answered me, and

said, The more you search, the more you shall marvel, for the world has fast to pass away,
27 And cannot comprehend the things that are promised to the righteous in time to come: for this world is full of unrighteousness and infirmities.
28 But as concerning the things whereof you ask me, I will tell you; for the evil is sown, but the destruction thereof is not yet come.
29 If therefore that which is sown, be not turned upside down; and if the place where the evil is sown pass not away, then cannot it come that is sown with good.
30 For the grain of evil seed has been sown in the heart of Adam from the beginning, and how much ungodliness has it brought up unto this time? And how much shall it yet bring forth until the time of threshing come.

Or, floor.

31 Ponder now by yourself, how great fruit of wickedness the grain of evil seed has brought forth.
32 And when the ears shall be cut down, which are without number, how great a floor shall they fill?

When Will the New Age Come?

33 Then I answered and said, How and when shall these things come to pass? wherefore are our years few and evil?
34 And he answered me, saying, Do you not hasten above the Most Highest: for your haste is in vain to be above him, for you have much exceeded.
35 Did not the souls also of the righteous ask question of these things in their chambers, saying, How long shall I hope on this fashion? when comes the fruit of the floor of our reward?
36 And unto these things Uriel the Archangel gave them answer, and said, Even when the number of seeds is filled in you: for he has weighed the world in the balance.
37 By measure has he measured the times, and by number has he numbered the times; and he does not move nor stir them, until the said measure be fulfilled.
38 Then I answered, and said, O Yahuah that bears rule, even we all are full of impiety.
39 And for our sakes peradventure it is that the floors of the righteous are not filled, because of the sins of them that dwell upon the earth.
40 So he answered me,

and said, Go your way to a woman with child, and ask of her, when she has fulfilled her nine months, if her womb may keep the birth any longer within her?

41 Then I said, No lord, that can she not. And he said unto me, In the grave, the chambers of souls are like the womb of a woman:

1 En. 22. Enoch witnessed these chambers within the Earth.

42 For like as a woman that travails, makes haste to escape the necessity of the travail: even so do these places haste to deliver those things that are committed unto them.

Cf. Rom. 8:22, Mt. 24:8 NIV.

43 From the beginning look what you desire to see, it shall be shown you.

How Much Time Remains?

44 Then I answered, and said, If I have found favor in your sight, and if it be possible, and if I be meet therefore,

45 Show me then whether there be more to come than is past, or more past than is to come.

46 What is past I know; but what is for to come I know not.

47 And he said unto me, Stand up upon the right side, and I shall expound the similitude unto you.

48 So I stood and saw, and behold an hot burning oven passed by before me: and it happened that when the flame was gone by, I looked, and behold, the smoke remained still.

49 After this there passed by before me a watery cloud, and sent down much rain with a storm, and when the stormy rain was past, the drops remained still.

50 Then he said unto me, Consider with yourself: as the rain is more than the drops, and as the fire is greater than the smoke: but the drops and the smoke remain behind: so the quantity which is past, did more exceed.

Or, measure.

51 Then I prayed, and said, May I live, you think, until that time? or what shall happen in those days?

Or, who shall be manuscript?

52 He answered me, and said, As for the tokens whereof you asked me, I may tell you of them in part; but as touching your life, I am not sent to show you, for I do not know it.

"For we know that the whole creation groaneth and travaileth in pain together until now." *Romans 8:22 KJV*

CHAPTER 5:

1 The signs of the times to come. 23 He asks why Elohim choosing but one people, did cast them off. 30 He is taught, that Yahuah's Judgments are unsearchable: 46 and that Yahuah does not all at once.

Signs of the End

1 Nevertheless as concerning the tokens, behold, the days shall come that they which dwell upon earth, shall be taken in a great number, and the way of truth shall be hidden, and the land shall be barren of faith.

Shall be found with great wealth.

2 But iniquity shall be increased above that which now you see, or that you have heard long ago.

Mt.24:12 **Messiah quotes 2 Esdras again.**

3 And the land that you see now to have root, shall you see wasted suddenly.

Or, that thou treadest upon and sees.

4 But if the Most High grant you to live, you shall see after the third trumpet, that the Sun shall suddenly shine again in the night, and the Moon thrice in the day.

Cf. Rev. 8:12. After the 3rd trumpet in Revelation at the sound of the 4th, 1/3 of the sun, moon and stars are smitten. 2 Esdras is the Origin of this Revelation

5 And blood shall drop out of wood, and the stone shall give his voice, and the people shall be troubled.

6 And even he shall rule whom they look not for that dwell upon the earth, and the fouls shall take their flight away together.

7 And the Sodomite sea shall cast out fish, and make a noise in the night, which many have not known: but they shall all hear the voice thereof.

Cf. Ez. 47:8-9.

8 There shall be a confusion also in many places, and the fire shall be oft sent out again, and the wild beasts shall change their places, and menstruous women shall bring forth monsters.

Or, slaked.

Cf. Mt. 24:19, Mk. 13:7. Likely a reference to Nephilim hybrids as the return of the days of Noah.

9 And salt waters shall be found in the sweet, and all friends shall destroy one another: then shall wit hide itself, and understanding withdraw itself into his secret chamber,

10 And shall be sought of many, and yet not be found: then shall unrighteousness and incontinency be multiplied upon earth.

11 One land also shall ask another, and say, Is righteousness that makes a man righteous, gone through you? And it shall say, No.

12 At the same time shall men hope, but nothing obtain: they shall labor, but their ways shall not prosper.

Or, be rejected.

13 To show you such tokens I have leave: and if you will pray again, and weep as now, and fast seven days, you shall hear yet greater things.

Conclusion of the Vision

14 Then I awaked, and an

extreme fearfulness went through all my body, and my mind was troubled, so that it fainted.

15 So the Angel that came to talk with me, held me, comforted me, and set me up upon my feet.

16 And in the second night it came to pass, that Salathiel the captain of the people came unto me, saying, Where have you been? and why is your countenance so heavy?

17 Know you not that Israel is committed unto you, in the land of their captivity?

18 Up then, and eat bread, and forsake us not as the shepherd that leaves his flock in the hands of cruel wolves.

19 Then I said unto him, Go your ways from me, and come not near me: And he heard what I said, and went from me.

20 And so I fasted seven days, mourning and weeping, like as Uriel the Angel commanded me.

Ezra's Second Prayer of Complaint

21 And after seven days, so it was that the thoughts of my heart were very grievous unto me again.

22 And my soul recovered the spirit of understanding, and I began to talk with the Most High again,

23 And said, O Yahuah, that bears rule of every wood of the earth, and of all the trees thereof, you have chosen your one only vine.

Cf. Jn. 15. **Messianic Prophecy.**

24 And of all lands of the whole world you have chosen one pit: and of all the flowers thereof, one Lily.

25 And of all the depths of the Sea, you have filled one river: and of all builded cities, you have hallowed Sion unto yourself.

26 And of all the fouls that are created, you have named one Dove: and of all the cattle that are made, you have provided one sheep.

27 And among all the multitudes of peoples, you have gotten one people: and unto this people whom you loved, you gave a law that is approved of all.

28 And now Yahuah, why have you given this one people over unto many? And upon the one root have you prepared others, and why have you scattered your only one people among many?

29 And they which did gainsay your promises, and believed not your covenants, have trodden them down.

Or, over.

30 If you did so much hate your people, yet should you

punish them with your own hands.

Response to Ezra's Complaints

31 Now when I had spoken these words, the Angel that came to me the night before, was sent unto me,
32 And said unto me, Hear me, and I will instruct you, hearken to the thing that I say, and I shall tell you more.
33 And I said, Speak on, my lord: then he said unto me, you are sore troubled in mind for Israel's sake: you love that people better than he that made them?
34 And I said, No lord, but of much grief have I spoken: For my heart pains me every hour, while I labor to comprehend the way of the Most High, and to seek out part of his judgment.
35 And he said unto me, You can not: and I said, wherefore lord? whereunto was I born then? or why was not my mother's womb then my grave, that I might not have seen the travel of Yacob, and the wearisome toil of the stock of Israel?
36 And he said unto me, Number me the things that are not yet come, gather me together the drops that are scattered abroad, make me the flowers green again that are withered.
37 Open me the places that are closed, and bring me forth the winds that in them are shut up, show me the image of a voice: and then I will declare to you the thing that you labor to know.
38 And I said, O Yahuah, that bearest rule, who may know these things, but he that has not his dwelling with men?
39 As for me, I am unwise: how may I then speak of these things whereof you ask me?
40 Then he said unto me, Like as you can do none of these things that I have spoken of, even so can you not find out my judgment, or in the end the love that I have promised unto my people.

Why Successive Generations Have Been Created

41 And I said, behold, O Yahuah, yet are you nigh unto them that be reserved til the end; and what shall they do that have been before me, or we (that be now) or they that shall come after us?
42 And he said unto me, I will liken my judgment unto a ring: like as there is no slackness of the last, even so there is no swiftness of the first.

43 So I answered and said, Could you not make those that have been made, and be now, and that are for to come, at once, that you might show your judgment the sooner?
44 Then he answered me, and said, The creature may not have above the maker, neither may the world hold them at once that shall be created therein.
45 And I said, As you have said unto your servant, that you which give life to all, has given life at once to the creature that you have created, and the creature bare it: even so it might now also bear them that now be present at once.
46 And he said unto me, Ask the womb of a woman, and say unto her, If you bring forth children, why do you not do it together, but one after another? Pray her therefore to bring forth ten children at once.
47 And I said, She cannot: but must do it by distance of time.
48 Then he said unto me, Even so have I given the womb of the earth to those that be sown in it, in their times.
49 For like as a young child may not bring forth the things that belong to the aged, even so have I disposed the world which I created.

When and How Will the End Come?

50 And I asked and said, Seeing you have now given me the way, I will proceed to speak before you: for our mother of whom you have told me that she is young, draws now nigh unto age.
51 He answered me and said, Ask a woman that bears children, and she shall tell you.
52 Say unto her, Wherefore are not they whom you have now brought forth, like those that were before, but less of stature?
53 And she shall answer you, They that be born in the strength of youth, are of one fashion, and they that are born in the time of age (when the womb fails) are otherwise.
54 Consider you therefore also, how that you are less of stature then those that were before you.
55 And so are they that come after you less than you, as the creatures which now begin to be old, and have passed over the strength of youth.

De-evolution is Biblical fact.

56 Then I said, Yahuah, I beseech thee, if I have found favor in thy sight, show your servant by whom you visit your creature.

CHAPTER 6:

1 Elohim's purpose is eternal. 8 The next world shall follow this immediately. 13 What shall fall out at the last. 31 He is promised more knowledge, 38 and reckon up the works of the creation, 57 and complain that they have no part in the world for whom it was made.

1 And he said unto me, in the beginning when the earth was made, before the borders of the world stood, or ever the winds blew,

Or, circle of the earth. Note: A circle is 2-dimensional. The ancient perspective was not that of a sphere.

2 Before it thundered and lightened, or ever the foundations of Paradise were laid,
3 Before the fair flowers were seen, or ever the moveable powers were established, before the innumerable multitude of Angels were gathered together,
4 Or ever the heights of the air were lifted up, before the measures of the firmament were named, or ever the chimnies in Sion were hot,
5 And before the present years were sought out, and before the inventions of them that now sin were turned, before they were sealed that have gathered faith for a treasure:
6 Then did I consider these things, and they all were made through me alone, and through none other: by me also they shall be ended, and by none other.

The Dividing of the Times

7 Then I answered and said, What shall be the parting assunder of the times? or when shall be the end of the first, and the beginning of it that follows?
8 And he said unto me, From Abraham unto Isaac, when Yacob and Esau were born of him, Yacob's hand held first the heel of Esau.

Cf. Gn.25:26. Or, from the beginning.

9 For Esau is the end of the world, and Yacob is the beginning of it that follows.

The War Scroll (iQM, 1Q33,4Q491-7,4Q471) identifies Edom as one of the "sons of Darkness" whom true Israel will fight to the very end. Edom is Esau. They will be consumed in the end of this world and those grafted into Yacob's covenant will be the beginning of the next world.

10 The hand of man is between the heel and the hand: other question, Ezra, ask you not.

More Signs of the End

11 I answered then and said, O Yahuah that bears rule, if I have found favor in thy sight,
12 I beseech you, show your servant the end of your tokens, whereof you showed me part the last night.
13 So he answered and said unto me, Stand up upon your feet, and hear a mighty sounding voice.

14 And it shall be as it were a great motion, but the place where you stand, shall not be moved.

Or, earthquake.

15 And therefore when it speaks be not afraid: for the word is of the end, and the foundation of the earth is understood.

16 And why? because the speech of these things trembles and is moved: for it knows that the end of these things must be changed.

17 And it happened that when I had heard it, I stood up upon my feet, and hearkened, and behold, there was a voice that spoke, and the sound of it was like the sound of many waters.

18 And it said, Behold, the days come, that I will begin to draw near, and to visit them that dwell upon the earth,

19 And will begin to make inquisition of them, what they be that have hurt unjustly with their unrighteousness, and when the affliction of Sion shall be fulfilled.

20 And when the world that shall begin to vanish away shall be finished: then will I show these tokens, the books shall be opened before the firmament, and they shall see all together.

Or, sealed.

21 And the children of a year old shall speak with their voices, the women with child shall bring forth untimely children, of three or four months old: and they shall live, and be raised up.

22 And suddenly shall the sown places appear unsown, the full storehouses shall suddenly be found empty.

23 And the trumpet shall give a sound, which when every man hears they shall be suddenly afraid.

Cf. 1 Cor. 15:52.

24 At that time shall friends fight one against another like enemies, and the earth shall stand in fear with those that dwell therein, the springs of the fountains shall stand still, and in three hours they shall not run.

Hydrothermal vents. Fountains of the Great Deep.

25 Whosoever remains from all these that I have told you, shall escape, and see my salvation, and the end of your world.

26 And the men that are received, shall see it, who have not tasted death from their birth: and the heart of the inhabitants shall be changed, and turned into another meaning.

27 For evil shall be put out, and deceit shall be quenched.

28 As for faith, it shall flourish, corruption shall be overcome, and the truth which has been so long without fruit, shall be declared.

Conclusion of the Second Vision

29 And when he talked with me, behold, I looked by little and little upon him before whom I stood.
30 And these words said he unto me, I am come to show you the time of the night to come.
31 If you will pray yet more, and fast seven days again, I shall tell you greater things by day, then I have heard.

See cap. 13. vers. 52.

32 For your voice is heard before the Most High: for the mighty has seen your righteous dealing, he has seen also your chastity, which you have had ever since your youth.
33 And therefore has he sent me to show you all these things, and to say unto you, Be of good comfort, and fear not.
34 And hasten not with the times that are past, to think vain things, that you may not hasten from the latter times.

The Third Vision

35 And it came to pass after this, that I wept again, and fasted seven days in like manner, that I might fulfill the three weeks which he told me.
36 And in the eighth night was my heart vexed within me again, and I began to speak before the Most High.
37 For my spirit was greatly set on fire, and my soul was in distress.

Yahuah's Work in Creation

38 And I said, O Yahuah, you spoke from the beginning of the creation, even the first day, and said thus, Let heaven and earth be made: and your word was a perfect work.

Cf. Gn. 1:1.

39 And then was the spirit, and darkeness, and silence were on every side; the sound of man's voice was not yet formed.
40 Then you commanded a fair light to come forth of your treasures, that your work might appear.
41 Upon the second day you made the spirit of the firmament, and commanded it to part assunder, and to make a division between the waters, that the one part might go up, and the other remain beneath.
42 Upon the third day you did command that the waters should be gathered in the seventh part of the earth: six parts have you dried up and kept them, to the intent that

of these some being planted of Elohim and tilled, might serve you.

43 For as soon as your word went forth, the work was made.

44 For immediately there was great and innumerable fruit, and many and diverse pleasures for the taste, and flowers of unchangable color, and odors of wonderful smell: and this was done the third day.

45 Upon the fourth day you commanded that the Sun should shine, and the Moon give her light, and the stars should be in order,

Cf. Gn. 1:14.

46 And gave them a charge to do service unto man, that was to be made.

Cf. Gn. 1:15; Dt. 4:19.

47 Upon the fifth day, you said unto the seventh part, where the waters were gathered, that it should bring forth living creatures, fouls and fishes: and so it came to pass.

Cf. Gn. 1:20.

48 For the dumb water, and without life, brought forth living things at the commandment of Elohim, that all people might praise your wondrous works.

49 Then did you ordain two living creatures, the one you called Enoch, and the other Leviathan,

Cf. Job 40:15 behemoth. Job 41:1 leviathan

50 And did separate the one from the other: for the seventh part (namely where the water was gathered together) might not hold them both.

51 Unto Enoch you gave one part which was dried up the third day, that he should dwell in the same part, wherein are a thousand hills.

52 But unto Leviathan you gave the seventh part, namely the moist, and has kept him to be devoured of whom you will, and when.

Cf. Ps. 74:14; Is. 27:1.

53 Upon the sixth day you gave commandment unto the earth, that before you it should bring forth beasts, cattle, and creeping things:

Cf. Gn. 1:25.

Why Do Yahuah's People Suffer?

54 And after these, Adam also whom you made lord of all your creatures, of him come we all, and the people also whom you have chosen.

55 All this have I spoken before you, O Yahuah, because you made the world for our sakes.

56 As for the other people which also come of Adam, you have said that they are nothing, but be like unto spittle, and have likened the abundance of them unto a drop that falls from a vessel.

57 And now, O Yahuah,

behold, these heathen, which have ever been reputed as nothing, have begun to be lords over us, and devour us:
58 But we your people (whom you have called your first born, your only begotten, and your fervent lover) are given into their hands.
59 If the world now be made for our sakes, why do we not possess an inheritance with the world? How long shall this endure?

15% Of the Earth Was Water Before the Flood

42 Upon the third day thou did command that the **waters should be gathered in the seventh part of the earth**: six parts has thou dried up and kept them...

47 Upon the fifth day, thou said **unto the seventh part, where the waters were gathered...**

50 And did separate the one from the other: for **the seventh part (namely where the water was gathered together)**...

52 But unto **Leviathan thou gave the seventh part**, namely the moist...

The World Ocean was formed by the Flood.

The Rivers from Eden can only be on the bottom of the ocean floor.
No modern river could fit.

Modern Rivers do not fit these Rivers from Eden as there was no rain before the Flood in Gen. 2:5. The Tigris, Modern Euphrates, Nile, Amazon, etc. all originate in precipitaion thus disqualified.

Genesis 2:10 KJV
And **a river went out of Eden to water the garden**; and from thence it was **parted**, and became into *four heads*.

The 60,000 km. continuous Mid-Ocean Ridge has exactly four intersections with Oceanic Trench System contiguous before the Flood.

PISON

NORTH AMERICA

The Philippines leads the world in gold, pearl and the onyx stone in all of history.

START 1

©2020 Map By The Levite Bible.

Gihon West 8:22

Genesis 2:11-12 KJV
The name of the first is **Pison**: that is it which **compasseth the whole land of Havilah**, where there is **gold**; And the gold of that land is **good**: there is **bdellium** and the **onyx stone**.

The Philippines is #1 in all 3 resources to this day and is the only fit.

Genesis 2:14b KJV
And the fourth river is Euphrates.

Cannot be the modern one.

It is the most significant and Hebrew reads East to West because all began in the East.

SOUTH AMERICA

RIVER FROM EDEN

PARAT

4 START

"If you drained all the water away, it would look exactly like a river system with bends and meanders, except there are no trees along the banks..."
– Dan Parsons, PhD, Sedimentologist, University of Hull, UK to BBC News (studies undersea rivers) [41]

"...waters should be gathered in the seventh part of the earth: six parts hast thou dried up..." *– 2 Esdras 6:42 KJVA (Cf. 2 Esdras 6:47, 6:49-52)*

Only 15% of Pre-Flood World was Water

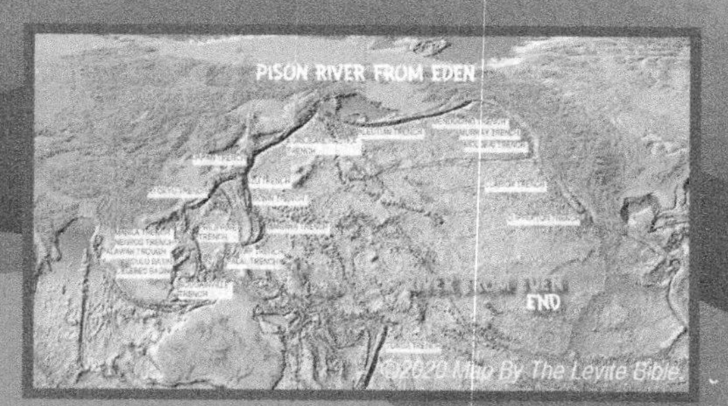

PRE-FLOOD WORLD RIVERS FROM EDEN THEORY

Confirmed By Jubilees

R FROM
DEN

Eden is the North Pole, the "middle" and "center of navel of earth." The River begins there and flows OUT.

EUROPE

Jubilees places Gihon on bottom of ocean floor and surrounding Africa.

Genesis 2:14a KJV
And the name of the third river is **Hiddekel**: that is it which goeth toward the **east of Assyria.**

The Tigris is "The River" in the Bible 27 times and NEVER Hiddekel. Daniel was in Iran during the period he had a vision on the Hiddekel and that was not the Tigris but the Iranian Persian Gulf.

LAND OF GOLD: Havilah, Ophir, Sheba, Tarshish, Elda

ASIA

ION

START

AFRICA

2

3

START

PISON

Defines East border of Shem and Elam

Genesis 2:13 KJV
And the name of the second river is **Gihon**: the same is it that **compasseth the whole land of Ethiopia.**

Ancient Ethiopia is coast to coast

Persian Gulf border

Gihon East border 8:15

GARDEN OF EDEN: Watered at End of Rivers from Eden

HIDDEKEL

"west to 'Afra...waters of Gihon, to the banks ..."
African Continental Shelf

AUSTRALIA

The Levite BIBLE

©2020 Map By The Levite Bible.

This is our theory.

VER FROM
EDEN

*All borders are approximations. This map not to scale.

NASA/Goddard Space Flight Center Map of the oceans drained. Emphasis added as we filled in the ridges and trenches with water. [15]

The flood breaketh out from the inhabitant; even the waters forgotten of the foot: they are dried up (Brought Low), they are gone away (shake) from men.." – Job 28:4 KJV
...Usually understood of (underground) streams. – Job 28:11 KJV

"...its roots (shall go down) to the Abyss
[and all the rivers of Eden shall water its branches]."
– Hymn 14, (formerly 10), The Thanksgiving Hymns. Qumran Scrolls (iQH, 1Q36,4Q427-32) [42]

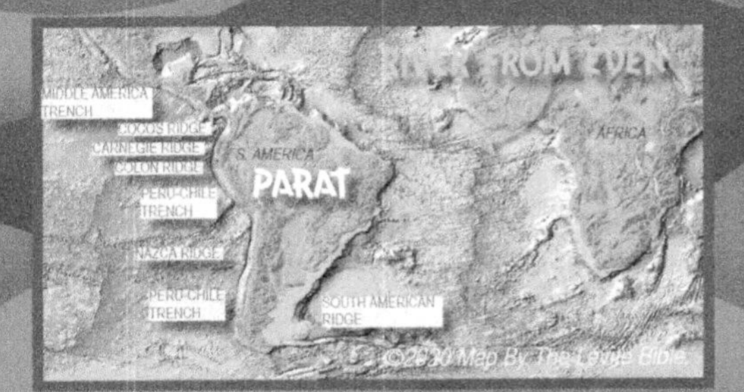

GARDEN OF EDEN

SHEM'S SOUTHEAST BORDER

MOUNTAINS OF FIRE

"Gunung Gunung Api" in Javanese

147 Volcanoes forming a natural geographic border between Shem and Ham in the Far East. [34]

GENESIS 3:24 KJV - EAST OF THE GARDEN

So he drove out the man; and he placed at the east of the garden of Eden Cherubims, and a flaming sword which turned every way, to keep the way of the tree of life.

SHEM

Whole land of the East and India.

Extends East til it reaches the GARDEN OF EDEN

PHILIPPINES

HAVILAH

GARDEN OF EDEN & OPHIR

east

north

Sabah, Malaysia

INDONESIA

From Africa West To Right of the Garden

PISON RIVER FROM EDEN

Philippine Trench

south

HAM

©2020 Map By The Levite Bible

West to Sea of Atel Indian Ocean

Then West to Sea of Ma'uk Atlantic Ocean

Then North to Gadir Cadiz, Spain

west

west

All borders are approximations. This map not to scale.

TESTING THE RESOURCES OF HAVILAH [31][32]

In all of history, the Philippines leads in gold mining since before 1000 B.C. and still remains #2 on earth in untapped gold reserves. There is no other land which competes. It is the ancient land of gold by historical record. [27]

PEARL

Bdellium is never a Biblical spice and all such spices are recorded in scripture. It is pearl. The Philippines has the largest pearls in all of history with no 2nd. [28]

"Puerto Princessa Pearl" 2006. 34 kg (75 lb.)

Ancient onyx especially in Egypt was known as alabaster used in ornamental construction. The Philippines has the strongest onyx and marble on earth in Romblon. [29]

Marine life is the true measure for the Land of Creation as it was not wiped out by the Flood. The Epicenter of Marine Biodiversity on ALL of earth is the Philippines in the Sulu Sea. [30]

Tubbataha Reef in the Sulu Sea.

In resources, history, geography, science, language and the Bible, this is Ophir.

See "The Search for King Solomon's Treasure: The Lost Isles of Gold and the Garden of Eden" for Evidences.

GENESIS 2:11-12 KJV

The name of the first is Pison: that is it which compasseth the whole land of Havilah, where there is gold; And the gold of that land is good: there is bdellium and the onyx stone.

HAVILAH [31][32]

= GARDEN OF EDEN

= LAND OF CREATION

= OPHIR

= PHILIPPINES

JUBILEES 3:32

Adam and his wife went forth from the Garden of Eden, and they dwelt in the land of 'Elda, in the land of their creation.

GARDEN SYSTEM IN THE END TIMES

The World Ocean will disppear in the end to restore the Rivers from Eden.

6:24
...the springs of the fountains shall stand still, and in **three hours they shall not run**.

Rev. 21:1
And I saw a new heaven and a new earth: for the first heaven and the first earth were passed away; and **there was no more sea**.

2:12 *(Cf. Rev. 2:7, 22:2, 22:14)*
They shall have the Tree of Life for an ointment of sweet sauour, they shall neither labor, nor be weary.

Sirach 24:29-31 *(Cf. 2 Enoch 8:4-7)*
For her thoughts are more than the sea, and her counsels profounder than the **great deep**. I also came out as a brook from a river, and as a **conduit into a garden**. I said, I will water my best garden, and will water abundantly my garden bed: and, lo, **my brook became a river, and my river became a sea**.

(Description of Pre-Flood world. The world ocean was formed by the Flood.)

CHAPTER 7:

4 The way is narrow. 12 When it was made narrow. 28 All shall die and rise again. 33 Messiah shall sit in judgement. 46 Elohim has not made Paradise in vain, 62 and is merciful.

Response to Ezra's Questions

1 And when I had made an end of speaking these words, there was sent unto me the Angel which had been sent unto me the nights before.

Elohim is a classification of heavenly being not exclusive to Yahuah and is plural.

2 And he said unto me, Up Ezra, and hear the words that I am come to tell you.

3 And I said, Speak on, my Elohim. Then said he unto me, The Sea is set in a wide place, that it might be deep and great.

4 But put the case the entrance were narrow, and like a river,

5 Who then could go into the Sea to look upon it, and to rule it? If he went not through the narrow, how could he come into the broad?

6 There is also another thing. A city is builded, and set upon a broad field, and is full of all good things.

Cf. Mt. 7:13-14. Narrow path ***Messiah quoted 2 Esdras.***

7 The entrance thereof is narrow, and is set in a dangerous place to fall, like as if there were a fire on the right hand, and on the left a deep water.

Or, steepe place.

8 And one only path between them both, even between the fire and the water, so small that there could but one man go there at once.

9 If this city now were given unto a man for an inheritance, if he never shall pass the danger set before it, how shall he receive this inheritance?

10 And I said, It is so, lord. Then he said unto me, Even so also is Israel's portion:

11 **Because for their sakes I made the world**: and when Adam transgressed my Statutes, then was decreed that now is done.

12 Then were the entrances of this world made narrow, full of sorrow and travail: they are but few and evil, full of perils, and very painful.

13 For the entrances of the elder world were wide and sure, and brought immortal fruit.

Or, greater

14 If then they that live, labor not to enter these straight and vain things, they can never receive those that are laid up for them.

Cf. Mt. 7; Jn. 15. Salvation is free but requires effort in relationship.

15 Now therefore why disquiet yourself, seeing you are but a corruptible man? and why are you moved, whereas you are but mortal?

Enter ye in at the strait gate: for wide is the gate, and broad is the way, that leadeth to destruction, and many there be which go in thereat:
Because strait is the gate, and narrow is the way, which leadeth unto life, and few there be that find it.

Matthew 7:13-14 KJV

The gate was not widened.
It remains narrow as does
the path to Salvation defined in
Matthew 7 and John 15 as relationship
with Yahusha. Even Christians will be
among those told to depart from Him
without true relationship.

Origin 2 Esdras 7:12-14

MESSIAH QUOTES
2 ESDRAS AGAIN

16 Why have you not considered in your mind this thing that is to come, rather than that which is present?

The Fate of the Ungodly

Cf. Dt. 8:1.

17 Then I answered, and said, O Yahuah, that bears rule, you have ordained in your Law, that the righteous should inherit these things, but that the ungodly should perish:

18 Nevertheless, the righteous shall suffer straight things, and hope for wide: for they that have done wickedly, have suffered the straight things, and yet shall not see the wide.

It is modern church doctrine to despise His Law generally yet the Bible never sets an expiration date for His Law which is also reinforced every time you see the word sin or lawlessness.

19 And he said unto me, There is no judge above Elohim, and none that has understanding above the Highest.

20 For there be many that perish in this life, because they despise the Law of Elohim that is set before them.

21 For Elohim has given straight commandment to such as came, what they should do to live, even as they came, and what they should observe to avoid punishment.

22 Nevertheless they were not obedient unto him, but spoke against him, and imagined vain things:

23 And deceived themselves by their wicked deeds, and said of the Most High, that he is not, and knew not his ways.

24 But his Law have they despised, and denied his covenants in his statutes have they not been faithful, and have not performed his works.

25 And therefore Ezra, for the empty, are empty things, and for the full, are the full things.

The Temporary Messianic Kingdom

26 Behold, the time shall come, that these tokens which I have told you, shall come to pass, and the bride shall appear, and she coming forth shall be seen, that now is withdrawn from the earth.

Cf. 1 Thes. 4:14-17; Dn. 12; Jn. 5:28-29; Rev. 20:12; Acts 24:15.

27 And whosoever is delivered from the forementioned evils, shall see my wonders.

Messianic Prophecy: The only exact prophecy of Messiah's birth by His name Yahusha and around 0 BC.

28 For my son YAHUSHA shall be revealed with those that be with him, and they that remain shall rejoice **within four hundred years**.

Messianic Prophecy: Yahusha's death predicted.

29 After these years shall my son Messiah die, and all men that have life.

30 And the world shall be turned into the old silence seven days, like as in the former judgements: so that no man shall remain.

Or, first beginning.

31 And after seven days, the world that yet awake not shall

Ezra predicted by name that Yahusha, the Son of Yahuah, would be born in around 0 B.C. as well as his death and resurrection so that men may have life. This is exact!

28 **For my son YAHUSHA shall be revealed** with those that be with him, and they that remain shall rejoice **within four hundred years**. 29 After these years shall my son Messiah die, and all men that have life.

– The Prophet Ezra, 400 B.C.

be raised up, and that shall die, that is corrupt.

32 And the earth shall restore those that are asleep in her, and so shall the dust those that dwell in silence, and the secret places shall deliver those souls that were committed unto them.

Cf. 1 Thes. 4:14-17; Dn. 12; Jn. 5:28-29; Rev. 20:12; Acts 24:15.

33 And the Most High shall appear upon the seat of judgment, and misery shall pass away, and the long suffering shall have an end.

34 But judgment only shall remain, truth shall stand, and faith shall wax strong.

Cf. Gn.18:13. Ex. 32:11.

35 And the work shall follow, and the reward shall be shown, and the good deeds shall be of force, and wicked deeds shall bear no rule.

Or, Archer.

No Intercession for the Ungodly

36 Then I said, Abraham prayed first for the Sodomites, and Moses for the fathers that sinned in the wilderness:

Cf. Gn. 18.

Cf. Ex. 32.

37 And Yahushua after him for Israel in the time of Achan,

Cf. 2 Sam. 24:17. 2 Chr. 6:14.

38 And Samuel; and David for the destruction: and Solomon for them that should come to the sanctuary.

39 And EliYahu for those that received rain, and for the dead that he might live.

Cf. 1 Ki.17:21, 18:42, 45. Elijah = EliYahu in Hebrew.

40 And Hezekiah for the people in the time of Sennacherib: and many for many.

Cf. 2 Ki. 19:15.

41 Even so now seeing corruption is grown up, and wickedness increased, and the righteous have prayed for the ungodly: wherefore shall it not be so now also?

42 He answered me and said, This present life is not the end where much glory does abide; therefore have they prayed for the weak.

43 But the day of doom shall be the end of this time, and the beginning of the immortality for to come, wherein corruption is past.

44 Intemperance is at an end, infidelity is cut off, righteousness is grown, and truth is sprung up.

45 Then shall no man be able to save him that is destroyed, nor to oppress him that has gotten the victory.

Cf. Rom. 5:18.

Lamentation over the Fate of Most People

46 I answered then and said, This is my first and last saying; that it had been better not to have given the earth unto Adam: or else when it was given him, to have restrained him from sinning.

31 And after seven days, the world that yet awake not shall be raised up, and that shall die, that is corrupt.

1 Enoch

10.12 ... bind them for seventy generations, under the hills of the earth, until the day of their judgment and of their consummation, until the judgment, which is for all eternity, is accomplished.

10.14 ...together they will be bound until the end of all generations.

(70 Generations = 7,000 years)

7 Days = 7,000 years

1 Day = 1,000 years: Jb. 4:30, 2 Pt. 3:8, Ps. 90:4

47 For what profit is it for men now in this present time to live in heaviness, and after death to look for punishment?
48 O Adam, what have you done? for though it was you that sinned, you are not fallen alone, but we all that come of you.
49 For what profit is it unto us, if there be promised us an immortal time, whereas we have done the works that bring death?
50 And that their is promised us an everlasting hope, whereas ourselves being most wicked are made vain?
51 And that there are laid up for us dwellings of health and safety, whereas we have lived wickedly?
52 And that the glory of the Most High is kept to defend them which have led a weary life, whereas we have walked in the most wicked ways of all?

Or, a chast life.

53 And that there should be shown a paradise whose fruit endures forever, wherein is security and medicine, since we shall not enter into it?

Or, fullness.

54 For we have walked in unpleasant places.
55 And that the faces of them which have used abstinence, shall shine above the stars, whereas our faces shall be blacker than darkness?
56 For while we lived and committed iniquity, we considered not that we should begin to suffer for it after death.

Or, intent.

57 Then he answered me and said, This is the condition of the battle, which man that is born upon the earth shall fight,
58 That if he be overcome, he shall suffer as you have said, but if he get the victory, he shall receive the thing that I say.
59 For this is the life whereof Moses spoke unto the people while he lived, saying, Choose you life that you may live.

Cf. Dt. 30:19.

60 Nevertheless they believed him not, nor yet the prophets after him, no nor me which have spoken unto them,
61 That there should not be such heaviness in their destruction, as shall be joy over them that are persuaded to salvation.

Cf. Rom. 2:4.

Ezra Appeals to Yahuah's Mercy

62 I answered then and said, I know, Yahuah, that the Most High is called merciful, in that he hath mercy upon them, which are not yet come into the world,

The remnant is found in Rev. doing exactly that turning to His Law again.

63 And upon those also that turn to his Law,
64 And that he is patient, and long suffer those that have sinned, as his creatures,
65 And that he is bountiful, for he is ready to give where needed,
66 And that is of great mercy, for he multiplies more and more mercies to them that are present, and that are past, and also to them which are to come.
67 For if he shall not multiply his mercies, the world would not continue with them that inherit therein.
68 And he pardons; for if he did not so of his goodness, that they which have committed iniquities might be eased of them, the ten thousand part of men should not remain living.
69 And being Judge, if he should not forgive them that are cured with his word, and put out the multitude of contentions,
70 There should be very few left peradventure in an innumerable multitude.

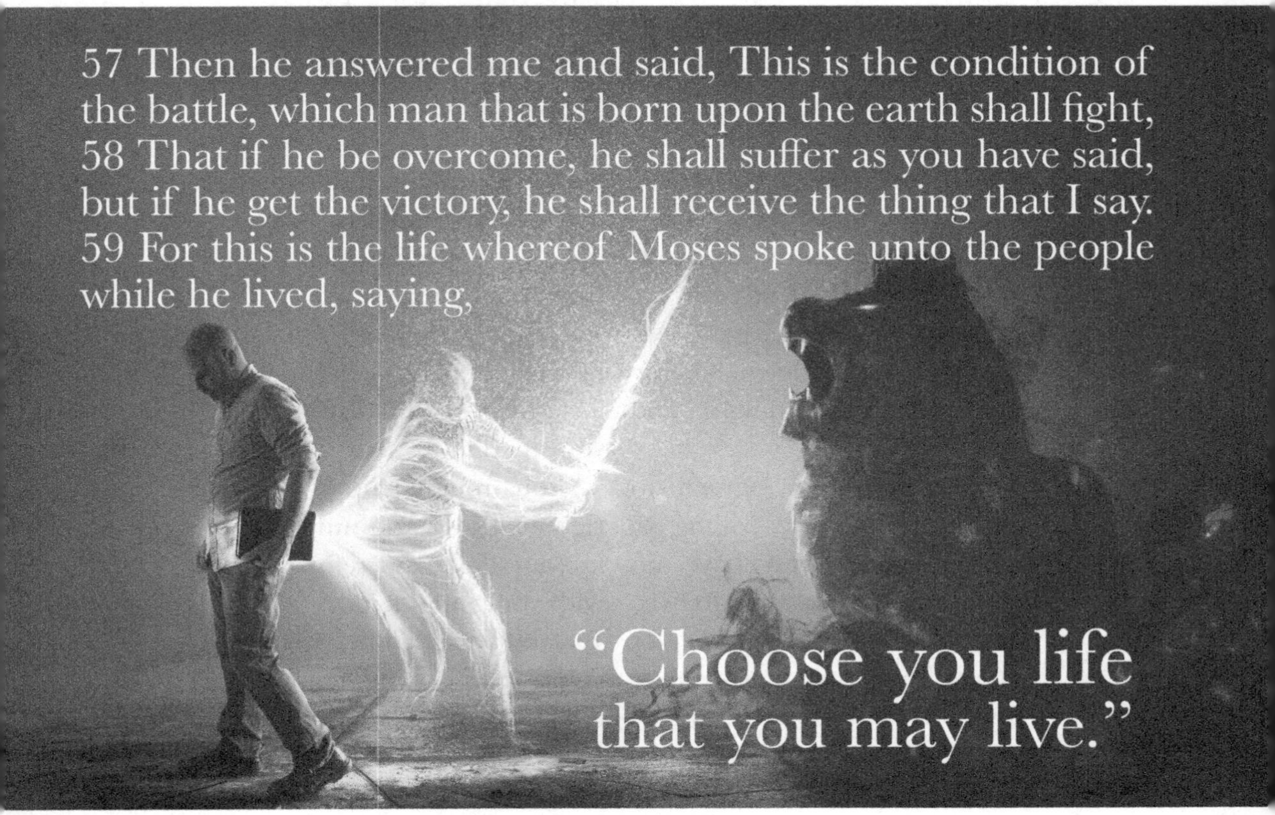

Or, created. Or, contempts.

57 Then he answered me and said, This is the condition of the battle, which man that is born upon the earth shall fight,
58 That if he be overcome, he shall suffer as you have said, but if he get the victory, he shall receive the thing that I say.
59 For this is the life whereof Moses spoke unto the people while he lived, saying,

"Choose you life that you may live."

CHAPTER 8:

1 Many created, but few saved. 6 He asks why Elohim destroys his own work, 26 and pray Elohim to look upon the people which only serve him. 41 Elohim answers that all seed comes not to Elohim, 52 and that glory is prepared for him and such like.

1 And he answered me, saying, The Most High hath made this world for many, but the world to come for few.

Mt. 20:16. Messiah quoted 2 Esdras.

2 I will tell you a similitude, Ezra, As when you ask the earth, it shall say unto you, that it gives much mold whereof earthen vessels are made, but little dust that gold comes of: even so is the course of this present world.

Ezra Again Appeals to Yah's Mercy

3 There be many created, but few shall be saved.

Mt. 20:16. Messiah quoted 2 Esdras.

4 So I answered and said, Swallow then down O my soul, understanding, and devour wisdom.

5 For you have agreed to give ear, and are willing to prophesy: for you have no longer space then only to live.

6 O Yahuah, if you suffer not your servant that we may pray before you, and you give us seed unto our heart, and culture to our understanding, that there may come fruit of it, how shall each man live that is corrupt, who bears the place of a man?

Or, to give us.

7 For you are alone, and we all one workmanship of your hands, like as you have said.

8 For when the body is fashioned now in the mother's womb, and you give it members, your creature is preserved in fire and water, and nine months does your workmanship endure your creature which is created in her.

Or, how is the body fashioned.

9 But that which keeps, and is kept, shall both be preserved: and when the time comes, the womb preserved, delivers up the things that grew in it.

10 For you have commanded out of the parts of the body, that is to say, out of the breasts milk to be given, which is the fruit of the breasts,

11 That the thing which is fashioned, may be nourished for a time, til you dispose it to your mercy.

12 You brought it up with your righteousness, and nurtured it in your Law, and reformed it with your judgment.

13 And you shall mortify it as your creature, and quicken it as your work.

Cf. Rom 8:11.

14 If therefore you shall destroy him which with so

great labor was fashioned, it is an easy thing to be ordained by your Commandment, that the thing which was made might be preserved.

Cf. Job 10:8. Ps.139:14.

15 Now therefore, Yahuah, I will speak (touching man in general, you know best) but touching your people, for whose sake I am sorry,

16 And for your inheritance, for whose cause I mourn, and for Israel, for whom I am heavy, and for Yacob, for whose sake I am troubled:

17 Therefore will I begin to pray before you, for myself, and for them: for I see the falls of us that dwell in the land.

18 But I have heard the swiftness of the Judge which is to come.

Messianic Prophecy.

19 Therefore hear my voice, and understand my words, and I shall speak before you: this is the beginning of the words of Ezra, before he was taken up: and I said;

Ezra's Prayer

20 O Yahuah, You that dwell in everlastingness, which beholds from above, things in the heaven, and in the air,

21 Whose Throne is inestimable, whose glory may not be comprehended, before whom the hosts of Angels stand with trembling,

22 (Whose service is conversant in wind and fire,) whose word is true, and sayings constant, whose Commandment is strong, and ordinance fearful,

23 Whose look dries up the depths, and indignation makes the mountains to melt away, which the truth witnesses:

24 O hear the prayer of your servant, and give ear to the petition of your creature.

25 For while I live, I will speak, and so long as I have understanding, I will answer.

26 O look not upon the sins of your people: but on them which serve you in truth.

27 Regard not the wicked inventions of the heathen: but the desire of those that keep your Testimonies in afflictions.

28 Think not upon those that have walked fainedly before you: but remember them, which according to your will have known your fear.

29 Let it not be your will to destroy them, which have lived like beasts: but to look upon them that have clearly taught your Law.

30 Take you no indignation at them which are deemed worse than beasts: but love them that always put their trust in your righteousness, and glory.

31 For we and our fathers do languish of such diseases; but because of us sinners, you shall be called merciful.

Are sick.

32 For if you have a desire to have mercy upon us, you shall be called merciful, to us namely, that have no works of righteousness.

Be willing.

33 For the just which have many good works laid up with you, shall out of their own deeds receive reward.

34 For what is man that you should take displeasure at him? Or what is a corruptible generation, that you should be so bitter toward it?

35 For in truth there is no man among them that be born, but he has dealt wickedly, and among the faithful, there is none which has not done amiss.

Cf. Rom. 3:23; 1 Ki. 8:46; 2 Chr. 6:36.

36 For in this, O Yahuah, your righteousness, and your goodness shall be declared, if you be merciful unto them which have not the confidence of good works.

Or, substance.

Response to Ezra's Prayer

37 Then he answered me, and said, Some things have you spoken aright, and according unto your words it shall be.

38 For indeed I will not think on the disposition of them which have sinned before death, before judgment, before destruction.

39 But I will rejoice over the disposition of the righteous, and I will remember also their pilgrimage, and the salvation, and the reward that they shall have.

Cf. Gn. 4:4.

40 Like as I have spoken now, so shall it come to pass.

41 For as the husbandman sows much seed upon the ground, and plants many trees, and yet the thing that is sown good in his season, comes not up, neither does all that is planted take root: even so is it of them that are sown in the world, they shall not all be saved.

42 I then answered, and said, If I have found grace, let me speak.

43 Like as the husbandman's seed perishes, if it come not up, and receive not the rain in due season, or if there come too much rain and corrupt it:

44 Even so perish man also which is formed with your hands, and is called your own image, because you are like unto him, for whose sake you have made all things, and likened him unto the husbandman's seed.

45 Be not wroth with us, but spare your people, and have mercy upon your own inheritance: for you are merciful unto your creature.

Ezra's Final Appeal for Mercy

46 Then he answered me, and said, Things present are for the present, and things to come, for such as be to come.
47 For you come far short, that you should be able to love my creature more than I: but I have oft times drawn near unto you, and unto it, **but never to the unrighteous**.
48 In this also you are marvelous before the Most High;
49 In that you have humbled yourself as it becomes you, and has not judged yourself worthy to be much glorified among the righteous.
50 For many great miseries shall be done to them, that in the latter time shall dwell in the world, because they have walked in great pride.
51 But understand you for yourself, and seek out the glory for such as be like you.
52 **For unto you is Paradise opened, the tree of life is planted**, the time to come is prepared, plentiousness is made ready, a city is built, and rest is allowed, yes perfect goodness and wisdom.

Cf. 2:12, Rev. 2:7, 22:2, 22:14. ***Believers in the end will once again partake of the Tree of Life and the Garden of Eden will be opened to them. Origin: 2 Esdras.***

53 The root of evil is sealed up from you, weakness and the moth is hidden from you, and corruption is fled into hell to be forgotten.
54 Sorrows are passed, and in the end is shown the treasure of immortality.

Or, grave.

55 And therefore ask you no more questions concerning the multitude of them that perish.
56 For when they had taken liberty, they despised the Most High, thought scorn of his Law, and forsook his ways.
57 Moreover, they have troden down his righteous,
58 And said in their heart, that there is no Elohim, yes and knowing that they must die.

Cf. Ps.14:1, 53:1. This is more profound today as the religion of Scientism or Atheism declares God is dead. They will be, He is not.

59 For as the things aforesaid shall receive you, so thirst and pain are prepared for them; for **it was not his will that men should come to nothing**.

Cf. 2 Pt. 3:9 Yahuah has never willed that any should perish. ***Origin: 2 Esdras.***

60 But they which be created, have defiled the Name of him that made them, and were unthankful unto him which prepared life for them.
61 And therefore is my judgment now at hand.
62 These things have I not shown unto all men, but unto you, and a few like you. Then I answered, and said,
63 Behold, O Yahuah, now have you shown me the multitude of the wonders which you will begin to do in the last times: but at what time, you have not shown me.

CHAPTER 9:

7 Who shall be saved, and who not. 19 All the world is now corrupted: 22 Yet Yahuah does save a few. 33 He complains that those perish which keep Elohim's Law: 38 and sees a woman lamenting in a field.

More about the Signs of the End

1 He then answered me, and said, Measure you the time diligently in itself: and when you see part of the signs past, which I have told you before,
2 Then shall you understand, that it is the very same time, wherein the Highest will begin to visit the world which he made.
3 Therefore when there shall be seen earthquakes and uproars of the people in the world:

Cf. Mt. 24:7.

4 Then shall you well understand, that the Most High spoke of those things from the days that were before you, even from the beginning.
5 For like as all that is made in the world has a beginning, and an end, and the end is manifest:
6 Even so the times also of the Highest, have plain beginnings in wonders and powerful works, and endings in effects and signs.
7 And every one that shall be saved, and shall be able to escape by his works, and by faith, whereby you have believed,

Jas. 2:18, 20, 26. "faith without works is dead." Faith is demonstrated through works as a sign of one's salvation.

8 Shall be preserved from the said perils, and shall see my salvation, in my land, and within my borders: for I have sanctified them for me, from the beginning.
9 Then shall they be in pitiful case which now have abused my ways: and they that have cast them away despitefully, shall dwell in torments.

Or, they shall marvel.

10 For such, as in their life have received benefits, and have not known me:

Cf. Mt. 7

11 And they that have loathed my law, while they had yet liberty, and when as yet place of repentance was open unto them, understood not, but despised it:
12 The same must know it after death by pain.
13 And therefore be not curious, how the ungodly shall be punished and when: but inquire how the righteous shall be saved, whose the world is, and for whom the world is created.

The Argument Recapitulated

14 Then I answered, and said,
15 I have said before, and now

do speak, and will speak it also hereafter: that there be many more of them which perish, then of them which shall be saved,

16 Like as a wave is greater than a drop.

17 And he answered me, saying: like as the field is, so is also the seed: as the flowers be, such are the colors also: such as the workman is, such

And Jesus answered and said unto them, Take heed that no man deceive you. For many shall come in my name, saying, I am Christ; and shall deceive many. And ye shall hear of wars and rumours of wars: see that ye be not troubled: for all these things must come to pass, but the end is not yet. For nation shall rise against nation, and kingdom against kingdom: and there shall be famines, and pestilences, and earthquakes, in divers places. All these are the beginning of sorrows.

Matthew 24:4-8 KJV

Origin 2 Esdras 9:1-7

MESSIAH QUOTES 2 ESDRAS AGAIN

also is the work: and as the husbandman is himself, so is his husbandry also: for it was the time of the world.

And now because the time of the world was come, when I was preparing the world.

18 And now when I prepared the world, which was not yet made, even for them to dwell in that now live, no man spoke against me.

But when the world was made, both now and then, the manners of every one created were corrupted by a never failing harvest, and a law unsearchable.

19 For then every one obeyed, but now the manners of them which are created in this world that is made, are corrupted by a perpetual seed, and by a law which is unsearchable, rid themselves.

20 So I considered the world, and behold there was peril, because of the devices that were come into it.

21 And I saw and spared it greatly, and have kept me a grape of the cluster, and a plant of a great people.

Or, grain.
Cf. Jn. 15.

22 Let the multitude perish then, which was born in vain, and let my grape be kept and my plant: for with great labor have I made it perfect.

Or, grain.

23 Nevertheless if you will cease yet seven days more (but you shall not fast in them.)

24 But go into a field of flowers, where no house is built, and eat only the flowers of the field, Taste no flesh, drink no wine, but eat flowers only.

25 And pray unto the Highest continually, then will I come and talk with you.

The Abiding Glory of the Mosaic Law

26 So I went my way into the field which is called Ardath, like as he commanded me, and there I sat amongst the flowers, and did eat of the herbs of the field, and the meat of the same satisfied me.

27 After seven days I sat upon the grass, and my heart was vexed within me, like as before.

28 And I opened my mouth, and began to talk before the Most High and said,

29 O Yahuah, you that shows yourself unto us, you were shown unto our fathers in the wilderness, in a place where no man treads, in a barren place when they came out of Egypt.

Cf. Ex. 19:9, 24:3. Dt. 4:12.
Or, comes.

30 And you spoke, saying, Hear me, O Israel, and mark my words, you seed of Yacob.

31 For behold I sow my law in you, and it shall bring fruit in you, and you shall be honored in it forever.

32 But our fathers which received the law, kept it not, and observed not your ordinances, and though the fruit of your law did not

Yahuah's Law cannot perish!

perish, neither could it, for it was yours:

33 Yet they that received it, perished, because they kept not the thing that was sown in them.

34 And lo, it is a custom when the ground has received seed, or the Sea a ship, or any vessel, meat or drink, that, that being perished wherein it was sown, or cast into,

35 That thing also which was sown or cast therein, or received, does perish, and remains not with us: but with us it has not happened so.

36 For we that have received the law perish by sin, and our heart also which received it.

Yahuah's Law cannot perish!

37 Notwithstanding **the law perishes not**, but remains in his force.

The Vision of a Weeping Woman

38 And when I spake these things in my heart, I looked back with my eyes, and upon the right side I saw a woman, and behold, she mourned, and wept with a loud voice, and was much grieved in heart, and her clothes were rent, and she had ashes upon her head.

39 Then I let my thoughts that I was in, go, and turned unto her,

40 And said unto her, Wherefore you weep? why are you so grieved in your mind?

41 And she said unto me, Sir, let me alone, that I may bewail myself, and add unto my sorrow, for I am sore vexed in my mind, and brought very low.

42 And I said unto her, What ails you? Tell me.

43 She said unto me, I your servant have been barren, and had no child, though I had an husband thirty years.

44 And those thirty years I did nothing else day and night, and every hour, but make my prayer to the Highest.

45 After thirty years, Elohim heard me your handmaid, looked upon my misery, considered my trouble, and gave me a son: and I was very glad of him, so was my husband also, and all my neighbors, and we gave great honor unto the Almighty.

The travailing woman is Israel in scripture.

46 And I nourished him with great travail.

47 So when he grew up, and came to the time that he should have a wife, I made a feast.

CHAPTER 10:

1 He comforts the woman in the field. 17 She vanishes away, and a city appears in her place. 40 The Angel declares these visions in the field.

The Vision of a Weeping Woman Continued

1 And it so came to pass, that when my son was entered into his wedding chamber, he fell down and died.

2 Then we all overthrew the lights, and all my neighbors rose up to comfort me, so I took my rest unto the second day at night.

Or country men citizens.

3 And it came to pass when they had all left off to comfort me, to the end I might be quiet: then I rose up by night and fled, and came hither into this field, as you see.

4 And I do now purpose not to return into the city, but here to stay, and neither to eat nor drink, but continually to mourn, and to fast until I die.

5 Then I left the meditations wherein I was, and spoke to her in anger, saying,

Or, speeches.

6 You foolish woman above all other, see you not our mourning, and what happened unto us?

7 How that Sion our mother is full of all heaviness, and much humbled, mourning very sore?

8 And now seeing we all mourn, and are sad, for we are all in heaviness, are you grieved for one son?

9 For ask the earth, and she shall tell you, that it is she, which ought to mourn, for the fall of so many that grow upon her.

10 For out of her came all at the first, and out of her shall all others come: and behold they walk almost all into destruction, and a multitude of them is utterly rooted out.

Or, abolished.

11 Who then should make more mourning than she that has lost so great a multitude, and not you which are sorry but for one?

12 But if you say unto me, My lamentation is not like the earth's, because I have lost the fruit of my womb, which I brought forth with pains, and bare with sorrows.

13 But the earth not so: for the multitude present in it, according to the course of the earth, is gone, as it came.

But the earth after the manner of the earth: whereinto the present multitude is gone again, as it came out.

14 Then I say unto you, Like as you have brought forth with labor: even so the earth also has given her fruit, namely man, ever since the beginning, unto him that made her.

15 Now therefore keep your

sorrow to yourself, and bear with a good courage that which has befallen you.

16 For if you shall acknowledge the determination of Elohim to be just, you shall both receive your son in time, and shall be commended amongst women.

17 Go your way then into the city, to your husband.

18 And she said unto me, That I will not do: I will not go into the city, but here I will die.

19 So I proceeded to speak further unto her, and said,

20 Do not so, but be counseled by me: for how many are the adversities of Sion? Be comforted in regard of the sorrow of Yerusalem.

21 For you see that our Sanctuary is laid waste, our Altar broken down, our Temple destroyed.

22 Our Psaltery is laid on the ground, our song is put to silence, our rejoicing is at an end, the light of our candlestick is put out, the Ark of our Covenant is spoiled, our holy things are defiled, and the Name that is called upon us, is almost profaned: our children are put to shame, our priests are burnt, our Levites are gone into captivity, our virgins are defiled, and our wives ravished, our righteous men carried away, our little ones destroyed, our young men are brought in bondage, and our strong men are become weak.

23 And which is the greatest of all, the seal of Sion has now lost her honor: for she is delivered into the hands of them that hate us.

24 And therefore shake off your great heaviness, and put away the multitude of sorrows, that the mighty may be merciful unto you again, and the Highest shall give you rest, and ease from thy labor.

25 And it came to pass while I was talking with her, behold her face upon a sudden shined exceedingly, and her countenance glistered, so that I was afraid of her, and mused what it might be.

26 And behold suddenly, she made a great cry very fearful: so that the earth shook at the noise of the woman.

27 And I looked, and behold, the woman appeared unto me no more, but there was a city built, and a large place shown itself from the foundations: then was I afraid, and cried with a loud voice, and said,

28 Where is Uriel the Angel, who came unto me at the first? for he has caused me to fall into many trances, and my

Chap.4.1. Or, into the multitude in a trance.

end is turned into corruption, and my prayer to rebuke.

Uriel's Interpretation of the Vision

29 And as I was speaking these words, behold, he came unto me, and looked upon me.
30 And lo, I lay as one that had been dead, and my understanding was taken from me, and he took me by the right hand, and comforted me, and set me upon my feet, and said unto me,
31 What ails you? And why are you so disquieted, and why is your understanding troubled, and the thoughts of your heart?
32 And I said, because you have forsaken me, and yet I did according to your words, and I went into the field, and lo I have seen, and yet see, that I am not able to express.
33 And he said unto me, Stand up manfully, and I will advise you.
34 Then I said, Speak on, my lord in me, only forsake me not, lest I die frustrated of my hope.
35 For I have seen, that I knew not, and hear that I do not know.
36 Or, is my sense deceived, or my soul in a dream?
37 Now therefore, I beseech you, that you will show your servant of this vision.

Or, trance.

38 He then answered me, and said, Hear me, and I shall inform you, and tell you wherefore you are afraid: for the Highest will reveal many secret things unto you.
39 He has seen that your way is right: for that you sorrow continually for your people, and make great lamentation for Sion.

Or, purpose.

40 This therefore is the meaning of the vision which you lately saw.
41 You saw a woman mourning, and you began to comfort her:
42 But now you see the likeness of the woman no more, but there appeared unto you a city built.
43 And whereas she told you of the death of her son, this is the solution.

Or, Interpretation.

44 This woman whom you saw, is Sion: and whereas she said unto you (even she whom you saw as a city built.)
45 Whereas I say, she said unto you, that she has been thirty years barren: those are the thirty years wherein there was no offering made in her.

Cf. Lev. 26:34, 2 Chr. 36:21. "So the land enjoyed it's Sabbath rest, lying desolate until the seventy years."

46 But after thirty years, Solomon built the city, and offered offerings: and then

Yahuah's presence in Yerusalem was to nourish His people with labor.

bare the barren a son.

47 And whereas she told you that she nourished him with labor: that was the dwelling in Yerusalem.

48 But whereas she said unto you, That my son coming into his marriage chamber, happened to have a fall, and died, this was the destruction that came to Yerusalem.

49 And behold, you saw her likeness, and because she mourned for her son, you began to comfort her, and of these things which have chanced, these are to be opened unto you.

50 For now the Most High sees, that you are grieved unfainedly, and suffer from your whole heart for her, so has he showed you the brightness of her glory, and the comeliness of her beauty.

51 And therfore I bade you remain in the field, where no house was built.

52 For I knew that the Highest would show this unto you.

53 Therefore I commanded you to go into the field, where no foundation of any building was.

54 For in the place wherein the Highest began to show his city, there can no man's building be able to stand.

55 And therefore fear not, let not your heart be afrighted, but go your way in, and see the beauty and greatness of the building, as much as your eyes be able to see:

56 And then shall you hear as much as your ears may comprehend.

57 For you are blessed above many others, and are called with the Highest, and so are but few.

Or, are called to be with.

58 But tomorrow at night you shall remain here.

59 And so shall the Highest show you visions of the high things, which the Most High will do unto them, that dwell upon earth in the last days. So I slept that night and another, like as he commanded me.

Or, last things.

Ezra laments the sacking of Yerusalem.

CHAPTER 11:

1 He sees in his dream an Eagle coming out of the Sea: 37 And a Lion out of a woods condemning and judging the Eagle.

The Vision of the Eagle

1 Then I saw a dream, and behold, there came up from the Sea an Eagle, which had twelve feathered wings, and three heads.

Cf. Rev. 13:1.

This Empire is of female identification. All 3 heads as the true power are known as she, her and mother.

2 And I saw, and behold, she spread her wings over all the earth, and all the winds of the air blew on her, and were gathered together.

3 And I beheld, and out of her feathers there grew other contrary feathers, and they became little feathers, and small.

4 But her heads were at rest: the head in the middle was greater than the other, yet it rested with the rest.

True power lies in the heads which rest and rise in the end.

5 Moreover I beheld, and lo, the Eagle flew with her feathers, and reigned upon earth, and over them that dwelt therein.

6 And I saw that all things under heaven were subject unto her, and no man spoke against her, no not one creature upon earth.

This must represent the largest world powers of history.

7 And I beheld, and lo, the Eagle rose upon her talons, and spoke to her feathers, saying,

8 Watch not all at once, sleep every one in his own place, and watch by course.

9 But let the heads be preserved for the last.

This Empire will conceal it's true power in it's 3 heads until the end. It has ruled for over 1,000 years but the heads are more recent history. They are hidden.

10 And I beheld, and lo, the voice went not out of her heads, but from the middle of her body.

This is the prince demon speaking from within known as Gog of Magog. However, though different names and countries rise and fall, this remains one single Empire in reality.

11 And I numbered her contrary feathers, and behold, there were eight of them.

12 And I looked, and behold, on the right side there arose one feather, and reigned over all the earth.

13 And so it was, that when it reigned, the end of it came, and the place thereof appeared no more: so the next following stood up and reigned, and had a great time.

14 And it happened, that when it reigned, the end of it came also, like as the first, so that it appeared no more.

15 Then came there a voice unto it, and said,

16 Hear, you that has born rule over the earth so long: this I say unto you, before you begin to appear no more.

17 There shall none after you attain unto your time, neither unto the half thereof.

18 Then arose the third, and reigned as the other before: and appeared no more also.

19 So it went with all the rest one after another, as that every one reigned, and then appeared no more.

20 Then I beheld, and lo, in process of time, the feathers that followed, stood up upon the right side, that they might rule also, and some of them ruled, but within a while they appeared no more:

These represent smaller Empires such as Spain, Portugal, etc. They reigned for a while but no longer.

21 For some of them were set up, but ruled not.

22 After this I looked, and behold, the twelve feathers appeared no more, nor the two little feathers:

23 And there was no more upon the Eagle's body, but three heads that rested, and six little wings.

24 Then saw I also that two little feathers divided themselves from the six, and remained under the head, that was upon the right side: for the four continued in their place.

25 And I beheld, and lo, the feathers that were under the wing, thought to set up themselves, and to have the rule.

26 And I beheld, and lo, there was one set up, but shortly it appeared no more.

27 And the second was sooner away then the first.

28 And I beheld, and lo, the two that remained, thought also in themselves to reign.

29 And when they so thought, behold, there awaked one of the heads that were at rest, namely it that was in the middle, for that was greater then the two other heads.

The British Empire remains the largest in history claiming 1/4 of the entire Earth. It is associated with the eagle and is a she.

30 And then I saw, that the two other heads were joined with it.

A trinity of world power. Financial, Military and Religion.

31 And behold, the head was turned with them that were with it, and did eat up the two feathers under the wing that would have reigned.

32 But this head put the whole earth in fear, and bare rule in it over all those that dwelt upon the earth, with much oppression, and it had the governance of the world more then all the wings that had been.

33 And after this I beheld, and lo the head that was in the midst, suddenly appeared no more, like as the wings.

Though the nation is still there, it's Empire power is no longer.

34 But there remained the two heads, which also in like sort ruled upon the earth, and over those that dwelt therein.

Britain essentially transferred it's Empire into the "New Atlantis" of the U.S.

35 And I beheld, and lo, the head upon the right side, devoured it, that was upon the left side.

The U.S. will be devoured by the Vatican.

A Lion Roused from the Forest

36 Then I heard a voice, which said unto me, Look before you, and consider the thing that you see.

37 And I beheld, and lo, as it were a roaring Lion, chased out of the wood: and I saw that he sent out a man's voice unto the Eagle, and said,

Messianic Prophecy. This is the Lion of Yahudah.

38 Hear you, I will talk with you, and the Highest shall say unto you,

39 Are you not it that remains of the four beasts, whom I made to reign in my world, that the end of their times might come through them?

Cf. Dan. 7.

This is the continuation of Daniel's vision. This is the fourth and terrible beast.

40 And the fourth came and overcame all the beasts that were past, and had power over the world with great fearfulness, and over the whole compass of the earth with much wicked oppression, and so long time dwelt he upon the earth with deceit.

41 For the earth have you not judged with truth.

42 For you have afflicted the meek, you have hurt the peaceable, you have loved liars, and destroyed the dwellings of them that brought forth fruit, and have cast down the walls of such, as did you no harm.

43 Therefore is your wrongful dealing come up unto the Highest, and your pride unto the Mighty.

44 The Highest also has looked upon the proud times, and behold, they are ended, and his abominations are fulfilled.

45 And therefore appear no more you Eagle, nor your horrible wings, nor your wicked feathers, nor your malicious heads, nor your hurtful claws, nor all your vain body:

46 That all the earth may be refreshed, and may return, being delivered from your violence, and that she may hope for the judgment, and mercy of him that made her.

Habakkuk 1:8-9 Fragment from Dead Sea Scrolls
*"Their horses are swifter than leopards and fleeter than evening wolves. Their horses step forward proudly and spread their wings; they fly from afar like an **eagle avid to devour**. All of them come for violence; the look on their faces is like the east wind (i, 8~9a)."*

LION OF YAHUDAH SPEAKS. EAGLE DISAPPEARS! *(12:31-33)*

Prophetic Commentary in Qumran, 0-100 A.D.
*"[Interpreted, this] concerns the **Kittim** who trample the earth with their horses and beasts. They come from afar, from the islands of the sea, to devour all the peoples **like an eagle** which cannot be satisfied, and they address [all the peoples] with anger and [wrath and fury] and indignation." [53]*
Kittim = Roman Empire = Eagle
*As this is the continuation of Daniel's fourth Beast in more detail, this is the new Roman Empire called the Holy Roman Empire which moves it's capitals even as evidenced in Ezra's vision. There is only one final empire and it is a mixture with the Roman Empire as it superceded it and must still remain until the end. Esdras even notes it is presumed to have disappeared and it's true power hidden. **Qumran was reading 2nd Esdras!***

OUR INTERPRETATION OF THE EAGLE HEADS:

CAME UP FROM THE SEA (11:1) Cf. Rev. 13:1

HEADS AT REST, CONCEALED UNTIL THE END.

UNITED STATES *"The New Atlantis" Known as Her.*

(1900-Present as Superpower)

LEFT HEAD RULES EARTH 2ND AND IS DEVOURED BY THE RIGHT.

Though not as large in territory, 40% of World Nations are occupied by the US Military in presence.

BRITAIN *"The empire on which the sun never sets"*

LARGER HEAD AWAKENS 1ST, RULES EARTH AND DISAPPEARS (1500-1900s). *SUBDUES 1/4TH OF THE EARTH. No longer an Empire. Known as she.*

VATICAN

Known as "Our mother."

REMAINS TO THE END WHEN MESSIAH (LION) REMOVES IT FROM POWER. 18:11 Never fell.

The true executor of the British Empire position in the world as a superpower. World power already dwindling as the final head takes it's position.

LEFT HEAD

RIGHT HEAD

Though smaller, the Vatican is the true power behind the final empire concealed or preserved til the end. It is the 2nd Beast who rises out of the Earth and False Prophet who prepares the way for the Anti-Messiah.

HEADS REIGN OVER EARTH

"LET THE HEADS BE PRESERVED FOR THE LAST"

THE FINAL EMPIRE: HOLY ROMAN EMPIRE

Wings & Feathers Rise and Fall from Power While Heads Rest. Same Empire.

The prince demon power behind all these is Gog of Magog whose seat is West and Central Europe. It is his voice which comes from the middle of the body of this Beast. This is why the voice came from the middle of the body and not the heads as this body is possessed.

Note: Though an antithesis, communism is the philosophy of a German son of a Rabbi. It was funded by the U.S. and Britain in the Bolshevik Revolution still falling into this same body of rule. The two opposing feathers are likely China and Russia.

This is the continuation of Daniel's prophecy of the 4 Beasts. This Eagle or Phoenix is the final Beast. The empire has existed since the Roman Empire fell but it is a mixture and partly weak as Daniel expresses and Ezra exposes the preservation or really, hiding of the true power over the ages until the end. The symbol of this Eagle has remained within the Holy Roman Empire and it's powers who have risen and fallen even royal houses in symbol for many centuries. We will leave such enumeration to others but the heads, we believe, can be firmly identified today.

CHAPTER 12:

3 The Eagle which he saw, is destroyed. 10 The vision is interpreted. 37 He is bid to write his visions, 39 and to fast, that he may see more. 46 He does comfort those, that were grieved for his absence.

1 And it came to pass while the Lion spake these words unto the Eagle, I saw:
2 And behold, the head that remained, and the four wings appeared no more, and the two went unto it, and set themselves up to reign, and their kingdom was small and full of uproar.
3 And I saw, and behold, they appeared no more, and the whole body of the Eagle was burnt, so that the earth was in great fear: then I awakened out of the trouble and trance of my mind, and from great fear, and said unto my spirit,
4 Lo, this have you done unto me, in that you search out the ways of the Highest.
5 Lo, yet I am weary in my mind, and very weak in my spirit: and little strength is there in me; for the great fear, wherewith I was affrighted this night.
6 Therefore I will now beseech the Highest, that he will comfort me unto the end.

The Interpretation of the Vision

7 And I said, Yahuah, that bears rule, If I have found grace before your sight, and if I am justified with you, before many others, and if my prayer indeed comes up before your face,
8 Comfort me then, and show me your servant the interpretation, and plain difference of this fearful vision, that you may perfectly comfort my soul.
9 For you have judged me worthy, to show me the last times.
10 And he said unto me, This is the interpretation of the vision.
11 The Eagle whom you saw come up from the sea, is the kingdom which was seen, in the vision of your brother Daniel.

Cf. Dan. 7:7.

12 But it was not expounded unto him, therefore now I declare it unto you.
13 Behold, the days will come, that there shall rise up a kingdom upon earth, and it shall be feared above all the kingdoms that were before it.
14 In the same shall twelve kings reign, one after another.
15 Whereof the second shall begin to reign, and shall have

more time than any of the twelve.

16 And this do the twelve wings signify which you saw.

17 As for the voice which you heard speak, and that you saw not to go out from the heads, but from the midst of the body thereof, this is the interpretation:

18 That after the time of that kingdom, there shall arise great strivings, and it shall stand in peril of falling: nevertheless it shall not then fall, but shall be restored again to his beginning.

The Vatican, power behind the Holy Roman Empire, is reported to have fallen from power. It never truly did.

19 And whereas you saw the eight small under feathers sticking to her wings, this is the interpretation:

20 That in him there shall arise eight kings, whose time shall be but small, and their years swift.

21 And two of them shall perish: the middle time approaching, four shall be kept until their ends begin to approach: but two shall be kept unto the end.

22 And whereas you saw three heads resting, this is the interpretation

23 In his last days shall the Most High raise up three kingdoms, and renew many things therein, and they shall have the dominion of the earth,

24 And of those that dwell therein with much oppression, above all those that were before them: therefore are they called the heads of the Eagle.

25 For these are they that shall accomplish his wickedness, and that shall finish his last end.

26 And whereas you saw that the great head appeared no more, it signifies that one of them shall die upon his bed, and yet with pain.

27 For the two that remain, shall be slain with the sword.

28 For the sword of the one shall devour the other: but at the last shall he fall through the sword himself.

29 And whereas you saw two feathers under the wings passing over the head, that is on the right side:

30 It signifies that these are they whom the Highest has kept unto their end: this is the small kingdom and full of trouble, as you saw.

Likely China and Russia.

31 And the Lion whom you saw rising up out of the wood, and roaring, and speaking to the Eagle, and rebuking her for her unrighteousness, with all the words which you has heard,

32 This is the Anointed which

2nd Coming of Messiah predicted. Origin: 2 Esdras.

the Highest has kept for them, and for their wickedness unto the end: he shall reprove them, and shall upbraid them with their cruelty.

33 For he shall set them before him alive in judgment, and shall rebuke them and correct them.

34 For the rest of my people shall he deliver with mercy, those that have been preserved upon my borders, and he shall make them joyful until the coming of the day of judgment, whereof I have spoken unto you from the beginning.

Cf. Gn. 3:15.

35 This is the dream that you saw, and these are the interpretations.

36 You only have been meet to know this secret of the Highest.

37 Therefore **write all these things that you have seen, in a book, and hide them**.

Cf. Dan. 12:4.

38 And teach them to the wise of the people, whose hearts you know may comprehend, and keep these secrets.

39 But you wait here yet seven days more, that it may be shown you whatsoever it pleases the Highest to declare unto you: And with that he went his way.

The People Come to Ezra

40 And it came to pass when all the people saw that the seven days were past, and I not come again into the city, they gathered them all together, from the least unto the greatest, and came unto me, and said,

41 What have we offended you? And what evil have we done against you, that you forsake us, and sit here in this place?

42 For of all the prophets you only are left us, as a cluster of the vintage, and as a candle in a dark place, and as a haven or ship preserved from the tempest:

Or, people.

43 Are not the evils which are come to us, sufficient?

44 If you shall forsake us, how much better had it been for us, if we also had been burnt in the midst of Sion.

45 For we are not better than they that died there. And they wept with a loud voice: then I answered them, and said,

46 Be of good comfort, O Israel, and be not heavy you house of Yacob.

47 For the Highest has you in remembrance, and the mighty has not forgotten you in temptation.

48 As for me, I have not forsaken you, neither am I departed from you: but am

come into this place, to pray for the desolation of Sion, and that I might seek mercy for the low estate of your Sanctuary.
49 And now go your way home every man, and after these days will I come unto you.
50 So the people went their way into the city, like as I commanded them:
51 But I remained still in the field seven days, as the Angel commanded me, and did eat only in those days, of the flowers of the field, and had my meat of the herbs.

This phoenix (eagle) will never rise from the ashes but disappear forever.

CHAPTER 13:

1 He sees in his dream a man coming out of the sea. 25 The declaration of his dream. 39 Trail of Northern Lost Tribes. 54 He is praised, and promised to see more.

The Man from the Sea

Messianic Prophecy of the Second Coming.

1 And it came to pass after seven days, I dreamed a dream by night.

2 And lo, there arose a wind from the sea that it moved all the waves thereof.

3 And I beheld, and lo, that man waxed strong with the thousands of heaven: and when he turned his countenance to look, all the things trembled that were seen under him.

Clouds.

Cf. Rev. 19:15, 21. Revelation indicates a sword from His mouth yet then mentions fire. **2 Esdras is it's origin.**

4 And whensoever the voice went out of his mouth, all they burnt, that heard his voice, like as the earth fails when it feels the fire.

Cf. Rev. 19:19. **2 Esdras is it's origin.**

5 And after this I beheld, and lo, there was gathered together a multitude of men out of number, from the four winds of the heaven, to subdue the man that came out of the sea.

Yahusha builds this mountain. It is likely the Heavenly Mt. Zion not necessarily the one in Israel named after it. The fact Ezra could not recognize the area supports this.

6 But I beheld, and lo, he had graved himself a great mountain, and flew up upon it.

7 But I would have seen the region, or place, whereout the hill was graven, and I could not.

8 And after this I beheld, and lo, all they which were gathered together to subdue him, were sore afraid, and yet do fight.

9 And lo, as he saw the violence of the multitude that came, he neither lift up his hand, nor held sword, nor any instrument of war.

10 But only I saw that he sent out of his mouth, as it had been a blast of fire, and out of his lips a flaming breath, and out of his tongue he cast out sparks and tempests,

Cf. Rev. 19:15, 21. Messiah consumes his enemies with eternal fire from his mouth.

11 And they were all mixed together; the blast of fire, the flaming breath, and the great tempest, and fell with violence upon the multitude, which was prepared to fight, and burnt them up every one, so that upon a sudden, of an innumerable multitude, nothing was to be perceived, but only dust and smell of smoke: when I saw this, I was afraid.

The Lost Tribes of Israel and the remnant of believers grafted into the kingdom.

12 Afterward saw I the same man come down from the mountain, and call unto him another peaceable multitude.

13 And there came much people unto him, whereof some were glad, some were sorry, some of them were bound, and other some brought of them that were

offered: then was I sick through great fear, and I awakened and said,

The Interpretation of the Vision

14 You have shown your servant wonders from the beginning, and have counted me worthy that you should receive my prayer:
15 Show me now yet the interpretation of this dream.
16 For as I conceive in my understanding, woe unto them that shall be left in those days; and much more woe unto them that are not left behind.

The movie is mistitled. Those left behind at this point are the believers. Those not, have been destroyed.

17 For they that were not left, were in heaviness.
18 Now I understand the things that are laid up in the latter days, which shall happen unto them, and to those that are left behind.
19 Therefore are they come into great perils, and many necessities, like as these dreams declare.
20 Yet is it easier for him that is in danger, to come into these things, then to pass away as a cloud out of the world, and not to see the things that happen in the last days. And he answered unto me, and said,

Or, this day.

21 The interpretation of the vision shall I show you, and I will open unto you, the thing that you have required.
22 Whereas you have spoken of them that are left behind, this is the interpretation.
23 He that shall endure the peril in that time, has kept himself: they that be fallen into danger, are such as have works, and faith towards the Almighty.
24 Know this therefore, that they which be left behind, are more blessed then they that be dead.

Cf. Mt. 24:29-30. "Immediately after the tribulation of those days..." Messiah time stamps the Rapture as after the Tribulation not before. Note: This is the opposite of the Rapture Doctrine. Believers will be left behind to the end and be blessed from it.

25 This is the meaning of the vision: Whereas you saw a man coming up from the middle of the Sea:
26 The same is he whom Elohim the Highest has kept a great season, which by his own self shall deliver his creature: and he shall order them that are left behind.
27 And whereas you saw, that out of his mouth there came as a blast of wind, and fire, and storm:
28 And that he held neither sword, nor any instrument of war, but that the rushing in of him destroyed the whole multitude that came to subdue him, this is the interpretation.

Note: Ezra knew Messiah would die, be raised and ascend to Heaven. He also, knew He would return as redeem the Earth. This is the origin of Revelation and tells the entire New Testament story 400 years before it happened.

29 Behold, the days come, when the Most High will begin to deliver them that are upon the earth.

30 And he shall come to the astonishment of them that dwell on the earth.

31 And one shall undertake to fight against another, one city against another, one place against another, one people against another, and one realm against another.

Cf. Mt. 24:7. **Messianic Prophecy.** *The Lost Tribes do not return until after Messiah returns. This is affirmed in Ez. 39:25. Ezra saw Messiah die, ascend into Heaven and His 2nd Coming.*

32 And the time shall be, when these things shall come to pass, and the signs shall happen which I showed you before, **and then shall my son be declared, whom you saw as a man ascending**.

33 And when all the people hear his voice, every man shall in their own land, leave the battle they have one against another.

34 And an innumerable multitude shall be gathered together, as you saw them willing to come, and to overcome him by fighting.

End Times Messianic Prophecy. His return.

35 But he shall stand upon the top of the mount Sion.

36 And Sion shall come and shall be shown to all men, being prepared and built, like as you saw the hill graven without hands.

Mt. Sion is built up in the end by Messiah. This is likely the heavenly New Jerusalem He constructs in Heaven.

37 And **this my son shall rebuke the wicked inventions of those nations**, which for their wicked life are fallen into the tempest,

38 And shall lay before them their evil thoughts, and the torments wherewith they shall begin to be tormented, which are like unto a flame: and **he shall destroy them without labor, by the law which is like unto fire**.

Cf. Mt. 5:17-20. The law from Messiah's mouth will destroy those in the end as fire. Thus, His law remains to the end as He said it would. One claiming He judges in the end without a Law to judge by is illiterate of scripture.

Trail of the Lost Tribes

39 And whereas you saw that he gathered another peaceable multitude unto him;

Cf. 1:38

40 Those are the **ten tribes**, which were carried away prisoners out of their own land, in the time of Osea the king, whom Salmanasar the king of Assyria led away captive, and he carried them over the waters, and so came they **into another land**.

Cf. 2 Ki. 17:3. In Assyria.

The Northern Tribes were in Assyria such as Nineveh on the East side of the Tigris. This means they crossed only the Euphrates and not the Tigris close to the Persian Gulf.

41 But they took this counsel amongst themselves, that they would **leave the multitude** of the heathen, and go forth into **a further country**, where never mankind dwelt,

Desert or wilderness.

42 That they might there keep their statutes, which they never kept in their own land.

Into Saudi Arabia's East coast.

43 And they **entered into Euphrates by the narrow passages of the River**.

There was no crossing Ishmael's portion of Saudi to the West thus, they must have taken to the sea.

44 For the Most High then showed signs for them, and held still the flood, til they

Though some are scattered some remain.

Cf. Ex.14:21; Jos. 3:15,16.

were passed over.

45 For through that country there was a great way to go; namely, of **a year and a half**: and the same region is called **Arsareth**.

Cf. 1:11

The Lost Tribes cannot return until the very end.

46 Then **dwelt they there until the latter time**; and now when **they shall begin to come**,

The Lost Tribes can only regather in peace not perpetual war.

47 The Highest shall stay the springs of the stream again, that they may go through: therefore you saw the multitude **with peace**.

Cf. 1:11, 38. These are the 2 provinces from Chapter 1 in the East. Some stayed in Assyria and the rest migrated likely by sea on a total 1.5 year journey.

48 But those that be left behind of your people, are they that are found within my borders.

49 Now when he destroys the multitude of the nations that are gathered together, he shall defend his people that remain.

50 And then shall he show them great wonders.

Gen. 2:4 ...Yahuah Elohim made (עשה: asah: aw-saw') the earth (ארץ: erets, eh'-rets) Land of Creation = Havilah. This is specifically the location of Creation.

51 Then I said, O Yahuah, that bears rule, show me this: Wherefore have I seen the man coming up from the midst of the Sea?

52 And he said unto me, Like as you can neither seek out, nor know the things that are in the deep of the sea: even so can no man upon earth **see my son**, or those that be with him, but in the day time.

Messianic Prophecy.

Only Ezra knew of this revelation in his day. However, John certainly received similar. This means if Ezra is the only to have seen this at the time of Yahuah saying so, this must be before John. There is no dating this book at the time of nor after the Apostles. Those scholars are not reading.

53 This is the interpretation of the dream which you saw, and whereby **you only are here lightened**.

54 For you have forsaken your own way, and applied your diligence unto my law, and sought it.

55 Your life have you ordered in wisdom, and have called understanding your mother.

56 And therefore I have shown you the treasures of the Highest: After another three days, I will speak other things unto you, and declare unto you mighty and wonderous things.

57 Then I went forth into the field giving praise and thanks greatly unto the Most High, because of his wonders which he did in time,

58 And because he governs the same, and such things as fall in their seasons, and there I sat three days.

Northern Kingdom of Israel Taken Captive to Assyria

(Modern Kurdistan)

...the king of Assyria led away captive, and he caried them over the waters, and so came they **into another land**. *(40)*

They never return to Samaria until the very end times.

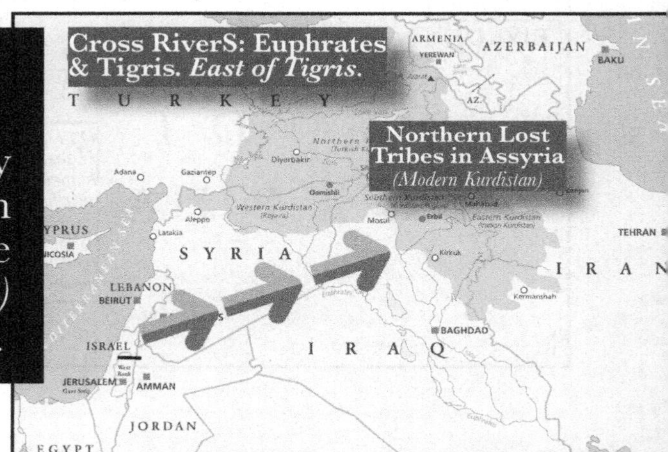

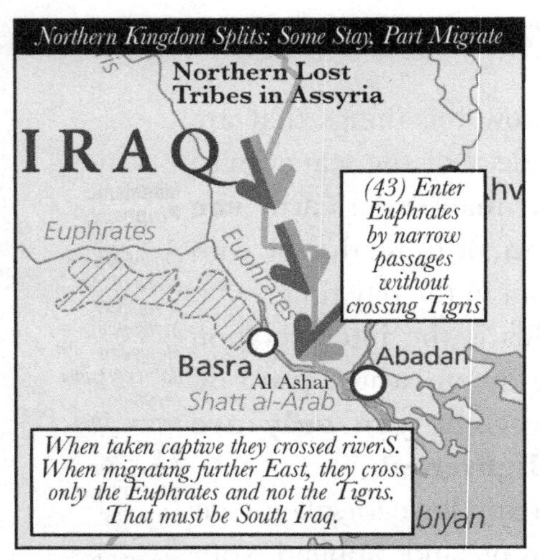

Northern Kingdom Splits: Some Stay, Part Migrate
Northern Lost Tribes in Assyria
IRAQ
(43) Enter Euphrates by narrow passages without crossing Tigris
Euphrates
Euphrates
Basra
Al Ashar
Abadan
Shatt al-Arab
When taken captive they crossed riverS. When migrating further East, they cross only the Euphrates and not the Tigris. That must be South Iraq.

Cross Euphrates Likely At Al Ashar, Iraq
Likely Crossing:
Al Ashar:
Hebrew: אשר
to go straight, go on, advance, guide, blessed, proceed
Bākhtarān
Jazīrah
Basrah
Al Ashar
Abadan
Al-Kuwayt
AL-KUWAYT
Strong's #833

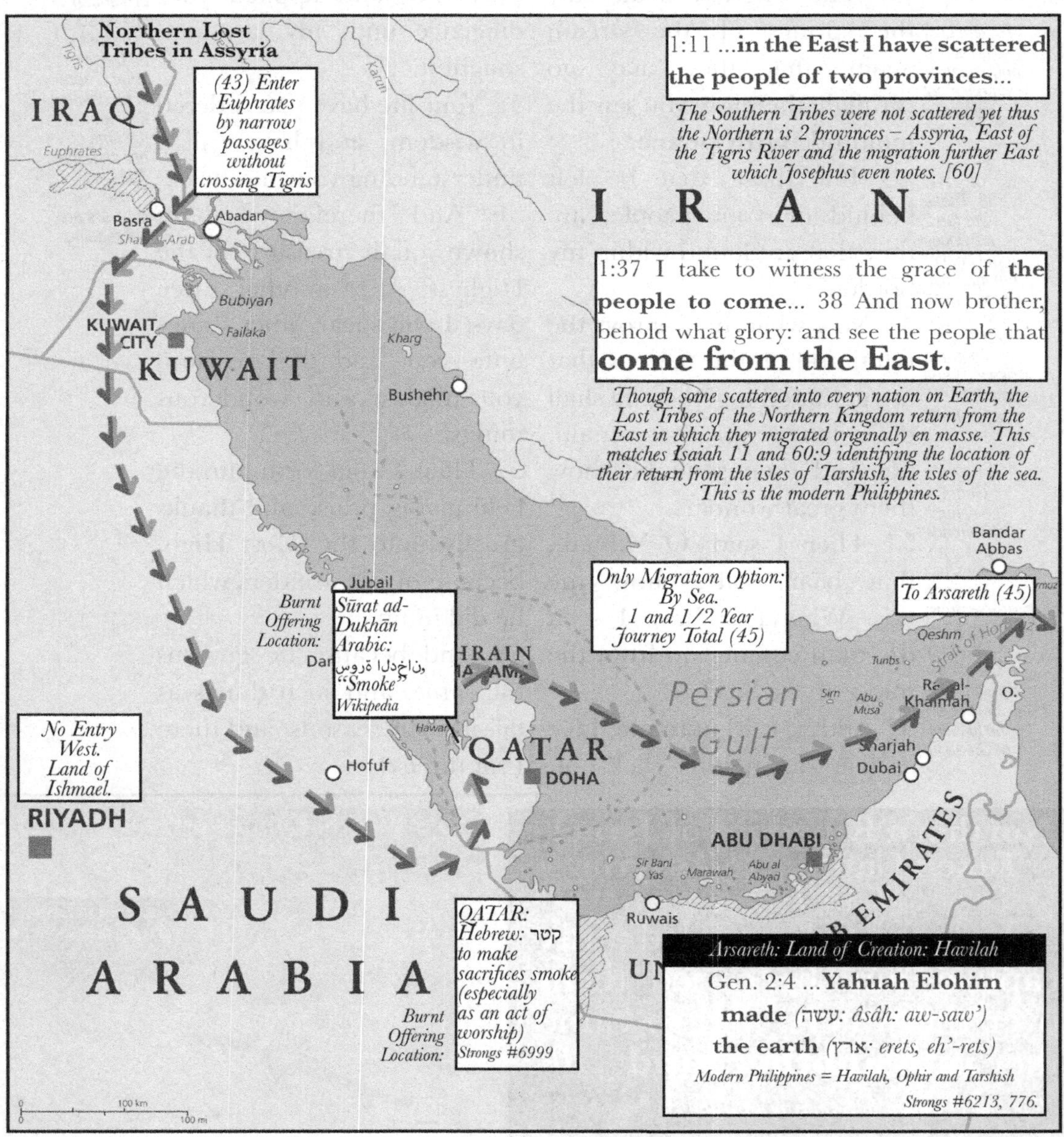

Northern Lost Tribes in Assyria
IRAQ
(43) Enter Euphrates by narrow passages without crossing Tigris
Euphrates
Basra
Abadan
Shatt al-Arab
Bubiyan
Failaka
KUWAIT CITY
KUWAIT
Kharg
Bushehr
1:11 ...in the East I have scattered the people of two provinces...
The Southern Tribes were not scattered yet thus the Northern is 2 provinces – Assyria, East of the Tigris River and the migration further East which Josephus even notes. [60]
IRAN
1:37 I take to witness the grace of the people to come... 38 And now brother, behold what glory: and see the people that come from the East.
Though some scattered into every nation on Earth, the Lost Tribes of the Northern Kingdom return from the East in which they migrated originally en masse. This matches Isaiah 11 and 60:9 identifying the location of their return from the isles of Tarshish, the isles of the sea. This is the modern Philippines.
Bandar Abbas
Jubail
Burnt Offering Location:
Sūrat ad-Dukhān
Arabic:
"Smoke"
Wikipedia
Only Migration Option: By Sea. 1 and 1/2 Year Journey Total (45)
To Arsareth (45)
Qeshm
Tunbs
Persian Gulf
Abu Musa
Ras al-Khaimah
Sharjah
Dubai
No Entry West. Land of Ishmael.
RIYADH
Hofuf
QATAR
DOHA
ABU DHABI
Sir Bani Yas
Marawah
Abu al Abyad
Ruwais
EMIRATES
SAUDI ARABIA
QATAR:
Hebrew: קטר
to make sacrifices smoke (especially as an act of worship)
Strongs #6999
Burnt Offering Location:
Arsareth: Land of Creation: Havilah
Gen. 2:4 ...Yahuah Elohim made (עשה: âsâh: aw-saw') the earth (ארץ: erets, eh'-rets)
Modern Philippines = Havilah, Ophir and Tarshish
Strongs #6213, 776.
100 km
100 mi

Isaiah 60:9 KJV

Who are these that fly as a cloud, and as the doves to their windows? **Surely the isles** *shall wait for me, and the* **ships of Tarshish** *first, to* **bring thy sons from far**, *their* **silver** *and their* **gold** *with them, unto the name of the LORD thy God, and to the Holy One of Israel, because he hath glorified thee.*

Isaiah 11:11-13 KJV

And it shall come to pass in that day, that the Lord shall set his hand again the second time to recover the remnant of his people, which shall be left, from **Assyria**, *and from* **Egypt**, *and from* **Pathros**, *and from* **Cush**, *and from* **Elam**, *and from* **Shinar**, *and from* **Hamath**, *and from* **the islands of the sea**. *And he shall set up an ensign for the nations, and shall assemble the outcasts of Israel, and gather together the dispersed of Judah from the four corners of the earth. The envy also of Ephraim shall depart, and the adversaries of Judah shall be cut off: Ephraim shall not envy Judah, and Judah shall not vex Ephraim.*

CHINA

CHINA SEA

ISAIAH 49:1 KJV
Listen, O isles, unto me; and hearken, ye people, from far; The LORD hath called me from the womb; from the bowels of my mother hath he made mention of my name. *(the isles of the sea in the Far East)*

PHILIPPINE SEA

ISAIAH 49:3 KJV
And said unto me, Thou art my servant, O Israel, in whom I will be glorified. *(the isles)*

SINAE

SEA OF SINIM

SOUTH CHINA SEA

LAND IN THE SEA OF SINIM

PHILIPPINES

ISAIAH 49:12 KJV
Behold, **these shall come from far**: and, lo, these from the **north** and from the **west (SEA)**; and these **from the land of Sinim**.

West: *yam:* ים: **SEA NOT WEST!**
sea (321x), west (47x), westward (21x), west side (4x), seafaring men (1x), south (1x), western (1x). {322 vs. 73 times? 4.5 times more likely "Sea"}

Sinim: Ciyniym: סינים
Sinim (1x): a people living at the extremity of the known world; may be identified with the inhabitants of southern ChinaSinim (1x): a people living at the extremity of the known world; may be identified with the inhabitants of southern China.

MALAYSIA

These are the islands in the South China Sea, the land in the Sea of Sinim. The Lost Tribes would have named this area and within the isles right next to the only desert where never mankind dwelt, is an area identified on this 1775 Map of the Ilocos Region of the Philippines, 3 times as Sinai. The Lost Tribes knew this was not Mt. Sinai which remains in Saudi Arabia but just as that was the destination in the First Exodus from Egypt, it would be the rightful name for the place in which they migrated during the Second Exodus.

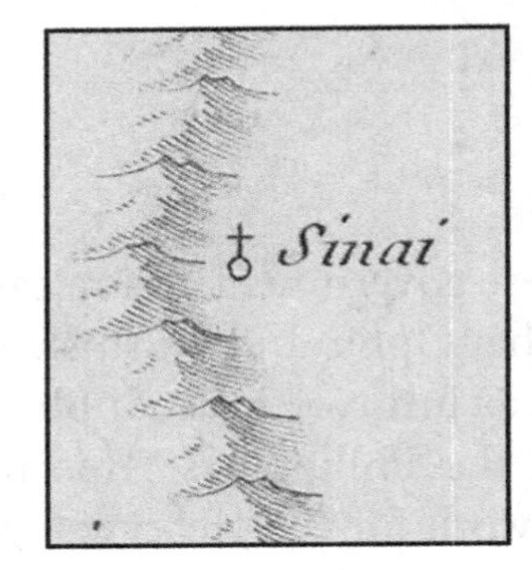

PLAN
DES PRINCIPAUX PORTS
DE
LA CÔTE D'ILLOCOS,
en l'Isle de Lucon.

Echelle d'une Lieue Marines de 20 au Degré.

Sinai: Hebrew: סיני: Modern Sinait
Near Laoag where the Lost Tribes of Israel may have landed in the desert, we oddly find three symbols of a second exodus. Today, the name has been changed adding a "t" on the end but on this 1775 French map, the area, the river and an island North are all labeled Sinai. Unto itself, this is perhaps coincidence. However, with all the overwhelming such references in the Philippines, this is certainly a Hebrew word. Vigan, originally Bi-Gan, is also a Hebrew possibility meaning come and go in the Garden.

"Plan des principaux ports de la Cote d'Illocos en l'Isle Lucon. (to accompany) Neptune Oriental. De d'Apres." Apres de Mannevillette, Jean-Baptiste-Nicolas-Denis d', 1707-1780. On display at Hotel Felicidad Vigan, Ilocos Sur. Published 1810. Depot Generale de la Marine. Public Domain.

The Mindset of the Age of Exploration from 1492:

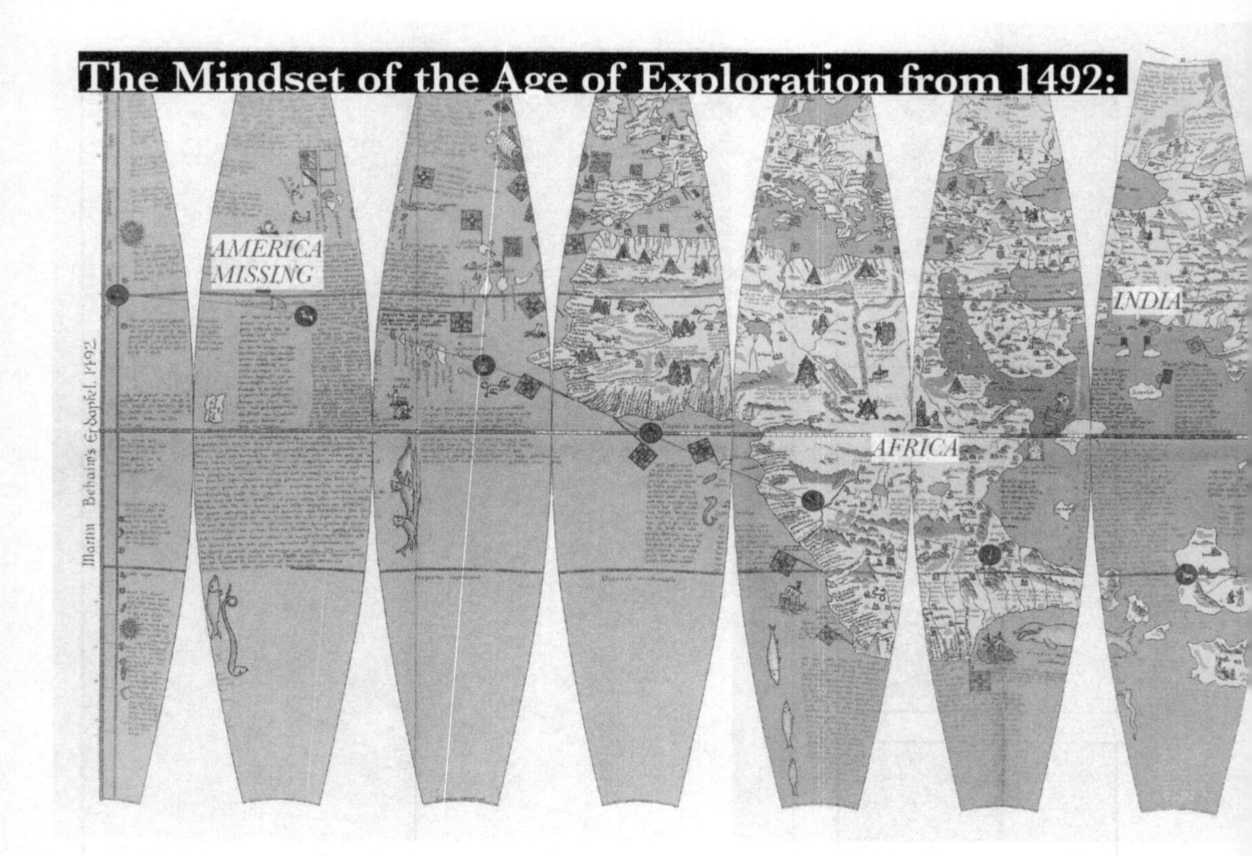

In the First World Globe commissioned by the Portuguese government and released in 1492, the mindset of the age of exploration was firm that Ophir and Tarshish, the land of Solomon's famed gold, were located in Southeast Asia just Northeast of Borneo and Southeast of China as an archipelago we now call the Philippines. This map identifies Luzon Island, Philippines as Chryse, the Greek word for the Hebrew Ophir and Mindanao as Argyre, the Greek word for the Hebrew Tarshish. The British were behind then and remain behind as they make claims only by ignoring this firm history and the Bible as well as Pomponius Mela*(43 AD)*, The Periplus of the Erythaean Sea*(70 AD)*, Dionysius the Tourist*(124 AD)*, etc. which have mapped Chryse*(Ophir)* South of the Tropic of Cancer in the Philippines all along. Magellan knew this and recorded it as well.

Columbus believed and noted in journals that this was his destination of Ophir and Tarshish, not America, this same year really using the same data of the most current Portuguese exploration which this mapping identifies. His research also concluded that these same islands housed the Garden of Eden and Arsareth, the land of the Lost Tribes of Northern Israel from 2 Esdras 13. Italian Jewish Scholar, Ferrisol, of the same era, records the very same in specifically identifying the Philippines as the location of the Lost Tribes who migrated according to 2 Esdras. This was soon buried by the British who began paying propagandists in at least 1625 such as Samuel Purchas. Their supposed cases all ignore the existance of the Philippines which is the only land that could even qualify as Ophir, Tarshish, the Garden of Eden and Arsareth.

See The Search for King Solomon's Treasure for details. www.OphirInstitute.com.

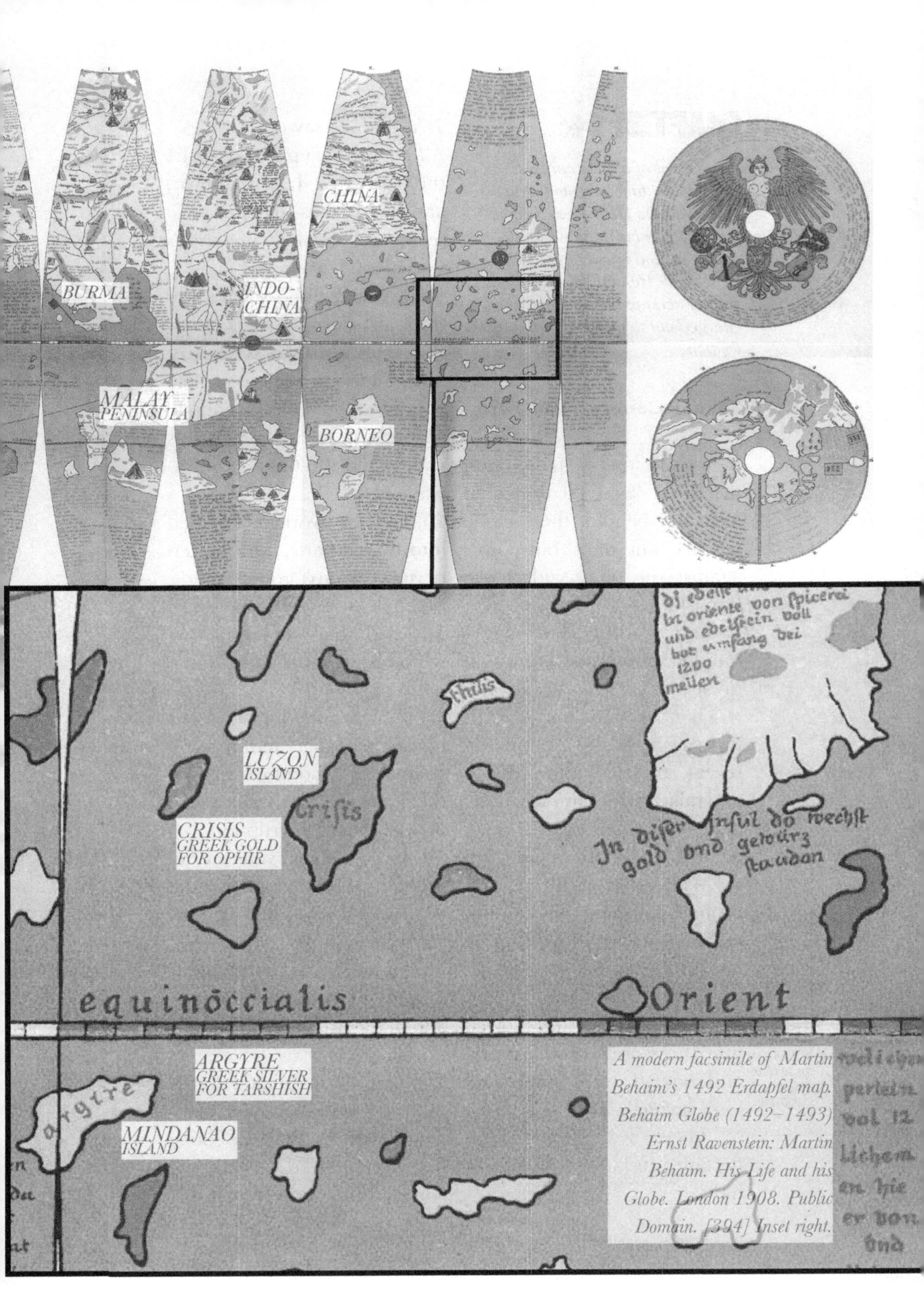

A modern facsimile of Martin Behaim's 1492 Erdapfel map. Behaim Globe (1492–1493) Ernst Ravenstein: Martin Behaim. His Life and his Globe. London 1908. Public Domain. [394] Inset right.

CHAPTER 14:

A voice out of a bush called Ezra, 10 and tells him that the world waxes old. 22 He desires, because the Law was burnt, to write all again, 24 and is bid to get swift writers. 39 He and they are filled with understanding: 45 but he is charged not to publish all that is written.

Yahuah Commissions Ezra

1 And it came to pass, upon the third day I sat under an oak, and behold, there came a voice out of a bush over against me, and said, Ezra, Ezra.

2 And I said, Here am I Yahuah, and I stood up upon my feet.

3 Then he said unto me, In the bush I did manifestly reveal myself unto Moses, and talked with him, when my people served in Egypt.

Cf. Ex. 3:2,8.

4 And I sent him, and led my people out of Egypt, and brought him up to the mount of Sinai, where I held him by me, a long season,

5 And told him many wonderous things, and showed him the secrets of the times, and the end, and commanded him, saying,

Moses knew the end times and you will not find much in the modern Torah because it is missing the book that has these clear prophecies – Jubilees.

6 These words shall you declare, and these shall you hide.

7 And now I say unto you,

8 That you lay up in your heart the signs that I have shown, and the dreams that you have seen, and the interpretations which you have heard:

9 For you shall be taken away from all, and from henceforth you shall **remain with my son**, and with such as be like you, until the times be ended.

10 For the world has lost his youth, and the times begin to wax old.

Imagine how much more the world has waxed old in more that 2,000 years.

11 For the world is divided into twelve parts, and the ten parts of it are gone already, and half of a tenth part.

12 And there remains that which is after the half of the tenth part.

This appears to refer to area or populations that are 100% pagan and not serving Yahuah. 10.5 of 12 total portions of the Earth are beyond hope. This leaves no room for the coming "Christian" evangelism because that is not the Biblical religion but still in basis the Catholic practice with Judaism, a non-Biblical religion as it's roots. The remnant is already figuring this out today. This is why we never reach the entire world, the Angel in Revelation does.

13 Now therefore set your house in order, and reprove your people, comfort such of them as be in trouble, and now renounce corruption.

14 Let go from you mortal thoughts, cast away the burdens of man, put off now the weak nature,

15 And set aside the thoughts that are most heavy unto you, and haste to flee from these times.

16 For yet greater evils than those which you have seen happen, shall be done hereafter.

Cf. Mt. 24:7.

17 For look how much the

1 ...behold, there came a voice out of
a bush over against me

world shall be weaker through age: so much the more shall evils increase upon them that dwell therein.

Mankind is not advancing despite what technology appears. Of course, examine those and much of those inventions are used to kill, steal and destroy. Even man physically is growing weaker and de-evolving not advancing.

18 For the truth is fled far away, and leasing is hard at hand: For now hastes the vision to come, which you have seen.

Ezra's Concern to Restore the Scriptures

19 Then I answered before you, and said,

20 Behold, Yahuah, I will go as you have commanded me, and reprove the people which are present, but they that shall be born afterward, who shall admonish them? thus the world is set in darkness, and they that dwell therein, are without light.

21 For your law is burnt, therefore no man knows the things that are done of you, or the works that shall begin.

Cf. 2 Ki. 25:9.

22 But if I have found grace before you, **send the Holy Ghost into me**, and I shall write all that has been done in the world, since the beginning, which were written in your Law, that men may find your path, and that they which will live in the latter days, may live.

The Law will be restored in the Latter Days according to Ezra and abundant scripture.

23 And he answered me, saying, Go your way, gather the people together, and say unto them, that they seek you not for fourty days.

24 But prepare you many box trees, and take with you Sarea, Dabria, Selemia, Ethanus and Asiel, these five which are ready to write swiftly.

Or, box tables to write on, See ver.44.

25 And come hither, and I shall light a candle of understanding in your heart, which shall not be put out, til the things be performed which you shall begin to write.

26 And when you have done, some things shall you publish, and some things shall you show secretly to the wise: tomorrow this hour shall you begin to write.

Ezra's Last Words to the People

27 Then I went forth as he commanded, and gathered all the people together, and said,

28 Hear these words, O Israel.

29 Our fathers at the beginning were strangers in Egypt, from whence they were delivered:

Cf. Gn. 47:4.

30 And received the **law of life** which they kept not, which you also have transgressed after them.

*Cf. Rom. 8:2. **This term referring to the Law originates in 2 Esdras.***

Cf. Acts 7:53.

31 Then was the land, even the

land of Sion, parted among you by lot, but your fathers, and you yourselves have done unrighteousness, and have not kept the ways which the Highest commanded you.

32 And for as much as he is a righteous judge, he took from you in time, the thing that he had given you.

33 And now are you here, and your brethren amongst you.

34 Therefore if so be that you will subdue your own understanding, and reform your hearts, you shall be kept alive, and after death you shall obtain mercy.

35 For after death, shall the judgment come, when we shall live again: and then shall the names of the righteous be manifest, and the works of the ungodly shall be declared.

Cf. Rev. 20:12.

36 Let no man therefore come unto me now, nor seek after me these fourty days.

The Restoration of the Scriptures

37 So I took the five men as he commanded me, and we went into the field, and remained there.

38 And the next day behold a voice called me saying, Ezra, open your mouth and drink that I give you to drink.

Cf. Ez. 3:2.

39 Then I opened my mouth, and behold, he reached me a full cup, which was full as it were with water, but the color of it was like fire.

40 And I took it, and drank: and when I had drunk of it, my heart uttered understanding: and wisdom grew in my breast, for my spirit strengthened my memory.

41 And my mouth was opened and shut no more.

42 The Highest gave understanding unto the five men, and they wrote the wonderful visions of the night, that were told, which they knew not: And they sat fourty days, and they wrote in the day, and at night they ate bread.

43 As for me I spoke in the day, and held not my tongue by night:

44 In fourty days they wrote two hundred and four books.

Or, 904.

45 And it came to pass when the fourty days were fulfilled, that the Highest spoke, saying, The first that you have written, publish openly, that the worthy and unworthy may read it.

46 But **keep the seventy last**, that you may deliver them only to such as be wise, among the people.

47 For in them is the spring of understanding, the fountains of wisdom, and the stream of knowledge.
48 And I did so.

Or, the light of knowledge.

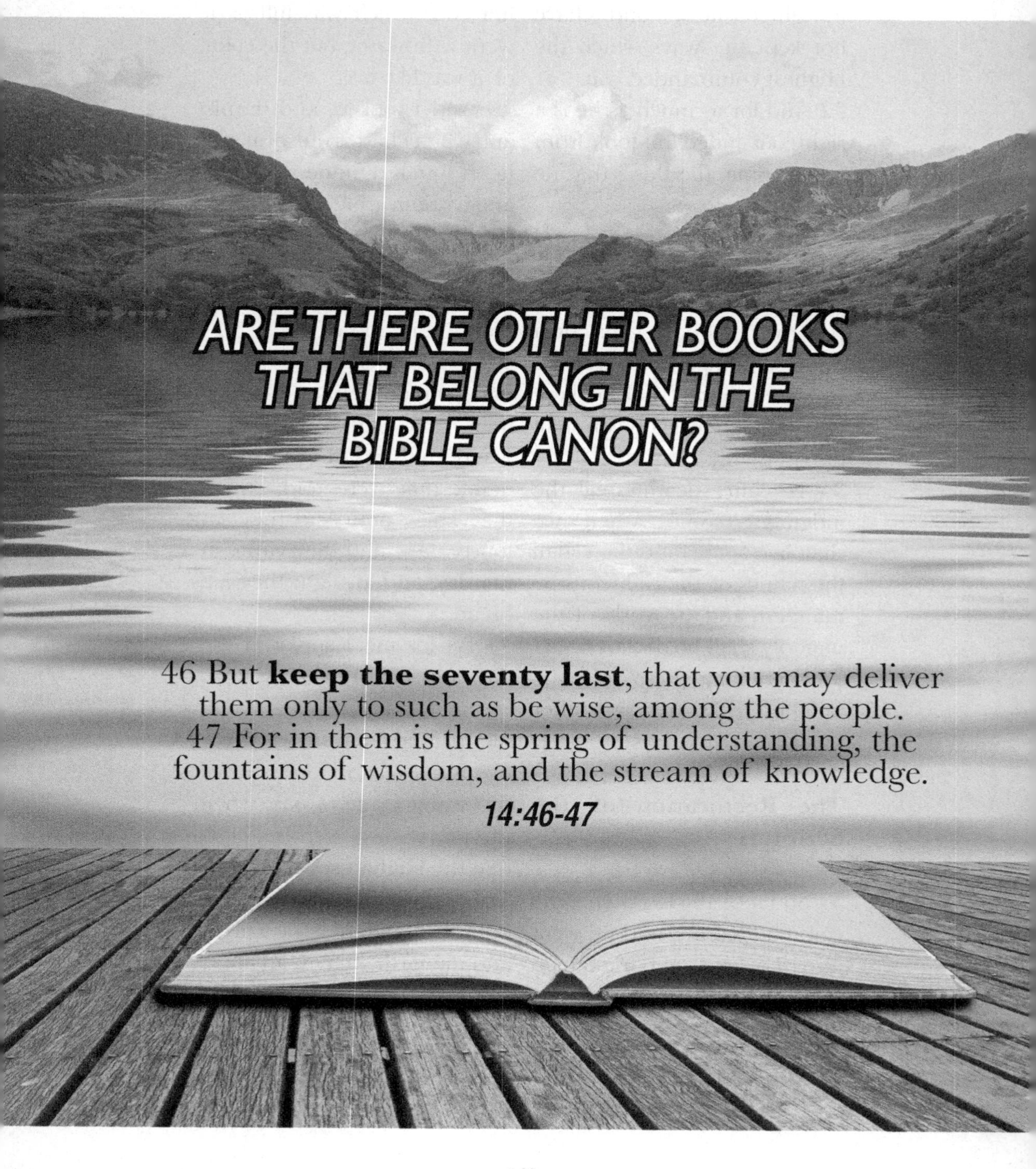

CHAPTER 15:

1 This prophecy is certain. 5 Elohim will take vengeance upon the wicked, 12 Upon Egypt, 28 An horrible vision. 43 Babylon and Asia are threatened.

Vengeance on the Wicked

1 Behold, speak in the ears of my people the words of prophesy, which I will put in your mouth, says Yahuah.
2 And cause them to be written in paper: for they are faithful and true.
3 Fear not the imaginations against you, let not the incredulity of them trouble you, that speak against you.
4 For all the unfaithful shall die in their unfaithfulness.
5 Behold, says Yahuah, I will bring plagues upon the world; the sword, famine, death, and destruction.
6 For wickedness has exceedingly polluted the whole earth, and their hurtful works are fulfilled.
7 Therefore says Yahuah,
8 I will hold my tongue no more as touching their wickedness, which they profanely commit, neither will I suffer them in those things, in which they wickedly exercise themselves: behold, the innocent and righteous blood cries unto me, and the souls of the just complain continually.

Cf. Gn. 4:10.

Rev. 6:10, 19:2.

9 And therefore says Yahuah, I will surely avenge them, and receive unto me, all the innocent blood from among them.
10 Behold, my people are led as a flock to the slaughter: I will not suffer them now to dwell in the land of Egypt.

Cf. Is. 53:7, Acts 8:32.

11 But I will bring them with a mighty hand, and a stretched out arm, and smite Egypt with plagues as before, and will destroy all the land thereof.
12 Egypt shall mourn, and the foundation of it shall be smitten with the plague and punishment, that Elohim shall bring upon it.
13 They that till the ground shall mourn: for their seeds shall fail, through the blasting, and hail, and with a fearful constellation.
14 Woe to the world, and them that dwell therein.
15 For the sword and their destruction draws near, and one people shall stand up to fight against another, and swords in their hands.
16 For there shall be sedition among men, and invading one another, they shall not regard their kings, nor princes, and the course of their actions

shall stand in their power.

17 A man shall desire to go into a city, and shall not be able.

18 For because of their pride, the cities shall be troubled, the houses shall be destroyed, and men shall be afraid.

19 A man shall have no pity upon his neighbor, but shall destroy their houses with the sword, and spoil their goods, because of the lack of bread, and for great tribulation.

20 Behold, says Elohim, I will call together all the Kings of the earth to reverence me, which are from the rising of the Sun, from the South, from the East, and Libanus: to turn themselves one against another, and repay the things that they have done to them.

21 Like as they do yet this day unto my chosen, so will I do also and recompense in their bosom, Thus says Yahuah Elohim;

In all of scripture Hell is an immediate burning with eternal fire. Esdras clarifies this is and immediate burning and their spirits are gone forever. Straw burns quickly and disappears.

22 My right hand shall not spare the sinners, and my sword shall not cease over them, that shed innocent blood upon earth.

23 The fire is gone forth from his wrath, and has consumed the foundations of the earth, and the sinners like the straw that is kindled.

24 Woe to them that sin and keep not my comandments, says Yahuah.

Yahuah warns to keep His command-ments even in the Last Days.

25 I will not spare them: go your way you children from the power, defile not my Sanctuary:

26 For Yahuah knows all them that sin against him, and therefore delivers them unto death and destruction.

27 For now are the plagues come upon the whole earth, and you shall remain in them, for Elohim shall not deliver you, because you have sinned against him.

A Terrifying Vision of Warfare

28 Behold an horrible vision, and the appearance thereof **from the East**.

Cf. Mal. 1:3 This is a likely reference to radical Islam.

29 Where the nations of the dragons of Arabia shall come out with many chariots, and the multitude of them shall be carried as the wind upon earth, that all they which hear them, may fear and tremble.

Persians.

30 Also the Carmanians raging in wrath, shall go forth as the wild boars of the wood, and with great power shall they come, and join battle with them, and shall waste a portion of the land of the Assyrians.

A portion of Assyria has well been wasted in modern times by Radical Islam.

31 And then shall the

dragons have the upper hand, remembering their nature, and if they shall turn themselves, conspiring together in great power to persecute them,

32 Then these shall be troubled, and keep silence through their power, and shall flee.

33 And from the land of the Assyrians, shall the enemy besiege them, and consume some of them, and in their host shall be fear, and dread and strife among their kings.

Or, against.

Judgment on Babylon

34 Behold clouds from the East, and from the North, unto the South, and they are very horrible to look upon; full of wrath and storm.

35 They shall smite one upon another, and they shall smite down a great multitude of stars upon the earth, even their own star; and blood shall be from the sword unto the belly.

Or, Pastern, or litter.

36 And dung of men unto the camels hoof.

37 And there shall be great fearfulness and trembling upon earth: and they that see the wrath, shall be afraid, and trembling shall come upon them.

38 And then shall there come great storms, from the South, and from the North, and another part from the West.

39 And strong winds shall arise from the East, and shall open it, and the cloud which he raised up in wrath, and the star stirred to cause fear toward the East and West wind, shall be destroyed.

40 The great and mighty clouds shall be lifted up full of wrath, and the star, that they may make all the earth afraid, and them that dwell therein, and they shall power out over every high and eminent place, an horrible star.

41 Fire and hail, and fleeing swords, and many waters, that all fields may be full, and all rivers with the abundance of great waters.

42 And they shall break down the cities, and walls, mountains and hills, trees of the wood, and grass of the meadows, and their corn.

43 And they shall go steadfastly unto Babylon, and make her afraid.

Or, destroy.

44 They shall come to her, and besiege her, the star and all wrath shall they power out upon her, then shall the dust and smoke go up unto the heaven: and all they that be about her, shall bewail her.

Cf. Rev 18:1-19. ***Origin of Revelation.***

45 And they that remain

under her, shall do service unto them that have put her in fear.

Judgment on Asia

46 And you Asia that are partaker of the hope of Babylon, and are the glory of her person:

Or, like unto Babylon.

47 Woe be unto you, you wretch, because you have made yourself like unto her, and have decked your daughters in whoredom, that they might please and glory in your lovers, which have always desired to commit whoredom with you.

48 You have followed her, that is hated in all her works and inventions: therefore says Elohim,

49 I will send plagues upon you: widowhood, poverty, famine, sword, and pestilence, to waste your houses with destruction and death.

50 And the glory of the power shall be dried up as flour, when the heat shall arise that is sent over you.

51 You shall be weakened as a poor woman with stripes, and as one chastised with wounds, so that the mighty and lovers shall not be able to receive you.

52 Would I with jealousy have so proceeded against you, says Yahuah,

53 If you had not always slain my chosen, exalting the stroke of your hands, and saying over their dead, when you were drunken,

Lat. death.

54 Set forth the beauty of your countenance.

55 The reward of your whoredom shall be in your bosom, therefore shall you receive recompense.

56 Like as you have done unto my chosen, says Yahuah; even so shall Elohim do unto you, and shall deliver you into mischief.

57 Your children shall die of hunger, and you shall fall through the sword: your cities shall be broken down, and all yours shall perish with the sword in the field.

58 They that be in the mountains shall die of hunger, and eat their own flesh, and drink their own blood, for very hunger of bread, and thirst of water.

59 You, as unhappy, shall come through the Sea, and receive plagues again.

60 And in the passage, they shall rush on the idle city, and shall destroy some portion of your land, and consume part of your glory, and shall return to Babylon that was destroyed.

61 And you shall be cast down by them, as stubble, and they shall be unto you as fire,
62 And shall consume you and your cities, your land and your mountains, all your woods and your fruitful trees shall they burn up with fire.
63 Your children shall they carry away captive, and look what you have, they shall spoil it, and mare the beauty of your face.

Or, blemish.

But thou, O Daniel, shut up the words, and seal the book, even to the time of the end: many shall run to and fro, and...

knowledge shall be increased.

THIS TIME HAS COME THAT ANCIENT KNOWLEDGE IS BEING RESTORED. *Not esoteric occult but His Torah which included Jubilees.*

DANIEL 12:4 KJV

CHAPTER 16:

1 Babylon and other places are threatened with plagues that cannot be avoided: 23 and with desolation. 40 The servants of Yahuah must look for troubles: 51 and not hide their sins, 74 but leave them, and they shall be delivered.

Further Denunciations

1 Woe be unto you, Babylon and Asia, woe be unto you Egypt and Syria.

2 Gird up yourselves with clothes of sack and hair, bewail your children, and be sorry, for your destruction is at hand.

3 A sword is sent upon you, and who may turn it back?

4 A fire is sent among you, and who may quench it?

5 Plagues are sent unto you, and what is he that may drive them away?

6 May any man drive away a hungry Lion in the wood? or may any one quench the fire in stubble, when it has begun to burn?

7 May one turn again the arrow that is shot of a strong archer?

8 The mighty Yahuah sends the plagues, and who is he that can drive them away?

9 A fire shall go forth from his wrath: and who is he that may quench it?

10 He shall cast lightnings, and who shall not fear? he shall thunder, and who shall not be afraid?

11 Yahuah shall threaten, and who shall not be utterly beaten to powder at his presence?

12 The earth quakes and the foundations thereof, the sea arises up with waves from the deep, and the waves of it are troubled, and the fish thereof also before Yahuah, and before the glory of his power.

13 For strong is his right hand that bends the bow, his arrows that he shoots are sharp, and shall not miss when they begin to be shot into the ends of the world.

14 Behold, the plagues are sent, and shall not return again, until they come upon the earth.

15 The fire is kindled, and shall not be put out, til it consume the foundation of the earth.

16 Like as an arrow which is shot of a mighty archer returns not backward: even so the plagues that shall be sent upon earth, shall not return again.

17 Woe is me, woe is me, who will deliver me in those days?

The Horror of the Last Days

Cf. Mt. 24:8. **Messiah quoted 2 Esdras again.**

18 The beginning of sorrows,

and great mournings, the beginning of famine, and great death: the beginning of wars, and the powers shall stand in fear, the beginning of evils, what shall I do when these evils shall come?

19 Behold, famine, and plague, tribulation and anguish, are sent as scourges for amendment.

20 But for all these things they shall not turn from their wickedness, nor be always mindful of the scourges.

21 Behold, victuals shall be so good cheap upon earth, that they shall think themselves to be in good case, and even then shall evils grow upon earth, sword, famine, and great confusion.

Or plagues.

22 For many of them that dwell upon earth, shall perish of famine, and the other that escape the hunger, shall the sword destroy.

23 And the dead shall be cast out as dung, and there shall be no man to comfort them, for the earth shall be wasted, and the cities shall be cast down.

24 There shall be no man left to till the earth, and to sow it.

25 The trees shall give fruit, and who shall gather them?

26 The grapes shall ripe, and who shall tread them? for all places shall be desolate of men.

27 So that one man shall desire to see another, and to hear his voice.

28 For of a city there shall be ten left, and two of the field which shall hide themselves in the thick groves, and in the clefts of rocks.

Cf. Rev. 6:16.

29 As in an orchard of olives, upon every tree there are left three or four olives:

30 Or, when as a vineyard is gathered, there are left some clusters of them that diligently seek through the vineyard:

31 Even so in those days there shall be three or four left by them that search their houses with the sword.

32 And the earth shall be laid waste, and the fields thereof shall wax old, and her ways and all her paths shall grow full of thorns, because no man shall travail therethrough.

33 The virgins shall mourn having no bridegrooms, the women shall mourn having no husbands, their daughters shall mourn having no helpers.

34 In the wars shall their bridegrooms be destroyed, and their husbands shall perish of famine.

Yahuah's People Must Prepare for the End

35 Hear now these things, and understand them, you servants of Yahuah.
36 Behold the word of Yahuah, receive it, believe not the gods of whom Yahuah spoke.
37 Behold, the plagues draw near, and are not slack.
38 As when a woman with child in the ninth month brings forth her son, within two or three hours of her birth great pains compass her womb, which pains, when the child comes forth, they slack not a moment,

Cf. Mt. 24:8; Mk. 13:8 NIV.

39 Even so shall not the plagues be slack to come upon the earth, and the world shall mourn, and sorrows shall come upon it on every side.
40 O my people, Hear my word: make you ready to the battle, and in those evils, be even as pilgrims upon the earth.
41 He that sells let him be as he that flees away: and he that buys, as one that will loose.
42 . He that occupies merchandise, as he that had no profit by it: and he that builds, as he that shall not dwell therein.
43 He that sows, as if he should not reap: so also he that plants the vineyard, as he that shall not gather the grapes.
44 They that marry, as they that shall get no children: and they that marry not, as the widowers.
45 And therefore they that labor, labor in vain.
46 For strangers shall reap their fruits, and spoil their goods, overthrow their houses; and take their children captives, for in captivity and famine shall they get children.
47 And they that occupy their merchandise with robbery, the more they deck their cities, their houses, their possessions and their own persons:
48 The more will I be angry with them for their sin, says Yahuah.
49 Like as an whore envies a right honest and virtuous woman:
50 So shall righteousness have iniquity, when she decks herself, and shall accuse her, to her face, when he comes that shall defend him that diligently searches out every sin upon earth.

The Power and Wisdom of Yahuah

51 And therefore be not like thereunto, nor to the works thereof.
52 For yet a little iniquity shall be taken away out of the

earth, and righteousness shall reign among you.

53 Let not the sinner say that he has not sinned: for Elohim shall burn coals of fire upon his head, which says before Yahuah Elohim and his glory, I have not sinned.

Cf. Rom. 3:23; 1Jn.1.10. ***Origin: 2 Esdras.***

54 Behold, Yahuah knows all the works of men, their imaginations, their thoughts, and their hearts:

Cf. Lk. 16:15.

55 Which spoke but the word, let the earth be made, and it was made: let the heaven be made, and it was created.

Cf. Gn.1.1.

56 In his word were the stars made, and he knows the number of them.

Cf. Ps. 146:4.

57 He searches the deep, and the treasures thereof, he has measured the Sea, and what it contains.

58 He has shut the Sea in the midst of the waters, and with his word has he hanged the earth upon the waters.

59 He spreads out the heavens like a vault, upon the waters has he founded it.

Cf. Job 22:14, 37:18.

60 In the desert has he made springs of water, and pools upon the tops of the mountains, that the floods might power down from the high rocks to water the earth.

61 He made man, and put his heart in the midst of the body, and gave him breath, life, and understanding.

62 Yes and the spirit of Almighty Elohim, which made all things, and searches out all hidden things in the secrets of the earth.

63 Surely he knows your inventions, and what you think in your hearts, even them that sin, and would hide their sin.

64 Therefore has Yahuah exactly searched out all your works, and he will put you all to shame.

65 And when your sins are brought forth you shall be ashamed before men, and your own sins shall be your accusers in that day.

66 What will you do? or how will you hide your sins before Elohim and his Angels?

67 Behold, Elohim himself is the judge, fear him: leave off from your sins, and forget your iniquities to meddle no more with them forever, so shall Elohim lead you forth, and deliver you from all trouble.

Impending Persecution of Yahuah's People

68 For behold, the burning wrath of a great multitude is kindled over you, and they shall take away certain of you, and feed you being idle with things offered unto idols.

Or, being unable to resist.

69 And they that consent unto them shall be had in derision, and in reproach, and trodden under foot.
70 For there shall be in every place, and in the next cities a great insurrection upon those that fear Yahuah.
71 They shall be like mad men, sparing none, but still spoiling and destroying those that fear Yahuah.
72 For they shall waste and take away their goods, and cast them out of their houses.
73 Then shall they be known who are my chosen, and they shall be tried, as the gold in the fire:

Promise of Divine Deliverance

74 Hear, O ye my beloved, says Yahuah: behold, the days of trouble are at hand, but I will deliver you from the same.
75 Be not afraid, neither doubt, for Elohim is your guide,
76 **And the guide of them who keep my commandments, and precepts**, says Yahuah Elohim; Let not your sins weigh you down, and let not your iniquities lift up themselves.

His commandments remain in the last days.

77 Woe be unto them that are bound with their sins, and covered with their iniquities: like as a field is covered over with bushes, and the path thereof covered with thorns, that no man may travel through.
78 It is left undressed, and is cast into the fire, to be consumed therewith.

Cf. John 15.
Or, shut out.

56 In his word were the stars made, and he knows the number of them.

THE
Levite
BIBLE
THE
Levite
BIBLE
LeviteBible.com

THE BOOK OF 1 ESDRAS

THE SECOND TEMPLE

THE Levite BIBLE

LeviteBible.com

CHAPTER 1:

1 Yosiah his charge to the Priests and Levites. 7 A great Passover is kept. 32 His death is much lamented: 34 His Successors. 53 The Temple, City, and people are destroyed. 56 The rest are carried unto Babylon.

Yosiah Celebrates the Passover

1 And Yosiah held the Feast of the Passover in Yerusalem unto his Yahuah, and offered the Passover the fourteenth day of the first month:

Cf. 2 Ki. 23:22; 2 Chr. 35:1.

2 Having set the Priests according to their daily courses, being arrayed in long garments, in the Temple of Yahuah.

3 And he spoke unto the Levites the holy ministers of Israel, that they should hallow themselves unto Yahuah, to set the holy Ark of Yahuah, in the house that king Solomon the son of David had built:

Cf. Ez. 40:46, 44:15, 48:11. The Levite Temple Priests remained holy just as Ezra. This book was in their library or what we would call today, Bible in Qumran/ Bethabara.

4 And said, You shall no more bear the Ark upon your shoulders: now therefore serve Yahuah your Elohim, and minister unto his people Israel, and prepare you after your families and kindreds.

5 According as David the king of Israel prescribed, and according to the magnificence of Solomon his son: and standing in the Temple according to the several dignities of the families of you the Levites, who minister in the presence of your brethren the children of Israel.

6 Offer the Passover in order, and make ready the sacrifices for your brethren, and keep the Passover according to the commandment of Yahuah, which was given unto Moses.

7 And unto the people that were found there, Yosiah gave thirty thousand lambs, and kids, and three thousand calves: these things were given of the kings allowance, according as he promised to the people, to the Priests, and to the Levites.

8 And Hilkiah, Zechariah, and Yehiel the governors of the Temple, gave to the Priests for the Passover, two thousand and six hundred sheep, and three hundred calves.

9 And Yeconiah, and Shemaiah, and Nethanel his brother, and Hashabiah, and Ochiel, and Yoram captains over thousands, gave to the Levites for the Passover five thousand sheep, and seven hundred calves.

Five hundred calves, Cf. 2 Chr.

10 And when these things were done, the Priests and Levites having the unleavened bread, stood in very comely order according to the kindreds,

11 And according to the

several dignities of the fathers, before the people, to offer to Yahuah, as it is written in the book of Moses: And thus did they in the morning.

Cf. 2 Chr. 35.12. And so of the bullocks.

12 And they roasted the Passover with fire, as appertains: as for the sacrifices, they sod them in brass pots, and pans with a good savor.

With good speed, or willingly, Cf. 2 Chr. 35:13.

13 And set them before all the people, and afterward they prepared for themselves, and for the Priests their brethren the sons of Aaron.

14 For the Priests offered the fat until night: and the Levites prepared for themselves, and the Priests their brethren the sons of Aaron.

15 The holy Singers also, the sons of Asaph, were in their order, according to the appointment of David, to with, Asaph, Zechariah, and Eddinus, who was of the king's retinue.

Cf. 2 Chr. 35:15. of David and Asaph, the kings seer.

16 Moreover the porters were at every gate: it was not lawful for any to go from his ordinary service: for their brethren the Levites prepared for them.

17 Thus were the things that belonged to the sacrifices of Yahuah accomplished in that day, that they might hold the Passover,

18 And offer sacrifices upon the altar of Yahuah, according to the commandment of king Yosiah.

19 So the children of Israel which were present, held the Passover at that time, and the feast of sweet bread seven days.

Unleavened.

20 And such a Passover was not kept in Israel since the time of the Prophet Samuel.

21 Yes all the kings of Israel held not such a Passover as Yosiah, and the Priests and the Levites, and the Yahudim held with all Israel that were found dwelling at Yerusalem.

22 In the eighteenth year of the reign of Yosiah was this Passover kept.

The End of Yosiah's Reign

23 And the works of Yosiah were upright before his Yahuah with an heart full of godliness.

24 As for the things that came to pass in his time, they were written in former times, concerning those that sinned, and did wickedly against Yahuah above all people and kingdoms, and how they grieved him exceedingly, so that the words of Yahuah rose up against Israel.

Or, were ungodly. Or, sensibly.

25 Now after all these acts of Yosiah, it came to pass that Pharaoh the king of

Egypt came to raise war at Carchamis upon Euphrates: and Yosiah went out against him.

Cf. 2 Chr. 35:20.

26 But the king of Egypt sent to him saying, What have I to do with you, O king of Yahudea?

27 I am not sent out from Yahuah Elohim against you: for my war is upon Euphrates, and now Yahuah is with me, yes Yahuah is with me hasting me forward: Depart from me and be not against Yahuah.

28 Howbeit Yosiah did not turn back his chariot from him, but undertook to fight with him, not regarding the words of the Prophet YirmiYahu, spoken by the mouth of Yahuah:

29 But joined battle with him in the plain of Megiddo, and the princes came against king Yosiah.

30 Then said the king unto his servants, carry me away out of the battle for I am very weak: and immediately his servants took him away out of the battle.

31 Then he got up upon his second chariot, and being brought back to Yerusalem, died, and was buried in his father's sepulchre.

32 And in all Yahudea they mourned for Yosiah, yes YirmiYahu the Prophet lamented for Yosiah, and the chief men with the women made lamentation for him unto this day: and this was given out for an ordinance to be done continually in all the nation of Israel.

The Last Kings of Yahudah

33 These things are written in the book of the stories of the kings of Yahudah, and every one of the acts that Yosiah did, and his glory, and his understanding in the law of Yahuah, and the things that he had done before, and the things now recited, are reported in the books of the Kings of Israel and Yahudea.

2 Kings and 2 Chronicles.

2 Kings and 2 Chronicles.

34 And the people took Yeconiah the son of Yosiah, and made him king instead of Yosiah his father, when he was twenty and three years old.

Cf. 2 Ki. 23:30; 2 Chr. 36:1.

35 And he reigned in Yahudea and in Yerusalem three months: and then the King of Egypt deposed him from reigning in Yerusalem.

36 And he set a tax upon the land of an hundred talents of silver, and one talent of gold.

37 The king of Egypt also made king Yehoiakim his brother king of Yahudea and

Yerusalem.

38 And he bound Yehoiakim and the nobles: but Zarius his brother he apprehended, and brought him out of Egypt.

39 Five and twenty years old was Yehoiakim when he was made king in the land of Yahudea and Yerusalem, and he did evil before Yahuah.

Cf. 2 Chr. 36:4. or Eliakim.

40 Wherefore against him Nebuchadnezzar the King of Babylon came up, and bound him with a chain of brass, and carried him unto Babylon.

41 Nebuchadnezzar also took of the holy vessels of Yahuah, and carried them away, and set them in his own temple at Babylon.

42 But those things that are recorded of him, and of his uncleanness, and impiety, are written in the Chronicles of the kings.

2 Chronicles.

43 And Yehoiachin his son reigned in his stead: he was made king being eighteen years old,

44 And reigned but three months and ten days in Yerusalem, and did evil before Yahuah.

45 So after a year Nebuchadnezzar sent, and caused him to be brought into Babylon with the holy vessels of Yahuah,

46 And made Zedekiah king of Yahudea and Yerusalem, when he was one and twenty years old, and he reigned eleven years:

The Fall of Yerusalem

47 And he did evil also in the sight of Yahuah, and cared not for the words that were spoken unto him, by the Prophet YirmiYahu from the mouth of Yahuah.

48 And after that king Nebuchadnezzar had made him to swear by the Name of Yahuah, he broke his oath and rebelled, and hardening his neck, and his heart, he transgressed the laws of Yahuah Elohim of Israel.

49 The governors also of the people and of the priests did many things against the laws, and passed all the pollutions of all nations, and defiled the Temple of Yahuah which was sanctified in Yerusalem.

50 Nevertheless, the Elohim of their fathers sent by his messenger to call them back, because he spared them and his tabernacle also:

51 But they had his messengers in derision, and look when Yahuah spoke unto them, they made a sport of his prophets,

52 So far forth that he being wroth with his people for

their great ungodliness, commanded the kings of the Chaldees to come up against them.

Babylon.

53 Who flew their young men with the sword, yes even within the compass of their holy Temple, and spared neither young man nor maid, old man nor child among them, for he delivered all into their hands.

54 And they took all the holy vessels of Yahuah, both great and small, with the vessels of the Ark of Elohim, and the king's treasures, and carried them away into Babylon.

55 As for the house of Yahuah they burnt it, broke down the walls of Yerusalem, set fire upon her towers.

56 And as for her glorious things, they never ceased til they had consumed and brought them all to nothing, and the people that were not slain with the sword, he carried unto Babylon:

57 Who became servants to him and his children, til the Persians reigned, to fulfill the word of Yahuah spoken by the mouth of YirmiYahu:

Cf. Jer. 25:11 and 29:10.

58 Until the land had enjoyed her Sabbaths, the whole time of her desolation shall she rest, until the full term of seventy years.

Or, Keep Sabbath.

Yerusalem ruins. Babylon sacks the city and the Temple.

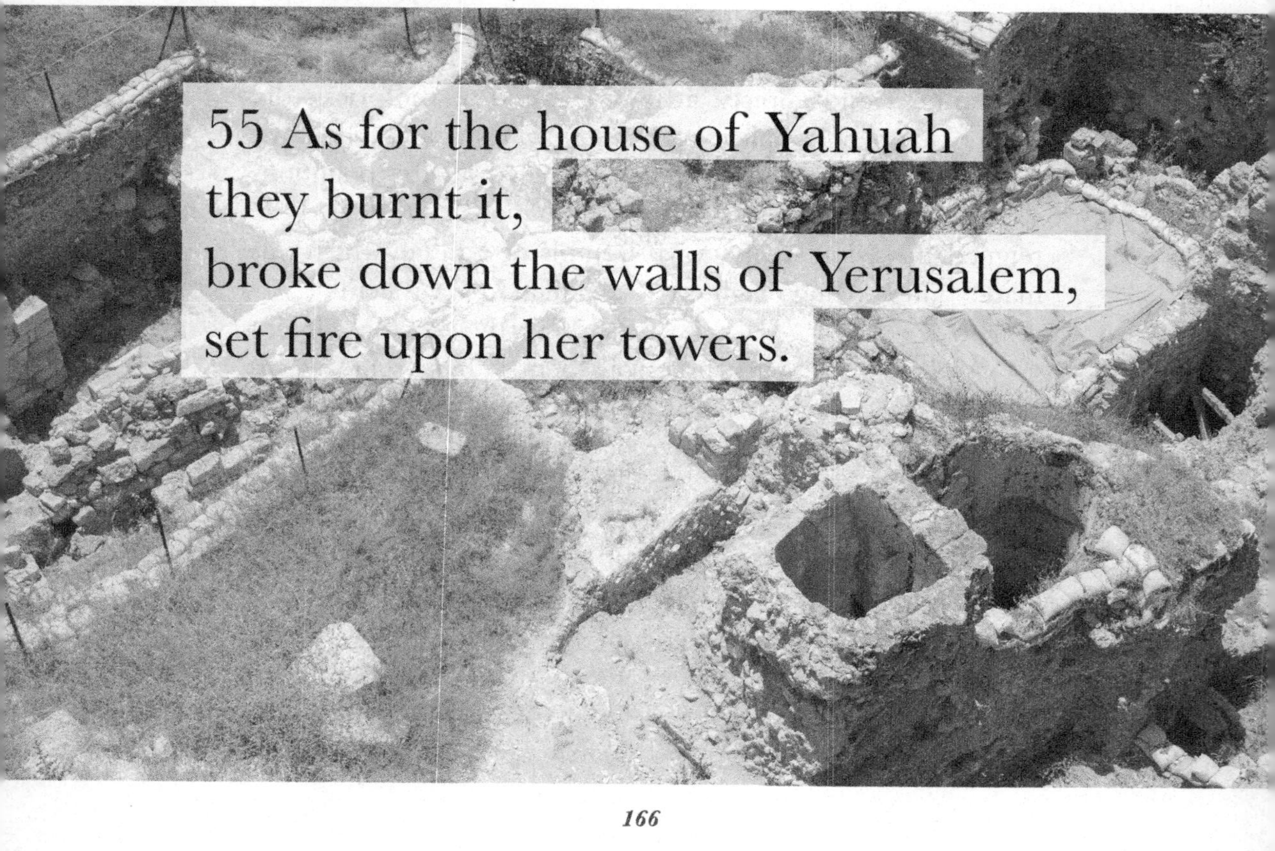

55 As for the house of Yahuah
they burnt it,
broke down the walls of Yerusalem,
set fire upon her towers.

CHAPTER 2:

1 Cyrus is moved by Elohim to build the Temple, 5 And gives leave to the Yahudim to return and contribute to it. 11 He delivers again the vessels which had been taken thence. 25 Artaxerxes (Cambyses) forbid the Yahudim to build any more.

Cyrus Permits the Exiles to Return

1 In the first year of Cyrus king of the Persians, that the word of Yahuah might be accomplished, that he had promised by the mouth of YirmiYahu:

Cf. 2 Chr. 36:22; Ezra 1:1.

2 Yahuah raised up the spirit of Cyrus the king of the Persians, and he made proclamation through all his kingdom, and also by writing,

3 Saying, Thus says Cyrus king of the Persians, Yahuah of Israel the Most High Yahuah, has made me king of the whole world,

4 And commanded me to build him an house at Yerusalem in Yahudea.

5 If therefore there be any of you that are of his people, let Yahuah, even his Lord be with him, and let him go up to Yerusalem that is in Yahudea, and build the house of Yahuah of Israel: for he is Yahuah that dwells in Yerusalem.

Or, this.

6 Whosoever then dwell in the places about, let them help him, those I say that are his neighbors, with gold and with silver,

7 With gifts, with horses, and with cattle, and other things, which have been set forth by vow, for the Temple of Yahuah at Yerusalem.

8 Then the chief of the families of Yahudea, and of the tribes of Benyamin stood up: the priests also and the Levites, and all they whose mind Yahuah had moved to go up, and to build an house for Yahuah at Yerusalem,

9 And they that dwelt round about them, and helped them in all things with silver and gold, with horses and cattle, and with very free gifts of a great number whose minds were stirred up thereto.

Hebr. substance, Cf. Ezr. 1:6.

10 King Cyrus also brought forth the holy vessels which Nebuchadnezzar had carried away from Yerusalem, and had set up in his temple of idols.

11 Now when Cyrus king of the Persians had brought them forth, he delivered them to Mithridates his treasurer:

12 And by him they were delivered to Sheshbazzar the governor of Yahudea.

Shash-bazar. Greek the first part of the word is corruptly joined to the word going before, Cf. Ezra 1:8.

13 And this was the number of them, a thousand golden cups, and a thousand of silver, censors of silver twenty.

Hebr. knives, Cf. Ezra 1:9, Ezra 1:10. but four hundred and ten.

nine, vials of gold thirty, and of silver two thousand four hundred and ten, and a thousand other vessels.

Cf. Ezra 1:11. but five thousand four hundred. 5,469 vessels of gold and silver. These mostly came from Ophir.

14 So all the vessels of gold, and of silver which were carried away, were five thousand, four hundred, threescore and nine.

15 These were brought back by Sheshbazzar, together with them of the captivity, from Babylon to Yerusalem.

Opposition to Rebuilding Yerusalem

Chaldean name for Cambyses, son of Cyrus. It cannot be the grandson of Darius.

16 But in the time of Artaxerxes king of the Persians, Bishlam, and Mithridates, and Tabeel, and Rehum, and Beltethmus, and Shimshai the scribe, with others that were in commission with them, dwelling in Samaria and other places, wrote unto him against them that dwelt in Yahudea and Yerusalem, these letters following.

Cf. Ezra 4:6. Bahumus and the name which follows, is but an epithet to the former, Ezra 4:9. Shimshai, Ezra 4:8. Note: These are Samaritans not Israelites. Some hold the title "scribe" and they will become the scribes and Sanhedrin in Yahudea after 165 B.C. when the Samaritans conquered the Temple and usurped the priesthood.

17 To King Artaxerxes our lord, Your servants Rehum the recorder, and Shimshai the scribe, and the rest of their counsel, and the Judges that are in Coelesyria and Phoenicia.

18 Be it now known to the lord the king, that the Yahudim that are come up from you to us, being come into Yerusalem (that rebellious and wicked city,) do build the market places, and repair the walls of it, and do lay the foundation of the Temple.

19 Now if this city, and the walls thereof be made up again, they will not only refuse to give tribute, but also rebel against kings.

20 And forasmuch as the things pertaining to the Temple, are now in hand, we think it meet not to neglect such a matter,

21 But to speak unto our lord the king, to the intent that if it be your pleasure, it may be sought out in the books of your fathers:

22 And you shall find in the Chronicles, what is written concerning these things, and shall understand that that city was rebellious, troubling both kings and cities:

23 And that the Yahudim were rebellious, and raised always wars therein, for the which cause even this city was made desolate.

24 Wherefore now we do declare unto you, (O lord the king) that if this city be built again, and the walls thereof set up anew, you shall from henceforth have no passage into Coelesyria and Phoenicia.

25 Then the King wrote back again to Rehum the recorder, to Beltethmus, to Shimshai the scribe, and to the rest that were in commission, and dwellers in Samaria and Syria, and Phoenicia, after this manner.

Note: *These are the enemies of Yahudea and the Bible. After defiling the Temple and usurping the priesthood, these Samaritans are the origin of the Pharisess which became Rabbinic Judaism.*

26 I have read the Epistle which you have sent unto me: therefore I commanded to make diligent search, and it has been found, that that city was from the beginning practicing against Kings.

27 And the men therein were given to rebellion, and war, and that mighty Kings and fierce were in Yerusalem, who reigned and exacted tributes in Coelesyria and Phoenicia.

28 Now therefore I have commanded to hinder those men from building the city, and heed to be taken that there be no more done in it,

29 And that those wicked workers proceed no further to the annoyance of Kings.

30 Then king Artaxerxes his letters being read, Rehum and Shimshai the scribe, and the rest that were in commission with them, moving in as towards Yerusalem with a troup of horsemen, and a multitude of people in battle array, began to hinder the builders, and the building of the Temple in Yerusalem ceased until the second year of the reign of Darius King of the Persians.

Or, a great number of souldiers.

Tomb of Cyrus the Great.

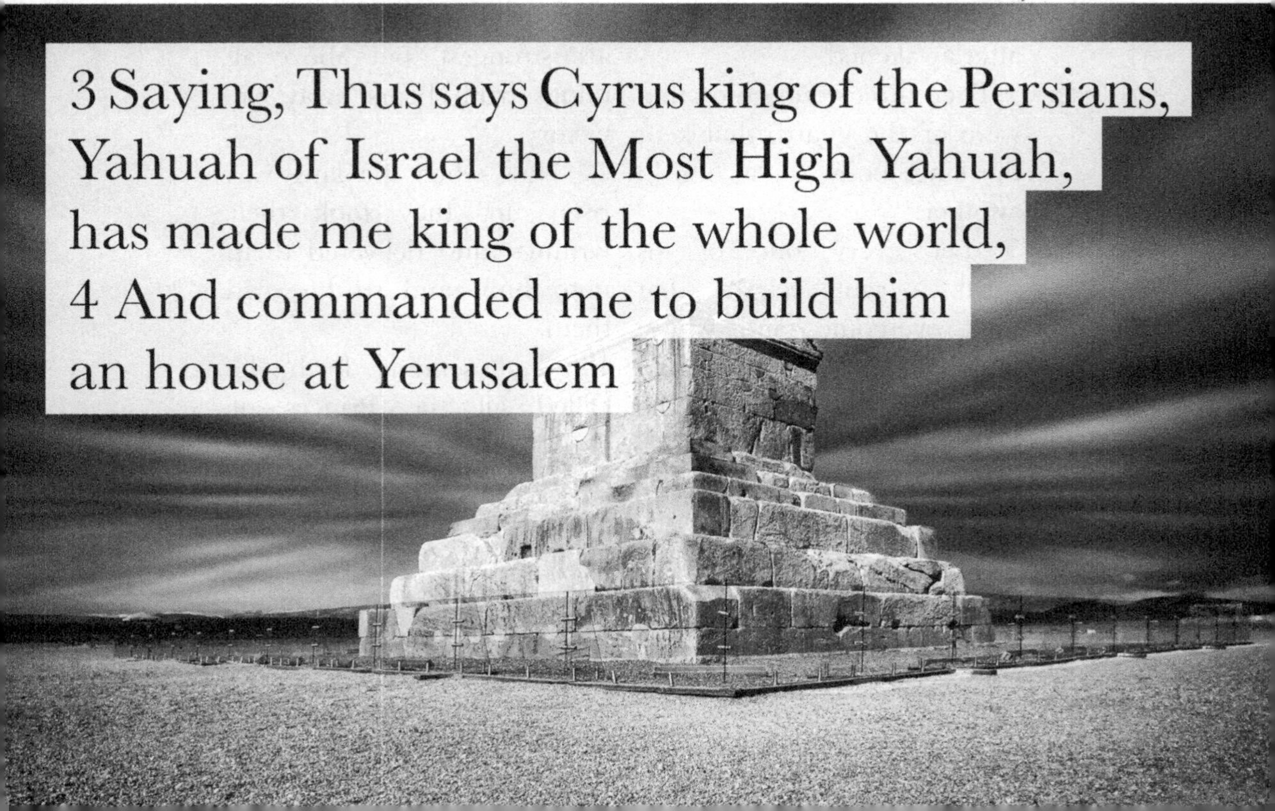

3 Saying, Thus says Cyrus king of the Persians, Yahuah of Israel the Most High Yahuah, has made me king of the whole world,
4 And commanded me to build him an house at Yerusalem

CHAPTER 3:

4 Three strive to excel each other in wise speeches. 9 They refer themselves to the judgment of the King. 18 The first declares the strength of Wine.

The Debate of the Three Bodyguards

1 Now when Darius reigned, he made a great feast unto all his Subjects and unto all his household, and unto all the princes of Media and Persia,
2 And to all the governors and captains, and lieutenants that were under him, from Yahudea unto Ethiopia, of an hundred twenty and seven provinces.
3 And when they ate and drank, and being satisfied were gone home, then Darius the king went into his bed chamber, and slept, and soon after awakened.
4 Then three young men that were of the guard, that kept the kings body, spoke one to another:
5 Let every one of us speak a sentence: he that shall overcome, and whose sentence shall seem wiser than the others, unto him shall the king Darius give great gifts, and great things in token of victory:
6 As to be clothed in purple, to drink in gold, and to sleep upon gold, and a chariot with bridles of gold, and an head-tire of fine linen, and a chain about his neck:
7 And he shall sit next to Darius, because of his wisdom, and shall be called, Darius his cousin.
8 And then every one wrote his sentence, sealed it, and laid it under king Darius' pillow,
9 And said, that when the king is risen, some will give him the writings, and of whose side the king, and the three princes of Persia shall judge, that his sentence is the wisest, to him shall the victory be given as was appointed.
10 The first wrote: Wine is the strongest.
11 The second wrote: The King is strongest.
12 The third wrote; Women are strongest, but above all things truth bears away the victory.
13 Now when the king was risen up, they took their writings, and delivered them unto him, and so he read them.
14 And sending forth, he called all the Princes of Persia and Media, and the governors, and the captains, and the lieutenants, and the chief officers,
15 And sat him down in the

royal seat of Judgment, and the writings were read before them:

Or, counsel.

16 And he said, Call the young men, and they shall declare their own sentences: so they were called, and came in.

17 And he said unto them, Declare unto us your mind, concerning the writings. Then began the first, who had spoken of the strength of wine;

The Speech about Wine

18 And he said thus: O you men, how exceeding strong is wine! It causes all men to err that drink it:

19 It makes the mind of the king, and of the fatherless child to be all one of the bondman and of the freeman, of the poor man and of the rich:

20 It turns also every thought into jollity and mirth, so that a man remembers neither sorrow nor debt:

21 And it makes every heart rich, so that a man remembers neither king nor governor, and it makes to speak all things by talents:

22 And when they are in their cups, they forget their love both to friends and brethren, and a little after draw out swords:

23 But when they are from the wine, they remember not what they have done.

24 O you men, is not wine the strongest, that enforces to do thus? And when he had so spoken, he held his peace.

Antique ceramic jugs, pots and vases in ancient city Ercolano of roman times ruined by volcano Vesuvius in Italy.

CHAPTER 4:

1 The second declares the power of a King. 14 The third, the force of women: 33 and of Truth. 41 The third is judged to be wisest, 47 and obtains Letters of the King to build Yerusalem. 58 He praises Elohim, and shows his brethren what he had done.

The Speech about the King

1 Then the second that had spoken of the strength of the King, began to say;

2 O you men, do not men excel in strength, that bear rule over Sea and land, and all things in them?

Or, have the command.

3 But yet the King is more mighty: for he is lord of all these things, and has dominion over them, and whatsoever he commands them, they do:

4 If you bid them to make war one against the other, they do it: if he send them out against the enemies, they go, and break down mountains, walls and towers.

5 They slay and are slain, and transgress not the King's commandment: if they get the victory, they bring all to the King, as well the spoil as all things else.

6 Likewise for those that are not soldiers, and have not to do with wars, but use husbandry; when they have reaped again, that which they had sown, they bring it to the King, and compel one another to pay tribute unto the King.

7 And yet he is but one man; if he command to kill, they kill, if he command to spare, they spare.

8 If he command to smite, they smite; if he command to make desolate, they make desolate; if he command to build, they build:

9 If he command to cut down, they cut down; if he command to plant, they plant.

10 So all his people and his armies obey him; furthermore he lies down, he eats and drinks, and takes his rest.

11 And these keep (watch) round about him, neither may any one depart, and do his own business, neither disobey they him in any thing.

Or, can.

12 O you men, how should not the King be mightiest, when in such sort he is obeyed? and he held his tongue.

The Speech about Women

13 Then the third, who had spoken of women, and of the truth (this was Zerubbabel) began to speak.

14 O you men, it is not the great King, nor the multitude of men, neither is it wine that excels; who is it then that rules them, or has the lordship over

Heb. is of force.

them, are they not women?

15 Women have born the King and all the people, that bear rule by sea and land.

16 Even of them came they: and they nourished them up that planted the vineyards from whence the wine comes.

17 These also make garments for men; these bring glory unto men, and without women cannot men be.

18 Yes and if men have gathered together gold and silver, or any other goodly thing, do they not love a woman, which is comely in favor and beauty?

19 And letting all those things go, do they not gape, and even with open mouth fix their eyes fast on her; and have not all men more desire unto her, then unto silver or gold, or any goodly thing whatsoever?

20 A man leaves his own father that brought him up, and his own country, and cleaves unto his wife.

21 He sticks not to spend his life with his wife, and remember neither father, nor mother, nor country.

22 By this also you must know, that women have dominion over you: do ye not labor and toil, and give and bring all to the woman?

23 Yes a man takes his sword, and goes his way to rob, and to steal, to sail upon the sea, and upon rivers,

24 And looks upon a lion, and goes in the darkness, and when he has stolen, spoiled and robbed, he brings it to his love.

25 Wherefore a man loves his wife better than father and mother.

26 Yes many there be that have run out of their wits for women, and become servants for their sakes:

Or, grown desperate.

27 Many also have perished, have erred, and sinned for women.

28 And now do you not believe me? Is not the King great in his power? Do not all regions fear to touch him?

29 Yet did I see him and Apame the Kings concubine, the daughter of the admirable Bartacus, sitting at the right hand of the King,

Josephus Antiq. lib. 11. cap. 4. Rabsaces Themasius.

30 And taking the crown from the King's head, and setting it upon her own head; she also slap the King with her left hand.

31 And yet for all this, the King gaped and gazed upon her with open mouth: if she laughed upon him, he laughed also: but if she took any displeasure at him, the King was faine to flatter, that

Or, here at. Or, be friends with him.

she might be reconciled to him again.
32 O you men, how can it be but women should be strong, seeing they do thus?

The Speech about Truth

33 Then the king and the princes looked one upon another: so he began to speak of the truth.
34 O you men, are not women strong? great is the earth, high is the heaven, swift is the Sun in his course, for he compasses the heavens round about, and fetches his course again to his own place in one day.
35 Is he not great that makes these things? Therefore great is the truth, and stronger than all things.
36 All the earth calls upon the truth, and the heaven blesses it, all works shake and tremble at it, and with it is no unrighteous thing.

Or, praises the truth. Athanas.

37 Wine is wicked, the king is wicked, women are wicked, all the children of men are wicked, and such are all their wicked works, and there is no truth in them. In their unrighteousness also they shall perish.
38 As for the truth it endures, and is always strong, it lives and conquers for evermore.
39 With her there is no accepting of persons, or rewards, but she does the things that are just, and refrains from all unjust and wicked things, and all men do well like of her works.
40 Neither in her judgment is any unrighteousness, and she is the strength, kingdom, power and majesty of all ages. Blessed be the Elohim of truth.
41 And with that he held his peace, and all the people then shouted and said, Great is truth, and mighty above all things.

Zerubbabel's Reward

42 Then said the king unto him, Ask what you will, more than is appointed in the writing, and we will give it to you, because you are found wisest, and you shall sit next to me, and shall be called my cousin.
43 Then he said unto the king, Remember your vow which you have vowed to build Yerusalem in the day when you came to the kingdom,
44 And to send away all the vessels that were taken away out of Yerusalem, which Cyrus set apart, when he vowed to destroy Babylon, and to send

Or, counsel.

The Edomites burnt the 1st Temple and join to defile the 2nd temple in Psalm 83 which occurred in 165 B.C.

them again thither.

45 You also have vowed to build up the Temple, which the Edomites burnt when Yahudea was made desolate by the Chaldees.

46 And now, O lord the king, this is that which I require, and which I desire of you, and this is the princely liberality proceeding from yourself: I desire therefore that you make good the vow, the performance whereof with your own mouth you have vowed to the king of heaven.

47 Then Darius the king stood up and kissed him, and wrote letters for him unto all the treasurers and lieutenants, and captains and governors that they should safely convey on their way, both him, and all those that go up with him to build Yerusalem.

48 He wrote letters also unto the lieutenants that were in Coelesyria and Phoenicia, and unto them in Lebanon, that they should bring Cedar wood from Lebanon unto Yerusalem, and that they should build the city with him.

49 Moreover he wrote for all the Yahudim that went out of his realm up into Yahudea, concerning their freedom, that no officer, no ruler, no lieutenant, nor treasurer, should forcibly enter into their doors,

Or, steward.

Edomites = Esau.

50 And that all the country which they hold, should be free without tribute, and that the Edomites should give over the villages of the Yahudim which then they held,

The Edomites occupied Yerusalem when Yahudea was taken into captivity. In Samaria for the Northern Tribes, there occurred no such order from any ruler and this is why they never returned to Samaria as it was occupied and that power structure also affirmed in this account. Yahudea is different as they return until after Messiah.

51 Yes that there should be yearly given twenty talents to your building of the Temple, until the time that it were built,

52 Another ten talents yearly, to maintain the burnt offerings upon the Altar every day (as they had a commandment to offer seventeen)

53 And that all they that went from Babylon to build the city, should have free liberty as well they as their posterity, and all the priests that went away.

54 He wrote also concerning the charges, and the priest's vestments wherein they minister:

55 And likewise for the charges of the Levites, to be given them, until the day that the house were finished, and Yerusalem builded up.

56 And he commanded to give to all that kept the city, pensions and wages.

Or, portions of land.

57 He sent away also all the vessels from Babylon that Cyrus had set apart, and all that Cyrus had given in commandment, the same he charged also to be done, and sent unto Yerusalem.

Zerubbabel's Prayer

58 Now when this young man was gone forth, he lifted up his face to heaven toward Yerusalem, and praised the king of heaven,
59 And said, From you comes victory, from you comes wisdom, and yours is the glory, and I am your servant.
60 Blessed are you who has given me wisdom: for to you I give thanks, O Yahuah of our fathers.
61 And so he took the letters, and went out, and came unto Babylon, and told it to all his brethren.
62 And they praised the Elohim of their fathers: because he had given them freedom and liberty
63 To go up, and to build Yerusalem, and the Temple which is called by his Name, and they feasted with instruments of music, and gladness seven days.

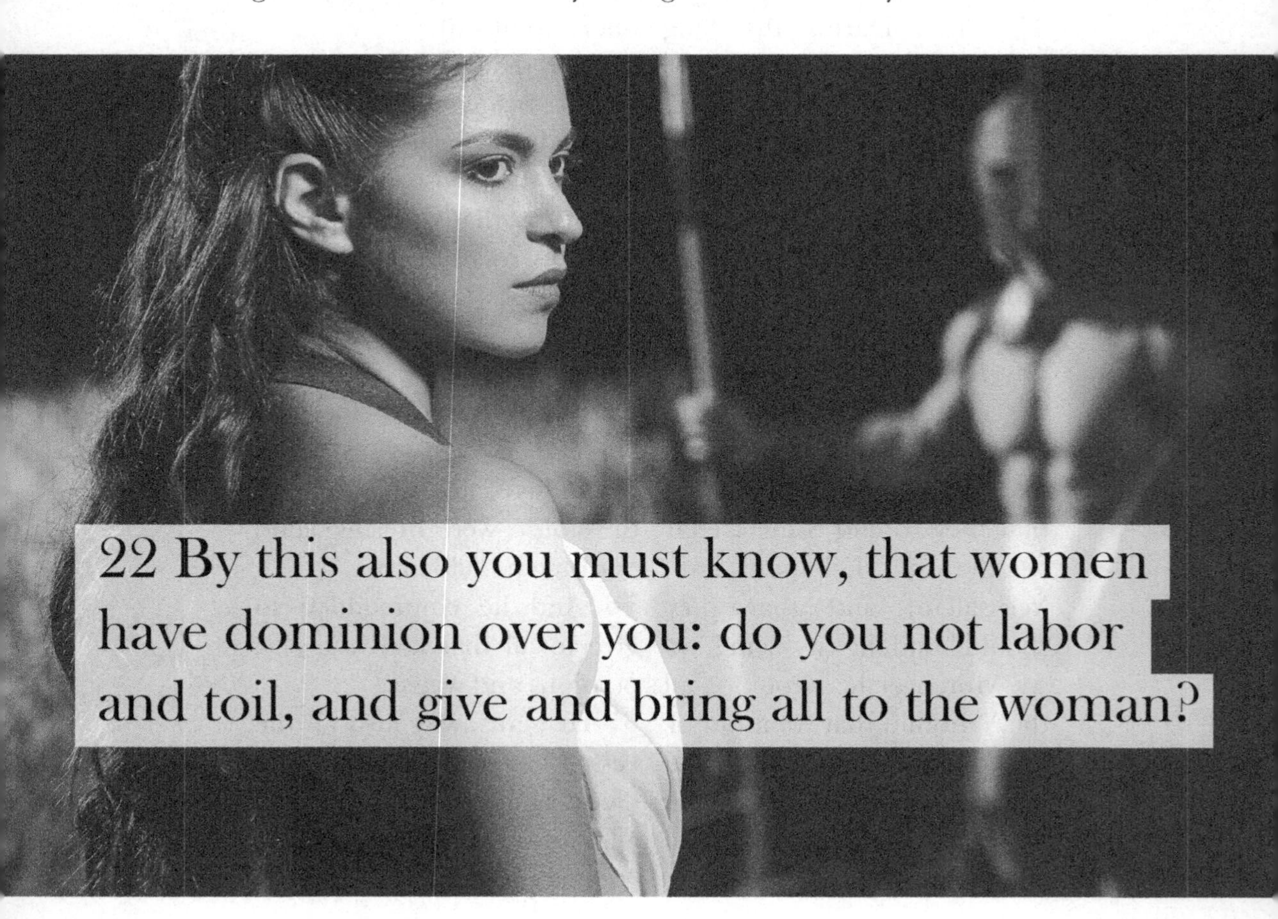

CHAPTER 5:

4 The names and number of the Yahudim that returned home. 50 The Altar is set up in his place. 57 The foundation of the Temple is laid. 73 The work is hindered for a time.

List of the Returning Exiles

1 After this were the principal men of the families chosen according to their tribes, to go up with their wives, and sons, and daughters, with their men-servants and maid-servants, and their cattle.
2 And Darius sent with them a thousand horsemen, til they had brought them back to Yerusalem safely, and with musical [instruments,] tabrets and flutes:
3 And all their brethren played, and he made them go up together with them.
4 And these are the names of the men which went up, according to their families, amongst their tribes, after their several heads.
5 The Priests the sons of Phinehas, the son of Aaron: Yahusha the son of Yozadak, the son of Seraiah, and Yoakim the son of Zerubbabel, the son of Shealtiel of the house of David, out of the kindred of Phares, of the tribe of Yahudah;

Yoachim and Zorobabel. This place is corrupt: For Yoachim was the son of Yosedech, Neh.12:10 and not Zorobabel, who was of the tribe of Yahudah.

6 Who spoke wise sentences before Darius the king of Persia, in the second year of his reign, in the month Nisan, which is the first month.

Zerubbabel.

Biblical month of Abib. Nisan is Babylonian not Hebrew.

7 And these are they of Yahudim that came up from the captivity, where they dwelt as strangers, whom Nebuchadnezzar the king of Babylon had carried away unto Babylon:
8 And they returned unto Yerusalem, and to the other parts of Yahudea every man to his own city, who came with Zerubbabel, with Yahusha, Nehemiah, and Seraiah, and Resaiah, Eneneus, Mordecai, Beelsarus, Aspharasus, Reeliah, Rehum, and Baanah their guides.
9 The number of them of the nation, and their governors: sons of Parosh two thousand an hundred seventy and two: the sons of Shephatiah four hundred seventy and two;
10 The sons of Arah seven hundred fifty and six:

Saraiah. Or Mispar., Or Reelaiah.

Parosh, Ezra 2:3. Neh. 7:9. where for brevity look for the true numbers of the particulars following: for here they vary much, and the names much more. Shephatia. Or, three hundred seventy two.

11 The sons of Pahath-moab, two thousand eight hundred and twelve:
12 The sons of Elam, a thousand two hundred fifty and four: the sons of Zattu, nine hundred fourty and five: the sons of Chorbe seven hundred and five: the sons of

Zacchai.

Bani, six hundred fourty and eight:

13 The sons of Bebai, six hundred twenty and three: the sons of Azgad, three thousand two hundred twenty and two:

Asgad.

14 The sons of Adonikam, six hundred sixty and seven: the sons of Biguai, two thousand sixty and six: the sons of Adin, four hundred fifty and four:

Bigui.

15 The sons of Ater, ninety and two: the sons of Kilan and Azetas, threescore and seven: the sons of Azaru, four hundred thirty and two.

Alerhezekia.

16 The sons of Annias, an hundred and one: the sons of Arom thirty two, and the sons of Bezai, three hundred twenty and three: the sons of Arsiphurith, an hundred and two:

Besai.

17 The sons of Baiterus, three thousand and five: the sons of Bethlomon, an hundred twenty and three.

Bethlehem.

18 They of Netophah fifty and five: they of Anathoth, an hundred fifty and eight: they of Bethasmoth, fourty and two:

Asmaneth.

19 They of Kiriatharim, twenty and five: they of Chephirah and Beeroth, seven hundred fourty and three: they of Pyra, seven hundred:

Kiriashiarim.

20 They of Chadiasans and Ammidians, four hundred twenty and two: they of Kirama and Geba, six hundred twenty and one:

Rama, Gabah.

21 They of Macalon, an hundred twenty and two: they of Betolio fifty and two: the sons of Niphish, an hundred fifty and six.

Michmas, Bethel, Maghbis.

22 The sons of Calamolalus and Ono, seven hundred twenty and five: the sons of Yerechus, two hundred fourty and five:

Lodhadid.

23 The sons of Senaah, three thousand three hundred and thirty:

24 The Priests, the sons of Yedaiah, the son of Yahusha, among the sons of Anasib, nine hundred seventy and two: the sons of Immer, a thousand fifty and two:

Yammar.

25 The sons of Pashhur, a thousand fourty and seven: the sons of Charme a thousand and seventeen.

Pashur, Harim, Or, 217. according to some copies.

26 The Levites: the sons of Yeshua, and Kadmiel, and Bannas, and Sudias, seventy and four.

Thus it is read, Ezra 2:40. the sons of Yeshua, and Cadmeel, of the sons of Hodowyah.

27 The holy singers: the sons of Asaph an hundred twenty and eight.

28 The porters: the sons of Shallum, the sons of Ater, the sons of Talmon, the sons of Akkub, the sons of Hatita, the sons of Shobai, in all an hundred thirty and nine.

Shebai.

Zich, Siaha, Agabah.

29 The servants of the Temple: the sons of Esau, the sons of Hasupha, the sons of Tabbaoth, the sons of Keros: the sons of Sua, the sons of Padon, the sons of Lebanah, the sons of Hagabah:

Shamlai, Giddes, Gahar.

30 The sons of Akkub, the sons of Uthai, the sons of Ketab, the sons of Hagab, the sons of Subai, the sons of Hana, the sons of Cathua, the sons of Geddur:

Reaiah, Rezin, Necodah, Gazam, Huzza, Pascah, Besai, Neumin, Nephusin, Bakbu, Hacupa, Harbur.

31 The sons of Yairus, the sons of Daisan, the sons of Noeba, the sons of Chezib, the sons of Gazera, the sons of Uzza, the sons of Phinoe, the sons of Hasrah, the sons of Basthai, the sons of Asnah the sons of Maani, the sons of Nephisim, the sons of Acuph, the sons of Hakupha, the sons of Asur, the sons of Pharakim, the sons of Bazluth.

Harsha, Barcos, Sisera, Thamai.

32 The sons of Mehida: the sons of Cutha, the sons of Charea, the sons of Barkos, the sons of Serar, the sons of Temah, the sons of Neziah, the sons of Hatipha.

Sophereth, Iaalah, Darcon, Goddet.

33 The sons of the servants of Solomon: the sons of Assaphioth, the sons of Peruda, the sons of Yaalah, the sons of Lozon, the sons of Isdael, the sons of Shephatiah:

Hatte, Phoceroth Hazzebaim, Ezra 2:25.

34 The sons of Agia, the sons of Pochereth-hazzebaim, the sons of Sabie, the sons of Sarothie, the sons of Masiah, the sons of Gas, the sons of Addus, the sons of Subas, the sons of Apherra, the sons of Barodis, the sons of Shaphat, the sons of Allon.

35 All the ministers of the Temple, and the sons of the servants of Solomon, were three hundred seventy and two.

36 These came up from Tel-melah, and Tel-harsha, Cherub leading them and Addan and Immer.

37 Neither could they show their families, nor their stock, how they were of Israel: the sons of Delaiah, the sons of Tobiah, the sons of Nekoda, six hundred fifty and two.

Persian false priests pretending to be Aaronic families were attempting infiltration even then. Likely Pharisees (Farsees/ Persians).

38 And of the **Priests that usurped the office of the Priesthood**, and were not found, the sons of Habaiah: the sons of Hakkoz, the sons of Yaddus, who married Agia one of the daughters of Barzillai, and was named after his name.

Hobaiah, Cos, Barzelai.

39 And when the description of the kindred of these men was sought in the Register, and was not found, they were **removed from executing the office of the Priesthood**.

Pharisees caught and removed. Cf. Rev. 2:9, 3:9.

40 For unto them said

Nehemiah, who also is Acharias, two of one. Neh.8:9 and 10:2. Chap. 2:63, Heb. Urim and Thummim.

Nehemiah, and Attharias, that they should not be partakers of the holy things, til there arose up an high Priest, clothed with Doctrine and Truth.

41 So of Israel from them of twelve years old and upward, they were all in number fourty thousand, besides men servants and women servants, two thousand three hundred and sixty.

42 Their men servants and handmaids were seven thousand three hundred fourty and seven: the singing men and singing women, two hundred forty and five.

Cf. Neh. 7:66.

43 Four hundred thirty and five camels, seven thousand thirty and six horses, two hundred fourty and five mules, five thousand five hundred twenty and five beasts used to the yoke.

Ezra 2:67, Asses.

44 And certain of the chief of their families, when they came to the Temple of Elohim that is in Yerusalem, vowed to set up the house again in his own place according to their ability:

45 And to give into the holy treasury of the works, a thousand pounds of gold, five thousand of silver, and an hundred priestly vestments.

46 And so dwelt the Priests, and the Levites, and the people in Yerusalem, and in the country: the Singers also, and the Porters, and all Israel in their villages.

Worship Begins Again

47 But when the seventh month was at hand, and when the children of Israel were every man in his own place, they came all together with one consent into the open place of the first gate, which is towards the East.

7th Month: Fall Feast Month

Or, before the East gate.

48 Then stood up Yahusha the son of Yozadak, and his brethren the Priests, and Zerubbabel the son of Shealtiel, and his brethren, and made ready the Altar of the Elohim of Israel,

49 To offer burnt sacrifices upon it, according as it is expressly commanded in the book of Moses the man of Elohim.

50 And there were gathered unto them out of the other nations of the land, and they erected the Altar upon his own place, because all the nations of the land were at enmity with them, and oppressed them, and they offered sacrifices according to the time, and burnt offerings to Yahuah both morning, and evening.

51 Also they held the feast of Tabernacles, as it is commanded in the law, and offered sacrifices daily as was meet:

52 And after, that the continual oblations, and the sacrifice of the Sabbaths, and of the new Moons, and of all holy feasts.

Or, daily sacrifice.

53 And all they that had made any vow to Elohim, began to offer sacrifices to Elohim from the first day of the seventh month, although the Temple of Yahuah was not yet built.

The Temple was not a requirement for burnt offerings.

Greek. halowed.

54 And they gave unto the Masons and Carpenters, money, meat and drink with cheerfulness.

55 Unto them of Sidon also and Tyre, they gave cares that they should bring Cedar trees from Lebanon, which should be brought by floats to the haven of Joppa, according as it was commanded them by Cyrus King of the Persians.

The Foundations of the Temple Laid

56 And in the second year and second month, after his coming to the Temple of Elohim at Yerusalem, began Zerubbabel the son of Shealtiel, and Yahusha the son of Yozadak, and their brethren and the priests, and the Levites, and all they that were come unto Yerusalem out of the captivity:

57 And they laid the foundation of the house of Elohim, in the first day of the second month, in the second year after they were come to Yahudea and Yerusalem.

58 And they appointed the Levites from twenty years old, over the works of Yahuah. Then stood up Yahusha and his sons, and brethren, and Kadmiel his brother, and the sons of Yeshua Emadabun, with the sons of Yoda the son of Iliadun, with their sons and brethren, all Levites, with one accord setters forward of the business, laboring to advance the works in the house of Elohim. So the workmen built the temple of Yahuah.

See Ezra 3:9. Or, overseers or encouragers of them that wrought in the house of Yahuah.

59 And the Priests stood arrayed in their vestments with musical instruments, and trumpets, and the Levites the sons of Asaph had Cymbals,

60 Singing songs of thanksgiving, and praising Yahuah according as David the king of Israel had ordained.

Or, after the manner of David king of Israel.

61 And they sung with loud voices songs to the praise of Yahuah: because his mercy and glory is forever in all Israel.

62 And all the people sounded trumpets, and shouted with a loud voice, singing songs of thanksgiving unto Yahuah for the rearing up of the house of Yahuah.

63 Also of the Priests and Levites, and of the chief of their families the ancients who had seen the former house, came to the building of this with weeping and great crying.

Cf. Ezra 3:12-13.

64 But many with trumpets and joy shouted with loud voice.

65 Insomuch that the trumpets might not be heard for the weeping of the people: yet the multitude sounded marvelously, so that it was heard a far off.

Or, discerned.

66 Wherefore when the enemies of the Tribe of Yahudah and Benyamin heard it, they came to know what that noise of trumpets should mean.

67 And they perceived, that they that were of the captivity did build the temple unto Yahuah Elohim of Israel.

These Samaritan replacements defiled the worship of YHWH by infusing it with their gods. Yahuah has always rejected this.

68 So they went to Zerubbabel and Yahusha, and to the chief of the families, and said unto

Asar-haddon, Chap.4:3. Cf. 2 Ki. 17:27-41.

***Note:** These are imposters who replaced the Northern Kingdom earlier and infused their gods into the worship of Yahuah falsely which He rejected. These are the origin of the Hasmoneans and Pharisees who would attack the Temple in 165 B.C.*

them, We will build together with you.

69 For we likewise, as you, do obey Yahuah, and do sacrifice unto him from the days of Esar-haddon the king of the Assyrians who brought us hither.

70 Then Zerubbabel and Yahusha, and the chief of the families of Israel said unto them, It is not for us and you to build together an house unto Yahuah our Elohim.

71 We ourselves alone will build unto Yahuah of Israel, according as Cyrus the King of the Persians has commanded us.

72 But the heathen of the land lying heavy upon the inhabitants of Yahudea, and holding them straight, hindered their building:

73 And by their secret plots, and popular persuasions, and commotions, they hindered the finishing of the building, all the time that king Cyrus lived, so they were hindered from building for the space of two years, until the reign of Darius.

***Note:** This passage calls those Samaritan heathens. They do not worship Yahuah. These are the origin of the Hasmoneans of Modi-in which is in Dan in Samaria not Yahudea.*

Until the second year of Darius. Ezra 4:5-7.

CHAPTER 6:

1 The Prophets stir up the people to build the Temple. 8 Darius is solicited to hinder it. 27 But he does further it by all means, 32 and threatens those that shall hinder it.

Work on the Temple Begins Again

1 Now in the second year of the reign of Darius, Haggai, and Zechariah the son of Iddo, the prophets prophesied unto the Yahudim, in Yahudea and Yerusalem in the Name of Yahuah Elohim of Israel which was upon them.

Or, which was called on them.

2 Then stood up Zerubbabel the son of Shealtiel, and Yahusha the son of Yozadak, and began to build the house of Yahuah at Yerusalem, the prophets of Yahuah being with them,and helping them.

3 At the same time came unto them Sisinnes the governor of Syria and Phoenicia, with Sathrabuzanes, and his companions, and said unto them,

Ezra 5:3. Or, Tatnai, Or, Shetherboznai.

4 By whose appointment do you build this house, and this roof, and perform all the other things? And who are the workmen that perform these things?

5 Nevertheless the Elders of the Yahudim obtained favor: because Yahuah had visited the captivity.

6 And they were not hindered from building until such time as signification was given unto Darius concerning them, and an answer received.

7 The copy of the letters which Sisinnes governor of Syria, and Phoenicia, and Sathrabuzanes with their companions rulers in Syria and Phoenicia, wrote and sent unto Darius, To king Darius, greeting.

8 Let all things be known unto our lord the King, that being come into the country of Yahudea, and entered into the city of Yerusalem, we found in the city of Yerusalem the ancients of the Yahudim that were of the captivity;

9 Building an house unto Yahuah, great, and new, of hewn and costly stones, and the timber already laid upon the walls.

10 And those works are done with great speed, and the work goes on prosperously in their hands, and with all glory and diligence is it made.

11 Then asked we these Elders, saying, By whose commandment build you this house, and lay the foundations of these works?

12 Therefore to the intent that we might give knowledge unto

you by writing, we demanded of them who were the chief doers, and we required of them the names in writing of their principal men.

13 So they gave us this answer: We are the servants of Yahuah which made heaven and earth.

14 And as for this house, it was builded many years ago, by a king of Israel great and strong, and was finished.

15 But when our fathers provoked Elohim unto wrath, and sinned against Yahuah of Israel which is in heaven, he gave them over into the power of Nebuchadnezzar king of Babylon of the Chaldees:

16 Who pulled down the house and burnt it, and carried away the people captives unto Babylon.

17 But in the first year that King Cyrus reigned over the country of Babylon, Cyrus the king wrote to build up this house.

18 And the holy vessels of gold and of silver, that Nebuchadnezzar had carried away out of the house at Yerusalem, and had set them in his own temple, those Cyrus the king brought forth again out of the temple at Babylon, and they were delivered to Zerubbabel and Sheshbazzar the ruler,

Or, Zorobabel, which is also Sanabassar the ruler, so as Zorobabel seemed to be added to the text, Ezra 1:8.

19 With commandment that he should carry away the same vessels, and put them in the Temple at Yerusalem, and that the Temple of Yahuah should be built in his place.

20 Then the same Sheshbazzar being come hither, laid the foundations of the house of Yahuah at Yerusalem, and from that time to this, being still a building, it is not yet fully ended.

21 Now therefore if it seem good unto the king, let search be made among the records of King Cyrus,

Or, rules.

22 And if it be found, that the building of the house of Yahuah at Yerusalem has been done with the consent of King Cyrus, and if our lord the king be so minded, let him signify unto us thereof.

Official Permission Granted

23 Then commanded king Darius to seek among the records at Babylon: and so at Ecbatana the palace which is in the country of Media, there was found a rule wherein these things were recorded.

Or, place.

24 In the first year of the reign of Cyrus, king Cyrus commanded that the house of Yahuah at Yerusalem should

be built again where they do sacrifice with continual fire.
25 Whose height shall be sixty cubits, and the breadth sixty cubits, with three rows of hewn stones, and one row of new wood of that country, and the expenses thereof to be given out of the house of king Cyrus.
26 And that the holy vessels of the house of Yahuah, both of gold and silver that Nebuchadnezzar took out of the house at Yerusalem, and brought to Babylon, should be restored to the house at Yerusalem, and be set in the place where they were before.
27 And also he commanded that Sisinnes the governor of Syria and Phoenicia, and Sathrabuzanes, and their companions, and those which were appointed rulers in Syria, and Phoenicia should be careful not to meddle with the place, but suffer Zerubbabel the servant of Yahuah, and governor of Yahudea, and the Elders of the Yahudim, to build the house of Yahuah in that place.
28 I have commanded also to have it built up whole again, and that they look diligently to help those that be of the captivity of the Yahudim, til the house of Yahuah be finished.
29 And out of the tribute of Coelesyria and Phoenicia, a portion carefully to be given these men, for the sacrifices of Yahuah that is, to Zerubbabel the governor, for bullocks, and rams, and lambs;
30 And also corn, salt, wine and oil, and that continually every year without further question, according as the Priests that be in Yerusalem shall signify, to be daily spent:
31 That offerings may be made to the Most High Elohim, for the king and for his children, and that they may pray for their lives.

Drink offerings.

32 And he commanded, that whosoever should transgress, yes, or make light of any thing afore spoken or written, out of his own house should a tree be taken, and he thereon be hanged, and all his goods seized for the king.
33 Yahuah therefore whose Name is there called upon, utterly destroy every king and nation, that stretches out his hand to hinder or damage that house of Yahuah in Yerusalem.
34 I Darius the king have ordained, that according unto these things it be done with diligence.

CHAPTER 7:

1 Sisinnes and others, help forward the building. 5 The Temple is finished, and dedicated. 10 The Passover is kept.

The Temple Is Dedicated

1 Then Sisinnes the governor of Coelesyria and Phoenicia, and Sathrabuzanes, with their companions, following the commandments of king Darius,

Ezra 6:13.

2 Did very carefully oversee the holy works, assisting the ancients of the Yahudim, and governors of the Temple.

3 And so the holy works prospered, when Haggai and Zechariah the Prophets prophesied.

Or, the decree.

4 And they finished these things, by the commandment of Yahuah Elohim of Israel, and with the consent of Cyrus, Darius, and Artaxerxes, kings of Persia.

Hebr. the third day, Ezra 6:15. **Note:** The Temple dedication or Feast of Dedication is a February event not December as Hanukkah has no precedence in scripture as a Feast Day. Messiah was in the Temple during the Feast of Dedication in February not December. Even the 1st Temple was Dedicated during Tabernacles in Oct (7th Hebrew Month).

5 And thus was the **holy house finished**, in the **three and twentieth day of the month Adar**, in the sixth year of Darius king of the Persians.

6 And the children of Israel: the Priests, and the Levites, and others that were of the captivity, that were added unto them, did according to the things written in the book of Moses.

7 And to the dedication of the Temple of Yahuah, they offered an hundred bullocks, two hundred rams, four hundred lambs;

8 And twelve goats for the sin of all Israel, according to the number of the chiefs of the tribes of Israel.

Or, tribes.

9 The Priests also and the Levites, stood arrayed in their vestments according to their kindreds, in the services of Yahuah Elohim of Israel, according to the book of Moses: and the porters at every gate.

Hebr. divisions, Esdr. 6:18.

The Passover

10 And the children of Israel that were of the captivity, held the Passover the fourteenth day of the first month, after that the Priests and the Levites were sanctified.

Or, with those that.

11 They that were of the captivity were not all sanctified together: but the Levites were all sanctified together,

12 And so they offered the Passover for all them of the captivity, and for their brethren the Priests, and for themselves.

13 And the children of Israel that came out of the captivity, did eat, even all they that had separated themselves from the abominations of the people of the land, and sought Yahuah. **14** And they kept the feast of unleavened bread seven days, making mercy before Yahuah, **15** For that he had turned the counsel of the King of Assyria towards them to strengthen their hands in the works of Yahuah Elohim of Israel.

Or, mind.

John 10:22 KJV
And it was at Jerusalem the feast of the dedication, and it was winter.

5 And thus was the holy house finished, in the three and twentieth day of the month Adar...

7 And to the dedication of the Temple of Yahuah, they offered...

Ezra 6:15 KJV
And this house was finished on the third day of the month Adar...

The 2nd Temple was dedicated in February during the Winter. This is the Feast of Dedication. The 1st Temple was dedicated on the Feast of Tabernacles in the 7th Month. There is no precedence for the modern Hanukkah in scripture nor a December celebration.

CHAPTER 8:

1 Ezra brings the King's Commission to build. 8 The copy of it. 28 He declares the names and number of those that came with him: 61 And his journey. 71 He laments the sins of his people, 96 And swears the Priests to put away their strange wives.

Ezra Arrives in Jerusalem

Esdras is the Latin form of Ezra.

1 And after these things, when Artaxerxes the king of the Persians reigned, came Ezra the son of Seraiah, the son of Azariah, the son of Hilkiah, the son of Shallum,

Azarias.

2 The son of Zadok, the son of Ahitub, the son of Amariah, the son of Uzzi, the son of Memeroth, the son of Zaraias, the son of Sauias, the son of Bukki, the son of Abishua, the son of Phineas, the son of Eleazar, the son of Aaron the chief Priest.

Azarias, Meraioth, Uzzi. Some copies want these three names, Heb. was first, Ezra 7:1.

3 This Ezra went up from Babylon, as a Scribe being very ready in the Law of Moses, that was given by the Elohim of Israel,

4 And the king did honor him: for he found grace in his sight in all his requests.

5 There went up with him also certain of the children of Israel, of the Priests, of the Levites, of the holy Singers, Porters, and Ministers of the Temple, unto Yerusalem,

Nethinims.

6 In the seventh year of the reign of king Artaxerxes, in the fifth month, (this was the king's seventh year) for they went from Babylon in the first day of the first month, and came to Yerusalem, according to the prosperous journey which Yahuah gave them.

Abib 1.

See Ezra 7:7-9.

Or, success.

7 For Ezra had very great skill, so that he omitted nothing of the Law and Commandments of Yahuah, but taught all Israel the Ordinances and Judgments.

The King's Mandate

8 Now the copy of the Commission which was written from Artaxerxes the King, and came to Ezra the priest and reader of the Law of Yahuah, is this that follows.

Or, decree.

9 King Artaxerxes unto Ezra the Priest and reader of the Law of Yahuah, send greeting.

10 Having determined to deal graciously, I have given order, that such of the nation of the Yahudim, and of the Priests and Levites being within our Realm, as are willing and desirous, should go with you unto Yerusalem.

11 As many therefore as have a mind thereunto, let them depart with you, as it has seemed good both to me, and my seven friends the

counselors,

12 That they may look unto the affairs of Yahudea and Yerusalem, agreeably to that which is in the Law of Yahuah.

13 And carry the gifts unto Yahuah of Israel to Yerusalem, which I and my friends have vowed, and all the gold and silver that in the country of Babylon can be found, to Yahuah in Yerusalem,

Or, go.

14 With that also which is given of the people, for the Temple of Yahuah their Elohim at Yerusalem: and that silver and gold may be collected for bullocks, rams and lambs, and things thereunto appertaining,

15 To the end that they may offer sacrifices unto Yahuah, upon the Altar of Yahuah their Elohim, which is in Yerusalem.

16 And whatsoever you and your brethren will do with the silver and gold, that do according to the will of your Elohim.

With the rest of, Ezra 7:18.

17 And the holy vessels of Yahuah which are given to you, for the use of the Temple of your Elohim which is in Yerusalem, you shall set before your Elohim in Yerusalem.

18 And whatsoever thing else you shall remember for the use of the Temple of your Elohim, you shall give it out of the king's treasury.

19 And I, king Artaxerxes, have also commanded the keepers of the treasures in Syria and Phoenicia, that whatsoever Ezra the priest, and the reader of the law of the Most High Elohim shall send for, they should give to him with speed,

20 To the sum of an hundred talents of silver: likewise also of wheat even to an hundred cors, and an hundred pieces of wine, and other things in abundance.

Or, measures or salt, Ezra 7:22.

21 Let all things be performed after the law of Elohim diligently unto the Most High Elohim, that wrath come not upon the kingdom of the King and his sons.

22 I command you also that you require no tax, nor any other imposition of any of the Priests or Levites, or holy singers, or porters, or ministers of the temple, or of any that have doings in this temple, and that no man have authority to impose anything upon them.

23 And you, Ezra, according to the wisdom of Elohim, ordain judges, and justices, that they may judge in all Syria and Phoenicia, all those that know the law of your Elohim, and those that know

Heb. of those that know Ezra 7:25.

Note: Artaxerxes is the same king in the story of Esther. There is no way this king turned on the Yahudim. Esther is false and not scripture. Ezra 7:26.

it not you shall teach.
24 And whosoever shall transgress the law of your Elohim, and of the king, shall be punished diligently, whether it be by death or other punishment, by penalty of money, or by imprisonment.

Ezra Praises Yahuah

25 Then said Ezra the Scribe, Blessed be the only Yahuah Elohim of my fathers, who has put these things into the heart of the king, to glorify his house that is in Yerusalem;
26 And has honored me in the sight of the king and his counselors, and all his friends and Nobles.
27 Therefore I was encouraged, by the help of Yahuah my Elohim, and gathered together men of Israel to go up with me:

The Leaders Who Returned

28 And these are the chiefs according to their families and several dignities, that went up with me from Babylon in the reign of king Artaxerxes.
29 Of the sons of Phineas, Gershom: of the sons of Ithamar, Gamael: of the sons of David; Hattush the son of Shecaniah:

Or, Daniel, Or, Chattus.

30 Of the sons of Parosh, Zechariah, and with him were counted, an hundred and fifty men:

Ezra 8:3, of the sons of Secheniah, of the sons of Parosh.

31 Of the sons of Pahath-moab, Eliehoenai son of Zerahiah, and with him two hundred men:

Zerachaiah.

32 Of the sons of Zattu, Shecaniah son of Yahaziel, and with him three hundred men, Of the sons of Adin, Obed son of Yonathan, and with him two hundred and fifty men.

Or, of the sons of Shecheniah the son of Yahaziel, Heb. fifty men.

33 Of the sons of Elam, Yeshaiah son of Gotholiah, and with him seventy men:

Or, Athaliah.

34 Of the sons of Shephatiah, Zeraiah son of Michael, and with him threescore and ten men:

Or, Zebadiah, Or, fourscore men.

35 Of the sons of Yoab, Obadiah son of Yehiel, and with him two hundred and twelve men:

Or, eighteen men.

36 Of the sons of Bani, Shelomith son of Yosiphiah, and with him an hundred and threescore men:
37 Of the sons of Bebai, Zechariah son of Bebai, and with him twenty and eight men:
38 Of the sons of Azgad, Yohanan son of Hakkatan, and with him an hundred and ten men:

Or, Az, gad, Or, Catan.

39 Of the sons of Adonikam the last, and these are the names of them, Eliphelet, Yeuel, and Shemaiah and with them seventy men:

Or, Shemaia, Or, sixty men.

40 Of the sons of Bigvai, Uthai son of Istalcurus, and with him seventy men:

41 And these I gathered together to the river, called Theras, where we pitched our tents three days, and then I surveyed them.

Or, to the river called Ahave. Ez. 8.11.

Or, be numbered the people and the priests: but found none of the sons of Levi.

42 But when I had found there, none of the priests and Levites,

43 Then sent I unto Eliezar, Iduel, Maasmas,

Or, Ariel, Or, Shemaiah.

44 And Elnathan, Shemaiah, Yarib, Nathan, Elnathan, Zechariah, and Meshullam principal men and learned.

Or, these mens names with their generations are rightly distinguished Ezra 8:16.

45 And I bade them that they should go unto Iddo the captain, who was in the place of the treasury:

Or, Casiphia.

46 And commanded them that they should speak unto Iddo, and to his brethren, and to the treasurers in that place, to send us such men as might execute the Priest's office in the house of Yahuah.

Or, the Nethinims at the place of Casiphia, Or, Machli.

47 And by the mighty hand of our Yahuah they brought unto us skillful men of the sons of Mahli, the son of Levi, the son of Israel, Sherebiah and his sons and his brethren, who were eighteen.

Sherebia Ezra 8:18.

48 And Asebia, and Hashabiah and Annunus and his brother Yeshaiah, of the descendants of Hananiah, and their sons were twenty men.

Or, also Hashabia, and with him Yeshaiah of the sons of Merari with his brethren Ezra 8:19.

49 And of the servants of the Temple whom David had ordained, and the principal men, for the service of the Levites (to wit) the servants of the Temple, two hundred and twenty, the catalogue of whose names were shown.

Ezra Proclaims a Fast

50 And there I vowed a fast unto the young men before our Yahuah, to desire of him a prosperous journey, both for us, and them that were with us: for our children and for the cattle:

Proclaimed, Heb. substance.

51 For I was ashamed to ask the king's footmen, and horsemen, and conduct for safeguard against our adversaries:

52 For we had said unto the king, that the power of Yahuah our Elohim, should be with them that seek him, to support them in all ways.

53 And again we besought our Yahuah, as touching these things, and found him favorable unto us.

The Gifts for the Temple

54 Then I separated twelve of the chiefs of the priests, Sherebiah and Hashabiah, and ten men of their brethren with them.

Serenias ad Hassibias.

55 And I weighed them the gold, and the silver, and the holy vessels of the house of our Yahuah, which the king and his counsel, and the princes, and all Israel had given.

56 And when I had weighed it, I delivered unto them six hundred and fifty talents of silver, and silver vessels of an hundred talents, and an hundred talents of gold,

57 And twenty golden vessels, and twelve vessels of brass, even of fine brass, glittering like gold.

Heb. two vessels, Ezra 8:27.

58 And I said unto them, Both you are holy unto Yahuah, and the vessels are holy, and the gold, and the silver is a vow unto Yahuah, the Yahuah of our fathers.

59 Watch, and keep them til you deliver them to the chiefs of the priests and Levites, and to the principal men of the families of Israel in Yerusalem into the chambers of the house of our Elohim.

60 So the priests and the Levites who had received the silver and the gold, and the vessels, brought them unto Yerusalem into the Temple of Yahuah.

The Return to Yerusalem

61 And from the river Theras we departed the twelfth day of the first month, and came to Yerusalem by the mighty hand of our Yahuah, which was with us: and from the beginning of our journey, Yahuah delivered us from every enemy, and so we came to Yerusalem.

Abib 12.

Dangers in the way.

62 And when we had been there three days, the gold and silver that was weighed, was delivered in the house of our Yahuah on the fourth day unto Meremoth the priest, the son of Uriah.

Or, unto Merimoth the son of Uriah the Priest.

63 And with him was Eleazar the son of Phinehas, and with them were Yozabad the son of Yeshua, and Moeth the son of Binnui, Levites: all was delivered them by number and weight.

Noadiah the son of Binnui.

64 And all the weight of them was written up the same hour.

65 Moreover they that were come out of the captivity offered sacrifice unto Yahuah Elohim of Israel, even twelve bullocks for all Israel, fourscore and sixteen rams,

66 Threescore and twelve lambs, goats for a peace

Heb. 77 lambs. 12 he goats for a sin offering, Ezra 8:31.

offering, twelve, all of them a sacrifice to Yahuah.

67 And they delivered the king's commandments unto the king's stewards, and to the governors of Coelesyria and Phoenicia, and they honored the people, and the Temple of Elohim.

68 Now when these things were done, the rulers came unto me, and said:

Ezra's Prayer

69 The nation of Israel, the princes, the priests, and Levites have not put away from them the strange people of the land: nor the pollutions of the Gentiles, to wit, of the Canaanites, Hittites, Pheresites, Jebusites, and the Moabites, Egyptians, and Edomites.

Ezra 9:2.

70 For both they, and their sons, have married with their daughters, and the holy seed is mixed with the strange people of the land, and from the beginning of this matter, the rulers and the great men have been partakers of this iniquity.

71 And as soon as I had heard these things, I rent my clothes, and the holy garment, and pulled off the hair from off my head, and beard, and sat down sad, and very heavy.

72 So all they that were then moved at the word of Yahuah Elohim of Israel, assembled unto me, while I mourned for the iniquity: but I sat still full of heaviness, until the evening sacrifice.

73 Then rising up from the fast with my clothes and the holy garment rent, and bowing my knees, and stretching forth my hands unto Yahuah:

74 I said, O Yahuah, I am confounded, and ashamed before your face;

75 For our sins are multiplied above our heads, and our ignorances have reached up unto heaven.

Greek. have abounded.

76 For ever since the time of our fathers we have been and are in great sin, even unto this day:

77 And for our sins and our fathers, we with our brethren, and our kings, and our priests, were given up unto the Kings of the earth, to the sword, and to captivity, and for a prey with shame, unto this day.

78 And now in some measure has mercy been shown unto us, from you, O Yahuah, that there should be left us a root, and a name, in the place of your Sanctuary.

79 And to discover unto us a light in the house of Yahuah our Elohim, and to give

Hebr. life, Ezra 9:8.

us food in the time of our servitude.

80 Yes, when we were in bondage, we were not forsaken of our Yahuah; but he made us gracious before the Kings of Persia, so that they gave us food;

81 Yes, and honored the Temple of our Yahuah, and raised up the desolate Sion, that they have given us a sure abiding in Yahudea, and Yerusalem.

82 And now, O Yahuah, what shall we say having these things? For we have transgressed your Commandments, which you gave by the hand of your servants the Prophets, saying,

83 That the land which you enter into to possess as an heritage, is a land polluted with the pollutions of the strangers of the land, and they have filled it with their uncleanness.

84 Therefore now shall you not join your daughters unto their sons, neither shall you take their daughters unto your sons.

85 Moreover you shall never seek to have peace with them, that you may be strong, and eat the good things of the land, and that you may leave the inheritance of the land unto your children for evermore.

86 And all that is befallen, is done unto us for our wicked works, and great sins: for you, O Yahuah, did make our sins light:

87 And did give unto us such a root: but we have turned back again to transgress your Law, and to mingle ourselves with the uncleanness of the nations of the land.

88 May you not be angry with us to destroy us, til you had left us neither root, seed, nor name?

Or, be not angry.

89 O Yahuah of Israel, you are true: for we are left a root this day.

90 Behold, now are we before you in our iniquities, for we cannot stand any longer by reason of these things before you.

The Plan for Ending Mixed Marriages

91 And as Ezra in his prayer made his confession, weeping, and lying flat upon the ground before the Temple, there gathered unto him from Yerusalem, a very great multitude of men, and women, and children: for there was great weeping among the multitude.

92 Then Shecaniah son of Yehiel, one of the sons of

Israel called out and said, O Ezra, we have sinned against Yahuah Elohim, we have married strange women of the nations of the land, and now is all Israel aloft.

Or, exalted, Dt. 28:13, Baruch 3.

93 Let us make an oath to Yahuah, that we will put away all our wives, which we have taken of the heathen, with their children,

94 Like as you have decreed, and as many as do obey the Law of Yahuah.

95 Arise, and put in execution: for to you does this matter appertain, and we will be with you: do valiantly.

96 So Ezra arose, and took an oath of the chief of the Priests, and Levites of all Israel, to do after these things, and so they sware.

Hebr. and of all Israel, Ezra 10:5.

CHAPTER 9:

3 Ezra assembles all the people. 10 They promise to put away the strange wives. 20 The names and number of them that did so. 40 The Law of Moses is read and declared before all the people. 49 They weep, and are put in mind of the Feast day.

The Expulsion of Foreign Wives

1 Then Ezra rising from the court of the Temple, went to the chamber of Yehohanan son of Eliashib,
2 And remained there, and did eat no meat nor drink water, mourning for the great iniquities of the multitude.
3 And there was a proclamation in all Yahudea and Yerusalem, to all them that were of the captivity, that they should be gathered together at Yerusalem:
4 And that whosoever met not there within two or three days according as the Elders that bare rule, appointed, their cattle should be seized to the use of the Temple, and himself cast out from them that were of the captivity.

Utterly destroyed, Josh.10:8.

5 And in three days **were all they of the tribe of Yahudah and Benyamin gathered together at Yerusalem** the twentieth day of the ninth month.

All Yahudea returned.

6 And all the multitude sat trembling in the broad court of the Temple, because of the present foul weather.
7 So Ezra arose up, and said unto them, You have transgressed the law in marrying strange wives, thereby to increase the sins of Israel.
8 And now by confessing give glory unto Yahuah Elohim of our fathers,
9 And do his will, and separate yourselves from the heathen of the land, and from the strange women.
10 Then the whole multitude cried, and said with a loud voice; Like as you have spoken, so will we do.
11 But forasmuch as the people are many, and it is foul weather, so that we cannot stand without, and this is not a work of a day or two, seeing our sin in these things is spread far:
12 Therefore let the rulers of the multitude stay, and let all them of our habitations that have strange wives, come at the time appointed,

Or, stand.

13 And with them the Rulers and Judges of every place, til we turn away the wrath of Yahuah from us, for this matter.
14 Then Yonathan the son of Asahel and Yahzeiah son

of Tikvah, accordingly took this matter upon them: and Meshullam and Levi and Shabbethai helped them.

15 And they that were of the captivity, did according to all these things.

16 And Ezra the Priest chose unto him the principal men of their families, all by name: and in the first day of the tenth month, they sat together to examine the matter.

17 So their cause that held strange wives, was brought to an end in the first day of the first month.

18 And of the Priests that were come together, and had strange wives, there were found:

19 Of the sons of Yahusha the son of Yozadak and his kindred, Maaseiah, Eliezar, Yarib, and Yodan.

Maasias, Gedaliah.

20 And they gave their hands to put away their wives, and to offer rams, to make reconcilement for their errors.

Hebr. a ram, Or, purification.

21 And of the sons of Immer: Hanani and Zebadiah and Maaseiah and Shemaiah and Yehiel and Azariah.

Harim, Maasiah, Yehiel, Uzziah

22 And of the sons of Pashhur: Elioenai, Maaseiah, Ishmael, and Nathanael, and Gedaliah, and Salthas.

Pashur, Yosabad, Elasah.

23 And of the Levites: Yozabad and Shimei, and Kelaiah, who was Kelita, and Pethahiah and Yahudah and Yonah.

Kelaiah, Kelitah.

24 Of the holy Singers: Eliashib and Zaccur.

25 Of the Porters: Shallum and Telem.

26 Of them of Israel, of the sons of Parosh: Ramiah, Izziah, Malchiyah, Miyamin, and Eleazar, and Asibias, and Benaiah.

Yesaiah, Miamin, Malchuah.

27 Of the sons of Elam: Mattaniah and Zechariah, Yezrielus and Abdi, and Yeremoth and EliYahu.

Yehiel.

28 And of the sons of Zamoth: Eliadas, Eliashib, Othoniah, Yeremoth, and Zabad and Zerdaiah.

Zattu, Elioenai, Mattaniah, Sabad, Aziza.

29 Of the sons of Bebai: Yehohanan and Hananiah and Zabbai and Emathis.

Athlai.

30 Of the sons of Mani: Olamus, Mamuchus, Adaiah, Yashub, and Sheal and Yeremoth.

Bani, Meshullam, Malluch.

31 And of the sons of Addi: Naathus and Moossias, Laccunus and Naidus, and Bescaspasmys and Sesthel, and Belnuus and Manasseas.

Of the names in vers. 31, 32, 34, 35, See Ezra 10:30, 31:34.

32 And of the sons of Annan, Elionas and Asaias and Melchias and Sabbaias and Simon Chosamaeus.

33 And of the sons of Hashum: Mattenai and Mattattah and Zabad and Eliphelet and

39 And they spoke unto Ezra the priest and reader, that he would bring the law of Moses, that was given of Yahuah Elohim of Israel. 40 So Ezra the chief priest, brought the law unto the whole multitude from man to woman, and to all the priests, to hear the law in the first day of the seventh month.

Manasseh and Shimei.
34 And of the sons of Bani: Yeremai, Momdius, Maerus, Yoel, Mamdai and Bedeiah and Waniah, Carabasion and Eliashib and Mamitanemus, Eliasis, Binnui, Elialis, Shimei, Shelemiah, Nethaniah: And of the sons of Ezora: Shashai, Azarel, Azael, Samatus, Zambris, Yoseph,
35 And of the sons of Nooma: Mazitias, Zabad, Iddo, Yoel, Benaiah.
36 All these had taken strange wives, and they put them away with their children.

Ezra Reads the Law to the People

37 And the priests, and Levites, and they that were of Israel dwelt in Yerusalem, and in the country, in the first day of the seventh month: so the children of Israel were in their habitations.

Or, villages.

38 And the whole multitude came together with one accord, into the broad place of the holy porch toward the East.

Neh. 8:1.

39 And they spoke unto Ezra the priest and reader, that he would bring the law of Moses, that was given of Yahuah Elohim of Israel.
40 So Ezra the chief priest, brought the law unto the whole multitude from man to woman, and to all the priests, to hear the law in the first day of the seventh month.

Feast of Trumpets.

41 And he read in the broad court before the holy porch from morning unto midday, before both men and women; and all the multitude gave heed unto the law.
42 And Ezra the priest, and reader of the law stood up, upon a pulpit of wood which was made for that purpose.
43 And there stood up by him Mattathiah, Shema, Ananias, Azariah, Uriah, Hezekiah, and Baalsamus, upon the right hand.

Or, Hilkiah, Or, Maasiah.

44 And upon his left hand stood Pedaiah, Mishael, Malchiyah, Lothasubus, Nabariah, and Zechariah.

Or, Hashum, See Neh. 8:4.

45 Then Ezra took the book of the law before the multitude: for he sat honorably in the first place in the sight of them all.

Heb. above them all.

46 And when he opened the law, they stood all straight up. So Ezra blessed Yahuah Elohim Most High, the Elohim of hosts Almighty.
47 And all the people answered Amen, and lifting up their hands they fell to the ground, and worshipped Yahuah.
48 Also Yahusha, Anniuth

and Sherebiah, Yadinus, Akkub, Shabbethai, Hodiah, Maiannas, and Kelita, Azariah and Yozabad, Hanan, Pelaiah, the Levites taught the law of Yahuah, making them withall to understand it.

Then Nehemiah and Ezra the priest and Scribe, and the Levites that instructed the people. said unto all the people. Neh. 8:9.

49 Then spoke Attharates unto Ezra the chief priest, and reader, and to the Levites that taught the multitude, even to all, saying,

50 This day is holy unto Yahuah; for they all wept when they heard the law.

51 Go then and eat the fat, and drink the sweet, and send part to them that have nothing.

Or, the poor.

52 For this day is holy unto Yahuah, and be not sorrowful; for Yahuah will bring you to honor.

53 So the Levites published all things to the people, saying: This day is holy to Yahuah, be not sorrowful.

54 Then they went their way, every one to eat and drink, and make merry, and to give part to them that had nothing, and to make great cheer,

55 Because they understood the words wherein they were instructed, and for the which they had been assembled.

BIBLIOGRAPHY:

Translation Originally From:

Books of 1st and 2nd Esdras from the Original, Authorized 1611 King James Bible. King James Bible Online. Original pages available as well. https://www.kingjamesbibleonline.org/

Other General Sources of Note:

The Complete Dead Sea Scrolls in English. Revised Edition. By Geza Vermes. Penguin Books. London, NY. Revised 2004. Originally Published 1962.

The Book of Jubilees: The Torah Calendar. By Timothy Schwab and Anna Zamoranos. 2020. Based on the Original Translation by R.H. Charles, 1903. Free eBook at www.bookofjubilees.org.

"Original Canon Series," "Flood Series," and "Solomon's Gold Series." The God Culture YouTube Channel. 2017-2020.

Cited, Numbered Sources:

1. ""The Canon of Scripture." Blue Letter Bible citing "What Everyone Needs To Know About The Bible." By Don Stewart. The Basic Bible Study Series. Publisher Dart Press, Orange, California. https://www.blueletterbible.org/faq/canon.cfm

2. Clark Pinnock, Biblical Revelation, Grand Rapids: Baker Book House, 1973, p. 104. See 1. Quoted by Blue Letter Bible.

3. 2014 Lecture at University of Chicago Divinity School sponsored by Jewish Federation of Chicago. Rachel Elior. Professor, Hebrew University of Jerusalem. https://www.youtube.com/watch?v=wLit979B60Y&t=3621s

4. Strong's Concordance "Awan" #H5770. Blue Letter Bible. (Note Ancient Hebrew never had a "V" so the word is Awan not Avan)

5. 1. "Where to See Some of the World's Oldest and Most Interesting Maps." By Jennifer Billock. Smithsonian Magazine. July 18, 2017. 2. "Geography and Ethnography: Perceptions of the World in Pre-Modern Societies." By Kurt A. Raaflaub & Richard J. A. Talbert. 2009. John Wiley & Sons. p. 147. 3. Map from: Wikimedia Commons. Map of the World from Sippar (Tell Abu Habba), Iraq, 6th century BCE. On display at the British Museum in London. By Osama Shukir Muhammed Amin.

8. "The Dead Sea Scrolls and the Christian Myth." Allegro.........

9. "The Mystery of the Essenes." By H. Spencer Lewis, F.R.C. From "The Mystical Life of Jesus." Rosicrucian Digest No. 2. 2007. p. 3.

10. "Natural History." Pliny the Elder. Book V. p. 277.

11. "The Life of Flavius Josephus." 1:2. The Genuine Works of Flavius Josephus the Jewish Historian. Translated from the Original Greek, according to Havercamp's accurate Edition.

12. 1770, Bonne Map of Israel. Rigobert Bonne 1727 – 1794. AdobeStock.

13. Madaba Mosaic Map(left), c. 6th century A.D. St. George's Church. Jordan. AdobeStock.

14. 1836, Tanner Map of Palestine, Israel, Holy Land. AdobeStock.

15. NASA/Goddard Space Flight Center Scientific Visualization Studio U.S. Department of Commerce, National Oceanic and Atmospheric Administration, National Geophysical Data Center, 2006, 2-minute Gridded Global Relief Data (ETOPO2v2). Horace Mitchell (NASA/GSFC): Lead Animator.

16. 1845, Chambers Map of Palestine, Israel, Holy Land. AdobeStock.

17. 1852, Philip Map of Palestine, Israel, Holy Land. AdobeStock.

18. Ein Gedi Photos: Chalcolithic Temple, Essene Synagogue, Tile mosaic Peacock symbols. AdobeStock.
19. Antiquities of the Jews — Book VIII, Chapter 6:4 and 7:1. Flavius Josephus. Larousse. 2001. p. 35.
20. "Enoch and Qumran Origins: New Light on a Forgotten Connection." Gabriele Boccaccini, Editor. William B. Erdemans Publishing Co. Grand Rapids, MI and Cambridge, UK. 2005. p. 137.
21. "The Complete Dead Sea Scrolls In English Revised Edition." "The Damascus Document." Translated By Geza Vermes, 2004, Penguin Classics Books. London, England. First Published 1962. Revised Edition 2004. p. 139.3. Flavius Josephus, Antiquities of the Jews, 18:16.
25. Strong's Concordance. Blue Letter Bible.
26. Ancient Hebrew Research Center. By Jeff A. Benner. Ancient-Hebrew.org. 2019.
27. Philippines #1 in Gold in History. The Search for King Solomon's Treasure. The Lost Isles of Gold and the Garden of Eden. By Timothy Schwab and Anna Zamoranos. 2020. 1. "Ancient Mining: Classical Philippine Civilization." Wikipedia. Extracted August 9, 2019. and "Cultural Achievements of Pre-Colonial Philippines." Wikipedia. Extracted August 9, 2019. 2. "The Edge of Terror: The Heroic Story of American Families Trapped in the Japanese-occupied Philippines." By Scott Walker. Thomas Dunne Books. St. Martin's Press. New York. Chap. 3 - The Gold Miners, 1901-1937. p. 44. 3. "Philippine Civilization and Technology," By Paul Kekai Manansala. Asia Pacific University. 4. "Encyclopedic Dictionary of Archaeology – Philippines, the." Compiled by Barbara Ann Kipfer, Ph.D. Kluwer Academic/ Plenum Publishers. New York, London, Moscow. 2000. p. 436. 5. "Miners Shun Mineral Wealth of the Philippines." By Donald Greenlees. NY Times. May 14, 2008. Citing The Fraser Institute. 6. "Trillion – Dollar Philippine Economic Goldmine Emerging From Murky Pit." By Ralph Jennings. Forbes Magazine. Apr. 5, 2015. 7. "Mining for Gold in the Philippines." By Nicole Rashotte. Gold Investing News. Sept. 10th, 2019.
28. Philippines #1 in Pearl. The Search for King Solomon's Treasure. The Lost Isles of Gold and the Garden of Eden. By Timothy Schwab and Anna Zamoranos. 2020. 1. "This $100 Million Pearl Is The Largest and Most Expensive in the World." By Roberta Naas. Forbes Magazine. Aug 23, 2016. 2. "Pinoy in Canada Discovers Strange Family Heirloom is Actually a Giant Pearl Worth $90 Million." Buzzooks.com. May 23, 2019.
29. Romblon Philippines Strongest Onyx. The Search for King Solomon's Treasure. The Lost Isles of Gold and the Garden of Eden. By Timothy Schwab and Anna Zamoranos. 2020. 1. "ROMBLON: 8 Awesome Places You Should Visit in Romblon!" Our Awesome Planet. Sept. 7, 2016. 2. "The Romblon Marble." Ellaneto Tiger Marble Trader, Romblon. 2010. 3. "Marvelous Marble" By Robert A. Evora. Manila Standard. Jan. 16, 2014.
30. "The Center of the Center of Marine Biodiversity on Earth." 1. "Environmental Biology of Fishes." K.E. Carpenter and V.G. Springer. 2005. 72: 467-480. 2. "Center of the Center of Marine Diversity." CNN. Apr. 30, 2012. 3. "100 Scientists Declare RP as World's 'Center of Marine Biodiversity." By Katherine Adraneda. June 8, 2006. The Philippine Star reporting on "Philippines Environmental Monitor, 2005" by the World Bank.
31. "Havilah." Hitchcock's Dictionary of Bible Names from BibleHub.org and KingJamesBibleDictionary.com, Strong's Concordance #H2341. Blue Letter Bible.
32. "Eve - Havah." Strong's Concordance #H2332. Blue Letter Bible.

33. European Russia. Wikipedia.
34. "Indonesia's Mountains of Fire." By Daniel Quinn. Indonesia Expat. June 30, 2014. Indonesia's Volcanological Survey. Laporan Kebencanaan Geologi. Apr. 2, 2019.
35. "Largest Islands of the World." WorldAtlas.com
41. "The giant undersea rivers we know very little about" By Richard Gray. BBC News. July 6, 2017. Citing Dan Parsons, PhD, Sedimentologist, University of Hull, UK.
42. "The Thanksgiving Hymns (iQH, 1Q36,4Q427-32). Hymn 14." The Complete Dead Sea Scrolls. By Geza Vermes. Penguin Classics. P. 278.
43. "Chapter Eight. Traditions Common To 4 Ezra And The Dead Sea Scrolls." By E.J.C. Tigchelaar and F. García Martínez. Qumranica Minora I. Qumran Origins and Apocalypticism. Series: Studies on the Texts of the Desert of Judah, Volume: 63. Publisher: Brill. 01 Jan 2007. 153–168.
44. F. García Martínez, "Qumran Origins and Early History: A Groningen Hypothesis," Folia Orientalia 25 (1989): 113–36.
45: "Bartacus." Encyclopedia of the Bible.
46. Josephus. "3.5". Antiquities of the Jews.
47. John Gower. "VII.1884-1899". Confessio Amantis translation is at Richard Brodie; Ellin Anderson (2009). "John Gower's Confessio Amantis Modern English version."
48. "4QProto-Esther[a]." The Complete Dead Sea Scrolls in English. Revised Edition. By Geza Vermes. Penguin Books. London, NY. Revised 2004. Originally Published 1962. p. 619
49. "Proto-Esther[d]." The Complete Dead Sea Scrolls in English. Revised Edition. By Geza Vermes. Penguin Books. London, NY. Revised 2004. Originally Published 1962. p. 620
50. "The missing link of Jewish European ancestry: contrasting the Rhineland and the Khazarian hypotheses." By Eran Elhaik. Department of Mental Health, Johns Hopkins University Bloomberg School of Public Health, MD, USA. Published by National Library of Medicine, Genome Biology and Evolution. 2013.
51. "Scythian, Ancient People." By The Editors of Encyclopaedia Britannica. Last Edited Nov. 2019.
52. "Royal concubines." 13-04-2015. worldhistory.biz.
53. "Commentary on Habakkuk." The Complete Dead Sea Scrolls in English. Revised Edition. By Geza Vermes. Penguin Books. London, NY. Revised 2004. Originally Published 1962. p. 510-511.
54. Commentary on Nahum, P. 505. The Complete Dead Sea Scrolls in English. Geza Vermes. Penguin Classics. Revised Edition. Published 1962. Revised 2004.
55. Commentary on Habukkuk, P. 515.The Complete Dead Sea Scrolls in English. Geza Vermes. Penguin Classics. Revised Edition. Published 1962. Revised 2004.
56. "Blessings (iQSb=iQ28b), The Blessing of the Prince of the Congregation." The Complete Dead Sea Scrolls in English. Geza Vermes. Penguin Classics. Revised Edition. Published 1962. Revised 2004. p. 389.
100 B.C. dating: J. T. Milik (DJD, I, 118-29).
57. "Mithraism: Worship, Practices, and Institutions." By Reinhold Merkelbach. The Editors of Encyclopaedia Britannica.
58. "The Pope and the Mithras Cult: Part II." By Jon Sorensen. Sept. 23, 2013. Catholic.com.
59. "Table Talk." By Martin Luther (1483-1546). P. 21. William Hazlitt, Esq. (Translator). Christian Classics Ethereal Library. Grand Rapids, MI.
60. "Antiquities of the Jews — Book XI." Josephus. Chapter 3.1. Chapter 11.133.

Over 300 pages. 6"x 9" Paperback.
© 2021

Most of us have been taught the Sabbath passed away. Is that what the Bible says? Review the evidence for yourself in this comprehensive Bible Case for Sabbath. This will change your life.

Coming Soon in Print and in eBook at:

OphirInstitute.com

International:

Philippines:

eBooks:

TheGodCulture.com

YouTube *The God Culture*

The God Culture - Original

THE MONUMENTAL CASE FOR

OPHIR, PHILIPPINES

The Full Case:
6" x 9" Paperback
384 pages, BW

Instructional Edition:
7" x 10" Paperback
256 pages, Color

Coffee Table Book:
10" x 12" Hardcover
200 pages, Color

The search for the ancient land of gold – Ophir, Sheba and Tarshish and the Garden of Eden found in the Philippines in history and the Bible. Learn how this restores understanding of prophecy for our age. Start your journey now.

SUPPORTED BY
300-PAGE SOURCEBOOK
Electronic Only.

Available in Print and in eBook at:

OphirInstitute.com

International:

Philippines:

eBooks:

amazon

TheGodCulture.com

YouTube *The God Culture*

The God Culture - Original

TheGodCulture.com

YouTube *The God Culture* f *The God Culture - Original*

Cracking the Dark Age Mysteries

Made in the USA
Las Vegas, NV
08 December 2024